QUITO 1599

QUITO 1599

City and Colony in Transition

DON P. Z ZA S.

DON

Kris Lane

 University of New Mexico Press, Albuquerque

A SERIES OF COURSE-ADOPTION BOOKS ON LATIN AMERICA:

Independence in Spanish America: Civil Wars, Revolutions, and Underdevelopment (revised edition)—Jay Kinsbruner, Queens College

Heroes on Horseback: A Life and Times of the Last Gaucho Caudillos—John Chasteen, University of North Carolina at Chapel Hill

The Life and Death of Carolina Maria de Jesus—Robert M. Levine, University of Miami, and José Carlos Sebe Bom Meihy, University of São Paulo

The Countryside in Colonial Latin America—edited by Louisa Schell Hoberman, University of Texas at Austin, and Susan Migden Socolow, Emory University

¡Que vivan los tamales! Food and the Making of Mexican Identity—Jeffrey M. Pilcher, The Citadel

The Faces of Honor: Sex, Shame, and Violence in Colonial Latin America—edited by Lyman L. Johnson, University of North Carolina at Charlotte, and Sonya Lipsett-Rivera, Carleton University

The Century of U.S. Capitalism in Latin America—Thomas F. O'Brien, University of Houston

Tangled Destinies: Latin America and the United States—Don Coerver, Texas Christian University, and Linda Hall, University of New Mexico

Everyday Life and Politics in Nineteenth Century Mexico: Men, Women, and War— Mark Wasserman, Rutgers, The State University of New Jersey

Lives of the Bigamists: Marriage, Family, and Community in Colonial Mexico—Richard Boyer, Simon Fraser University

Andean Worlds: Indigenous History, Culture, and Consciousness Under Spanish Rule, 1532–1825—Kenneth J. Andrien, Ohio State University

The Mexican Revolution, 1910–1940—Michael J. Gonzales, Northern Illinois University

SERIES ADVISORY EDITOR: LYMAN L. JOHNSON,
UNIVERSITY OF NORTH CAROLINA AT CHARLOTTE

To the people of Ecuador and Colombia,

in hopes of better times

Library of Congress Cataloging-in-Publication Data

Lane, Kris E., 1967–

Quito 1599 : city and colony in transition / Kris Lane.— 1st ed.

p. cm. — (Diálogos)

Includes bibliographical references and index.

ISBN 0-8263-2356-1 (cloth : alk. paper) — ISBN 0-8263-2357-X

(pbk. : alk. paper)

1. Quito (Ecuador)—History—16th century.

2. Quito (Audiencia)—History.

3. Quito (Ecuador)—Economic conditions—16th century.

4. Quito (Ecuador)—Race relations.

5. Quito (Ecuador)—Social life and customs—16th century.

I. Title.

II. Diálogos (Albuquerque, N.M.)

F3781.3 .L36 2002

986.6'13—dc21

2002004203

CONTENTS

List of Illustrations

Figures

Maps

Graphs

What I find in history is that people are more likely to deceive themselves than to succeed in deceiving others—though I grant some spectacular exceptions to this rule.

—*Charles Gibson (addressing the American Historical Association in Dallas, Texas, 1977)*

PREFACE

The portrait on the cover of this book was painted and signed in 1599, but
it appears as fresh and startling today as it must have looked some four
hundred years ago. At the center is a coffee-colored man with a
Shakespearean goatee and a penetrating gaze. His light-brown eyes and
what appear to be streaks of gray hair suggest the wisdom of an elder and
the pride of an accomplished warrior. An inscription above his head
identifies him as "Don Francisco de Arobe, 56 Años," the Spanish title
"don" in this case signifying "native lord." On either side stand, peering
over his shoulders, two beardless youths of similar complexion and eye
color. Their gazes, slightly elevated, cross the frame. On the left but
significantly to don Francisco's right is "Don Pedro, 22," to his left the
younger "Don Domingo, 18."

Father and sons stand guard with iron-tipped lances of hard palm-
wood held gracefully in their right hands. The implicit message: we hereby
promise to defend Your Majesty's domain against all foes. The men's noses,
ears, and lips are studded with strange crescents and balls and tubes of gold.
Beneath starched white ruffs flow finely bordered ponchos and capes of
brocaded silk, their drape lovingly rendered by the painter: here a foil-like
blue, there bronze, now bright orange against velvety black. Only don
Francisco's poncho appears to be woolen, perhaps fashioned from imported
Spanish broadcloth. The three are further adorned with matching shell
necklaces, and don Francisco holds a supple, black felt hat with copper
trim. Don Domingo holds a more pedestrian sombrero, (shown in full on
title page) and all three appear to be wearing fitted doublets of contemporary, late-Renaissance European style. These are all but hidden, nestled
beneath flowing Chinese overgarments, which are, in turn, cut in a
distinctly Andean fashion.

The bright backdrop of this unusual portrait suggests swirls of clouds,
perhaps a tropical sunset, but looking down one wonders if a second panel
(now lost) rendered feet and foreground. On the right-hand side is a

framed architectural element containing a dedication to Philip III, just-crowned "King of Spain and the Indies" (see title page). The caption also states that the painting was commissioned by a Quito judge, Dr. Juan del Barrio de Sepúlveda. Beneath this frame, in a tiny patch of light-blue sky, is the abbreviated signature of the artist, Andrés Sánchez Gallque, a native of Quito who had hispanicized his surname (possibly "Sangolquí") to match his new, hybrid persona. His remarkable 1599 portrait of the Arobes was rediscovered in a storehouse early in the last century, and is now proudly displayed in Madrid's Museo de América. We do not know if the young king ever saw his gift.

Sánchez Gallque's masterpiece conveys a sort of staged majesty, yet its unusual realism and extraordinary attention to detail render it all the more enigmatic for the twenty-first-century viewer.[1] Who are these men? Why are they dressed this way? Why the strange jewelry and iron-tipped lances? Why were they painted in this pose? And why in 1599? Some years ago, as a naïve graduate student in search of a compelling topic, this painting alone motivated me to study early colonial Ecuador and Colombia. At the time these and other, similar questions seemed simple enough. I have since learned to appreciate the limitations, disappointments, and occasional epiphanies of historical research. Despite much hard digging some of the answers, or at least their bronchial subtleties, will remain mysterious. Fragments that have begun to coalesce I offer here, tentatively.

Despite its prominence in the title, *Quito 1599* is not intended as a "snapshot," or synchronic analysis of this particular city and region in this particular year. As the experience of researching the Sánchez Gallque painting demonstrates, the records all but prohibit such an approach.[2] Rather, what follows is a series of overlapping narratives, document-derived explorations, as it were, into that lost colonial world inhabited by don Francisco and his two sons. Their portrait will serve as a kind of touchstone. The point is not to simply marvel at quaint antiquities or tropical landscapes, but rather to attempt to evoke the many spirits, some would say mentalities, of these men's age, to ask the diverse inhabitants of circa-1599 Quito—women, children, and men of many classes, ethnicities, and colors—how the world (and occasionally, the afterworld) appeared to them. What opportunities and limitations did they face?

This is the personal or "microhistorical" side of *Quito 1599*. As will become quickly evident, I have unabashedly embraced storytelling in more than a few places. The "transition" of the subtitle, on the other hand, refers mostly to certain long- and short-range diachronic patterns of political economy that steered but did not for the most part determine (I am now convinced) individual careers. These include the geographical expansion and contraction of Quito's domain, some dramatic demographic changes, particularly among indigenous populations, and relatively abrupt shifts in production and trade, most of which were noticed and remarked on by contemporary observers. Other patterns and changes I describe below probably remained hidden from contemporary view.

Though at times it may make for an uncomfortable ride, I have opted to straddle these two approaches—the synchronic "micro" and the diachronic "macro"—in order to emphasize the importance of analyzing multiple perceptions of and responses to what may appear to us, in retrospect, a straightforward evolution of political, economic, and social structures. Considering the myriad and often only barely accessible mentalities at play in Quito at the turn of the seventeenth century, I am frequently forced to simply set the stage as best I can, offer plausible suggestions, and ultimately capitulate to the reader's imagination.

I am fully aware that the moral and philosophical concerns of Spain's overseas administrators, church leaders, and colonial subjects in the age of the Arobes and of Philips II and III are not ours, and I have attempted to avoid unfair or anachronistic judgments in examining these distant lives. Nevertheless *Quito 1599* does ask why—to the extent one can fathom, given the nature of the record—these particular colonial subjects (and also some of those who successfully and totally rejected the Spanish imperial yoke) did what they did. For this reason, throughout the narrative the related issues of human captivity and the quest for liquid wealth in the form of gold recur. I am particularly interested in exploring the different ways in which these universal themes of Western, and to a certain extent, world history were viewed and contested in this early American colonial context.

The choice is not arbitrary. After a number of years spent reviewing the extraordinarily large and diverse manuscript record of this period it is my view that gold-lust and human captivity in various forms were central pillars—perhaps *the* central pillars—of life in early Quito, city and colony. The European side of both issues alone is remarkably rich with paradoxes, most centering on contemporary Christian (specifically, reformed Roman Catholic) views of sin and redemption, but I have also attempted to glean evidence of alternative and what might be called subaltern and even rebel points of view. Here modern ethnographies and linguistic studies have been helpful, yet the reader will no doubt find that when all is said and done these other, less-familiar voices remain distressingly faint. To date no corpus of indigenous-language colonial documents has been discovered here.

In today's world, particularly in the Americas, where all of us are descendants of either voluntary or forced migrants or of the peoples they came to supplant, all colonial history is relevant. In prosperity and poverty we live with the legacies—some positive, some negative—of Spanish, Portuguese, French, English, Dutch, and other European colonial enterprises. Relentless exploitation of mineral wealth, for example, a project that dates to Columbus's time, continues to scar and pollute vast portions of both American continents and more than a few islands. In the case of gold, there remains no significant practical justification.

On the other hand, in part as a result of colonial ecological interpenetration, this hemisphere now feeds the world (not forgetting, of course, that surplus food production also entails great environmental and social costs). Meanwhile, the socioeconomic and psychological aftereffects of colonial slavery; apartheidlike segregation and genocide of indigenous peoples; "hypermasculine" domestic tyranny; and generally unequal wealth distribution—to name but a few more legacies with roots traceable to the colonial period—have proved remarkably resilient. Memories of this painful past/present, though often repressed for centuries, may be "recovered" at any time, with potentially explosive results. The current pan-indigenous movement in Ecuador is a case in point.

I do not pretend to have a formula for reconciliation in the postcolonial world, and I do not envision this book as some kind of exorcism of colonial demons. Still, an inevitable by-product of colonial histories, whether in reading or writing them, is emotional confrontation. Some of the events described below, particularly in chapters 2 and 3, cannot help but provoke rage and sadness. Many are simply puzzling. How do we understand without rushing to judgment?

In recent years historians and other analysts suggested that understand-ing "contact" was key. They argued that modern pan-American sociological patterns (notably racism, sexual exploitation of poor women, child labor, and other pathologies) had roots traceable to the heady years surrounding 1492. Thus conquest and initial encounters in various parts of the Americas drew (and continue to draw) much-deserved attention. While acknowledging the trap of reductionism, whereby history becomes a blunt political cudgel, we now see much more clearly how the seeds of several of these colonial legacies were planted. Likewise, all American conquests are now assumed ambivalent.[3] On the other hand, many persistent or recurrent patterns do not seem to be rooted in the early encounter, or even in the wars of conquest. Looking well beyond 1492, to the period some historians have dubbed "crystallization" (in Spanish South America roughly 1580–1600, earlier in Mexico), one discovers several striking features.

First glance at this period, usually associated with transition from Renaissance to Baroque ideals in most of Europe, has long provoked déjà vu, a sense that the institutions and patterns of culture here emerging would define the rest of the colonial and much of the national period in many places. Stunned by the multitude of apparent colonial continuities, particularly in regions of dense indigenous or African-descended populations, observers of Latin America, both foreign and domestic, have long argued that the region's future somehow got mired in a Baroque swamp. Even today, Marxist revolutionaries and neoliberal technocrats alike agree that positive change requires a final escape from the despotism of this supposedly stagnant colonial past.

A closer look at the period itself, however, reveals a multitude of fractal whorls spinning at every edge—and often within and around the various colonial centers themselves. At least in Quito, rather than "crystallization" (a.k.a. "fossilization") one sees an unsettling yet compelling historical analogue of fluid dynamics. For the historian who strains to examine the chaos of everyday life up close there are patterns, and they sometimes appear to crystallize—but only to metamorphose unexpectedly and flow into something else. In short, the dead certainties of the center (Lima, Mexico City, Seville) seem far less convincing at the mercurial or unstable periphery. Perhaps the fact that Quito was not the apple of King Philip's eye is part of what makes it all the more intriguing.

Quito 1599 is my attempt to navigate a section of one such peripheral, or at least second-tier colonial history during a key period of transition. To linger just above its eddies, as it were, is, among other things, to gauge the many and changing tinctures of colonial relations of power, what some might call the surge and reflux of hegemony and counter-hegemony at the often violent edge of empire.[4] Oddly, Spain's troubled and constantly changing relationship with the rest of Europe and the near East at about this time was to some extent mirrored by contemporary Quito's successes and failures at its own periphery. Certain features of the so-called early modern world-system, such as forced labor and precious metals extraction for export, were also duly replicated at Quito's margins, only to be snuffed out or diverted by "Indian rebels" and other willful locals. Other aspects of Quito's early political economy, such as the nearly industrial-scale production of textiles for another colonial market of enormous consumptive capacity, do not seem to jibe at all with world-systems theory.

Although I concentrate much attention on the periphery and attempt to avoid the oversimplification of at least the cruder sort of world-systems analysis, at the same time I do not deny the importance of centers (administrative, commercial, religious, etc.) and their gravitational fields. I simply fear too much respect for them obscures subtler motions and pulls at the margins that in aggregate—or even individually—may have had as much import in the long run. To embrace this patterned chaos is, I think, to challenge ourselves with the notion that other worlds might have been, that the present is not simply a predictable outgrowth of the past.

I have accumulated many debts in the course of this project and wish I could offer more than these few words as restitution. First of all, in Ecuador I thank historians Guillermo Bustos and Rosemarie Terán for nearly a decade of unflagging encouragement and friendship, and I am grateful to sociologist Luís Guerrón for introducing me to them and to the country. To Tamara Estupiñán, for her boundless generosity, enthusiasm, and encouragement as we tracked similar quarry in the archives. Also in Ecuador Dr. Christiana Borchart de Moreno for her guidance and suggestions, and also for listening to more mining stories than most people could stand. Thanks to Professors Enrique Ayala Mora and César Montúfar for inviting me to share my research in seminars at the Universidad Andina Simón Bolívar in Quito. Likewise Dr. Heraclio Bonilla, for his always penetrating commentary and useful suggestions, and for inviting me to share my findings at the Graduate School of the Universidad Nacional de Colombia in Bogotá.

In the United States I thank Professors Robert J. Ferry, John D. Hoag, and Davíd Carrasco at the University of Colorado, Boulder, for helping me build an empirical base and also for filling my knapsack with disquiet, or at least lifelong questions regarding colonial history. At the University of Minnesota I learned still more about the practice of history from my Ph.D. adviser, Professor Stuart B. Schwartz; his rare combination of wit, insight, and productive energy remain a constant inspiration. My experience at Minnesota was further enriched by courses and exchanges with Professors William D. and Carla Rahn Phillips, Ward Barrett, Robert McCaa, Edward Farmer, Dennis Valdés, Jean O'Brien, and Stephen Gudeman. Thanks also to Professor John J. TePaske of Duke University for encouraging me to examine Quito's smeltery ledgers. They yielded unexpected treasures. At the University of Wisconsin, Madison, I thank Professors Carmén Chuquín and Frank Salomon for introducing me to yet another Ecuador through the study of Imbabura Quichua. Professors Karen Vieira Powers of Northern Arizona University and Kimberly Gauderman of the University of New Mexico have also been great supporters and occasional archive mates.

Many thanks are also due the ever-helpful staffs of the National History and Municipal Archives in Quito, especially Doña Grecia Vasco de Escudero, and to Dr. Hedwig Hartmann and Yolanda Poloe of the Archivo Central del Cauca in Popayán. In Spain I thank the staffs of the Archive of the Indies in Seville and the National Library in Madrid. In Williamsburg I thank the staff of the interlibrary loan office at the College of William and Mary's library. Other debts were incurred during informal field research in Ecuador and Colombia. In Peguche, Ecuador, I thank Narciso and Fanny Conejo, and especially Doña Antonia Conejo, for boarding and bearing with a gringo blockhead struggling to learn their native tongue. I also thank the many gold miners and their families of Zaruma and Nambija, Ecuador, and Barbacoas and Chisquío, Colombia, for so graciously inviting me into their worlds, both above and underground. I also sincerely thank the volcanos Sangay, Tungurahua, and Guagua Pichincha for not erupting as I lingered stupid with hypoxia and curiosity in their steaming craters. (All three belched commemorative smoke and fire in 1999.)

Study in Ecuador and Colombia was funded by a Fulbright/IIE pre-dissertation fellowship (1994–95), followed by two William and Mary Summer research grants (1998 and 2000). Research in Spain was funded by an Early Modern Studies Grant from the University of Minnesota (1995) and a National Endowment for the Humanities Summer Stipend (1999). Thanks also to the Reves and Charles Centers at the College of William and Mary for funding two outstanding undergraduate students to accompany me to the archives and mines of Ecuador during the summers of 1998 and 2000. Those students, Christopher Mercer and Alicia Caleb, I thank especially for sharing their fresh impressions of a world I had come to think I knew. Mr. Mercer also read the manuscript and offered helpful suggestions. Thanks also to my supportive colleagues in the History Department at the College of William and Mary, particularly Judith Ewell, and to graduate-student readers Catharine Dann, Scott Ebhardt, and Paul Grady. David Holtby, Lyman Johnson, and the entire production staff at the University of New Mexico Press have been extraordinarily accommodating and helpful at every step. Above all, I thank my *dos vidas,* Pamela and Ximena, for reminding me that there was more to life than mucking through gold mines and unpacking *legajos,* literally and figuratively. Their love makes it all worthwhile.

A few words on names and terms: as is to be expected in a book on the colonial Andes, a variety of Spanish, Quechua, and other non-English words appear throughout the text. I have attempted to translate them as needed. Also, I have opted to follow modern Quechua orthography, which incorporates *k*s and *w*s. "Inca" is now "Inka," for example, and "Atahualpa," "Atawallpa." As will be seen in the introduction, I use the term "Spaniard" with caution; it meant different things to different people in colonial times, none perfectly consistent with modern concepts of nationality. "Indigenous," "native American," and "Amerindian" are terms used more or less interchangeably to refer to the peoples encountered by and sometimes conquered by the "Spaniards." "Andean" refers to native highlanders, as opposed to say, Amazonian or coastal lowland peoples. More precise terms, like "Pijao" or "Jivaroan," are used whenever possible.

Bogotá

Quito

Lima

Cuzco

La Paz

Potosí

Salvador

Santiago

Buenos Aires

*Pacific
Ocean*

*Atlantic
Ocean*

Area claimed by the Audiencia of Quito, c. 1599. Map drawn by Carol Cooperrider.

INTRODUCTION

When they visited the city of Quito in 1599 don Francisco de Arobe and his two sons must have temporarily lost their breath. First the altitude, over 2,800 meters, or about 9,200 feet, above sea level, rarely fails to slow even the fittest newcomer. Second, the landscape, particularly the high mountains—a half-dozen snow-capped volcanos towering over 5,000 meters (16,500-plus feet)— could hardly have contrasted more sharply with the lush, steamy jungle left behind in coastal Esmeraldas. Naturally defended by deep ravines and perched upon the flanks of mighty Pichincha Volcano, Quito the city was itself a breathtaking contrast in warmth and cold, darkness and light.

Even in the largest and airiest structures of the early colonial period, Spanish and indigenous interiors alike tended to be cavelike, a feature exaggerated in part by the constant high angle of the sun. But the cool darkness inside the city's tightly packed thatch-roofed *bohíos* and tile-roofed residential quadrants, churches, offices, and stores was offset by numerous sun-drenched plazas and patios. At night or on rainy days residents and visitors piled on layers of clothing or blankets to ward off the chill. Outside on clear days, especially around noon, one could appreciate the ingenious variety of head-coverings devised by indigenous women and men to keep the sun from scorching their scalps. From the mountains cold, clear water spilled down in quantity, to be channeled to city, mill, and field. Nearby the green, grassy valleys of Añaquito and Chillos, dotted with plump creole cattle, promised unlimited bounty, at least for some.

Although no census or even rough contemporary estimate survives, Quito in 1599 was clearly a second-tier Spanish American city, seat of a bishopric but permanent home to perhaps only about ten thousand people. Most, probably half or more, were native Andeans, their numbers swelling to some thirty thousand when taken to include the twenty-five-odd villages falling within the city's "five-league" jurisdiction in the surrounding countryside. The city was divided into seven parishes, the

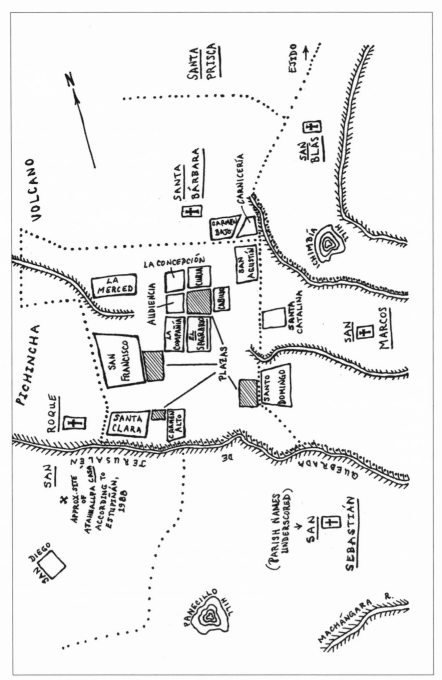

Plan of the City of Quito. Map by Kris Lane, after Martin Minchom, *The People of Quito, 1690–1810: Change and Unrest in the Underclass* (Boulder: Western Press, 1994), p. 22.

largest of which pertained to the cathedral chapter, or Sagrario; others were named for Saints Sebastian, Blas, Barbara, Mark, Prisca, and Roque.[1]

By 1599 these *barrios,* or neighborhoods, were already somewhat segregated according to income, color, and ethnicity, and some hint of Inka-era moiety ("upper half/lower half") divisions may have also lingered. Parish records and other sources suggest many of the indigenous residents of the city and near hinterland were recent immigrants from the northern and southern highlands. Some came also from ports like Guayaquil and Manta, and from the wetter hill country east or west of the city. African and locally born slaves seem to have numbered only in the hundreds, certainly no more than a thousand, and free people of color far fewer, perhaps a hundred. Despite their small numbers, people of African descent did much to shape both city and colony by 1599 and would continue to do so. Several were linked to indigenous persons by ties of godparentage. Symbolically, African slavery was the baseline against which all contemporary notions of freedom and captivity were measured.

Europeans, overwhelmingly Spanish in heritage but including a handful of Portuguese, French, Italian, Greek, Flemish, and German individuals, constituted perhaps a quarter of Quito's urban population; of these, two-thirds or more were men. Such diverse groups of male immigrants were even more characteristic of the gold camps. "Spanish" defined a person rather loosely in this early-modern imperial rather than national age, and it would be perhaps more accurate to note immigrants' regional origins, their "little homeland," or *patria chica.* As in most of early Spanish America, Andalusians, Extremadurans, and Basques were most visible in Quito, followed by natives of New and Old Castile, Galicia, Catalonia, and other Spanish kingdoms. Some "Spaniards" migrated from other colonies, including the Canary Islands, but most were locally born. The remainder of Quito's residents were deemed *mestizos,* mulattos, *zambaigos,* and *montañéses* by scribes, churchmen, and crown officials, usually with more than a hint of disdain. "Mestizo," "mulatto," and "zambaigo" (later shortened to "zambo") were terms applied to indigenous-European, African-European, and indigenous-African offspring, respectively; illegitimacy was strongly implied in all three cases. "Montañés," on the other hand, was a socio-racial term usually reserved for Andean-Europeans born of a church-sanctioned marriage, as between

Dry season above Cayambe, Ecuador

an indigenous noblewoman and a conquistador. We know almost nothing of how these persons of "mixed" heritage, male or female, defined themselves.

Be that as it may, Quito's fast-growing bi- or multiracial population, mostly Andean-European at this time, represented both a bridge between and a breach of prescribed ethnic categories. Some would be absorbed into the "Spanish" world, or *república de españoles* (though, as will be seen, color still mattered there). Others might be absorbed into the indigenous one, or *república de indios* (where European or African admixture might be forgotten).² Still others escaped or were cast out of both spheres to fend for themselves. Thankfully, both city and colony made space for mestizos, mulattos, zambaigos, and other multiracial individuals to form interstitial "colonial" identities all their own, often as petty merchants in the case of women and artisans or majordomos in the case of men. The Afro-indigenous Arobes of Esmeraldas represented yet another option, that of the autonomous frontier dweller found throughout the Americas.

Though inconsistent, what could be called racial discrimination was already very much in evidence in Quito and environs by 1599. For example, persons of indigenous, African, and so-called mixed parentage were technically barred from joining regular religious orders by about 1580. Undaunted, in response they formed their own sodalities, or lay sister- and brotherhoods devoted to particular saints and causes. The depth of the mixed, black, and indigenous populations' devotion, expressed frequently and lavishly in public and private acts and ceremonies, often shamed their fairer-skinned social superiors. Less fortunate were the city's many mixed-heritage soldiers, veterans of "Indian wars" and other quasi-official armed conflicts. They would be jettisoned to the fringes to face the crown's myriad internal and external enemies.

Many Quitos

Traditionally, the Kingdom of Quito, like modern Ecuador, has been divided into three regions: the Coast, Sierra, and *Oriente,* or Amazonian Lowlands. As any geographer will attest, this is a pitiful oversimplification. In truth, it is impossible to describe in a nutshell the stunningly diverse topography of the equatorial Andean wedge of South America now called Ecuador, southern Colombia, and northernmost Peru. Still, even a crabbed sketch of this complex and dramatic landscape will aid in understanding the flow of human interactions within it. Below is a summary of greater Quito's climate, surface features, and human occupation up to 1599. Of critical importance in the sociopolitical category was the interaction between aboriginal chiefdoms and the late-arriving Inka state; though modified, these relationships shaped Spanish-indigenous affairs in the generations between conquest and 1599, even in areas the Inkas themselves had not penetrated.

Geography and Climate

In and around Quito every day, like every night, lasts a monotonously perfect twelve hours. Between about 2,200 and 3,000 meters above sea level the diurnal flux in temperature is so minimal and the mean so pleasant (unchanging lows of 8–10 degrees centigrade, or c. 40–45°F, highs 18–22, or c. 60–70°F) as to suggest an endless spring or autumn. Though immediately charming, the effect on long-term visitors from higher latitudes can be disconcerting, creating in some a sense of timelessness and immutability. Though semiannual shifts in temperature and humidity are fairly significant on the coast, exposed as it is to alternating warm and cool ocean currents, in the highlands from the cities of Popayán to Loja a sunny day in January hardly differs from a sunny day in June. As a result, the equatorial Andes is one of the few regions on earth where solstice festivals feel at once necessary and inappropriate—inappropriate because of the eternal equinox, necessary because there do seem to be distinct seasons.

Typical of the tropics these seasons are dry and wet, in Quito and environs corresponding roughly to northern hemisphere summer and fall-winter-spring, respectively. There is often a dry break in the long wet season during the month of December, as well. Whereas the climates of highland Mexico and Peru tend to be at best semiarid, much of Ecuador and southern Colombia (thanks to the phenomenon of equatorial low pressure) remains bankably wet almost year-round. The coast floods annually, in El Niño years disastrously, and the steep and generally young and volcanic north Andes and their foothills are prone to tremendous landslides when saturated. In most years geophysical curses are turned to blessings: vulcanism and massive erosion, though often enough deadly and disruptive, serve also to periodically replenish well-watered bottomlands. Indeed, flooding and tectonic events are rather frequent for most tastes, but never so much as to prevent significant human settlement and growth, in a word, adaptation to a sometimes challenging environment.

Staple foods of Upper Amazonia, the coastal lowlands, and some inter-Andean valleys include manioc, plantains (introduced), and sweet potatoes, while in the highlands assorted tubers like the native potato, *mashua, oca,* and *melloco* are basic. To these starches are added beans, squash, and a variety of native fruits, often harvested more than once a year. More like Mexico than Peru, however, in the north Andes maize is and has long been the crop of choice in virtually all ecological zones. Even today dried ears of the hearty *choclo* variety hang in the husk from the rafters of highland indigenous dwellings.[3] Treasured cobs were brought to Quito

Polylepis trees in high páramo, Imbabura Province, Ecuador

from Central America at some point in the very distant prehistoric past, perhaps overland or via the once-thriving coastwise raft traffic (*balsa,* or "raft" wood is native to the Ecuadorian coast). Pre-Columbian condiments consisted primarily of salt, gathered from both inland mineral springs and seaside pans, and potent red capsicum peppers. According to various conquest-era chroniclers, a lightly salted and "peppered" maize gruel was considered a fine meal for indigenous peoples of all classes.

Unlike central Peru, in the north Andes agricultural terracing was minimal, but crop yields were improved by relatively small-scale irrigation works and raised fields.[4] As ethnohistorians and archaeologists continue to discover, throughout the region control of prime maizefields was *the* hallmark of political success. Native lords of modern Imbabura Province, Ecuador, for example, lived atop earthen quasi-pyramids overlooking such fields. In Quito's cool highlands Old World cultigens like wheat, oats, and barley—none, incidentally, as nourishing as native *quinua*—would thrive, making these "neo-European" ecological niches all the more attractive to bread-addicted Europeans and their grain-chomping mounts.

Lower intermontane valleys like the Cauca, Patía, Chota, Guayllabamba, Patate, Jubones, and Catamayo, though hotter, drier, and more prone to breed mosquitoes, yielded coca leaves, cotton, and capsicum peppers. It was the nearness and heavy exploitation of these valleys that led to the development of a compact, stair-step ecological exchange system now called "microverticality." The Spanish would try their hand at multi-tier exploitation as well, introducing Mediterranean sugarcane to great effect in almost all the hot inter-Andean valleys, where it is still grown today. Experimental vineyards and olive groves generally withered. Never subject to frost, the hot valleys were a paradise for fungi and insects, great enemies of viticulture (and horticulture generally), but abundant mushrooms, grubs, and snails made good snacks for lucky cotton, coca, and pepper pickers.

Aside from epidemic disease and human "macro-parasites," the most significant ecological consequences of European invasion came with animals, large and small. Native north Andeans had few domestic ones, a possible clue to their apparent good health prior to the arrival of Europeans. The llama and alpaca were rare in contrast to Peru, but small household dogs and Guinea pigs (the Quechua *cuy*) are still ubiquitous

Cuyes, or guinea pigs, Imbabura Province, Ecuador

well into Colombia. Unlike their hapless counterparts in Mexico, Quito's native dogs appear to have been spared the stew pot, and cuy were more a source of fertilizer than food (eaten only on ritual occasions). Meat in fact appears to have been something of a luxury associated, like the control of maize—and, far more importantly, maize beer—with chiefly status.

Still, even commoners desiring animal protein or temporarily fallen on hard times could count on an abundance of game in the region's omnipresent hills and wooded ravines. Deer and rabbits were frequently caught grazing in the foggy *páramo,* the vast, grassy moorlands typical above c. 3,300 meters. By 1599 this fragile ecological zone would be wholly transformed by Spanish-introduced sheep, horses, and cattle; dryer valleys like the Guayllabamba would be denuded by goats. Their scrawny descendants may still be seen searching out scarce leaves at canyon's edge today.[5] Less frequently seen among wild animals though presumably more abundant than today were the shy and corpulent wooly mountain tapir, or

Creole cattle and sheep grazing below Chimborazo

danta, the magnificent spectacled bear, and the majestic Andean condor. Among the highland *runa,* or Quechua-speaking majority of Ecuador and southernmost Colombia, all three came to be endowed with mythical properties, powerful agents in human affairs alongside capricious rainbows and the leprechaunlike *chuzalungu.*

Social Formations

At one time ancient Americans must have hunted tapirs, bears, and other animals in the north Andes, but they left scant trace. "Otavalo Man" (only a skull remains) was once thought to be some thirty thousand years old, touted as evidence in the most extreme case of an independent South American human evolution. Recent analysis shows the ancient Otavalan to have been decidedly "post-Clovis," in fact a maize eater from about the middle of Peru's Chavín Horizon (c. 500 B.C.E.).[6] Maize agriculture dates back some three millennia in the equatorial highlands, but archaeological evidence points to older and more interesting developments along the coast.

This cradle of Ecuadorian civilization follows a strip of land trending northwestward from modern El Oro to Esmeraldas Province centered on Guayas and Manabí.[7] Here sedentary life apparently grew not so much from agriculture as from exploitation of abundant marine resources. One of the Americas' most ancient ceramic traditions (c. 3000 B.C.E.), named for the coastal hamlet of Valdivia, is characterized by playful, elaborately coiffured female figurines of amulet size.

Almost two thousand years after Valdivia, coinciding roughly with the late Olmec culture of isthmian Mexico, began the period of greatest florescence among Ecuador and southwest Colombia's coastal chiefdoms. Sometimes called the "Regional Developmental" period (c. 500 B.C.E.–500 C.E.), this was the age of the La Tolita–Tumaco goldsmiths, makers of the fabulous "antique" jewelry worn by Don Francisco de Arobe and his sons.

The more extensive Jama-Coaque, Guangala, and Jambelí culture areas to the south are somewhat better known than La Tolita. Still, given the poor rate of organic preservation on the wet coast and continued plunder of sites little is known of these apparent chiefdoms save what can be surmised from their evocative and occasionally frightening terra cotta figurines. We do know that highly efficient raised-field agriculture covered fifty thousand hectares in the Daule and Guayas river basins by the first century of the common era, strong evidence of dense populations and political sophistication.

An enduring enigma regarding coastal societies like La Tolita–Tumaco is the extent of their overseas trade networks. Stylistic connections have been made between the ceramic traditions of coastal Ecuador and some western Mesoamerican ones (shaft-tombs and other traits were also shared), and much unequivocal evidence of trade with coastal Peru has been found. As noted above, raft wood was readily available on Ecuador's coast, and native *Spondylus* and other shells, both whole and in bead form, were in high demand abroad. Peruvian imports included copper implements and so-called axe money, but what goods Mesoamericans might have exchanged with early Ecuadorians (besides maize cobs) remains unclear.

Remnants of the vanished religions and ideologies of war and trade that permeated these coastal cultures may survive in the folklore of the modern Tsáchela, Chachi, and Awa-Kwaiker peoples of the Pacific piedmont.[8]

It was only in the millennium or so preceding the arrival of the Spanish (c. 500–1500 C.E.) that highland groups chose to organize into discrete political-cultural units, in size and extent of influence resembling somewhat the chiefdoms of the earlier coast. Meanwhile, political consolidation and generalized population growth seem to have taken place on the long-exploited but still fertile plains of Guayas and Manabí. Shaft-tombs became more common in this era both on the coast and in the northern highlands, particularly in the modern Province of Carchi, Ecuador, and Nariño Department, Colombia. Most of what is known of the so-called Carchi chiefdoms has been reconstructed from excavations of a few pristine tombs. Human sacrifice was practiced to the extent that retainers and select wives appear to have been asked or forced to accompany their lords in the journey to the hereafter.

As for equatorial Upper Amazonia, still thickly forested and less studied by archeologists than the coast, after c. 1000 C.E. ceramic and other evidence, including numerous mounds and platforms, suggest complex human settlement along the upper Napo and Upano rivers. This is only a beginning. In general, archaeologists and geographers have recently argued for more densely populated and politically complex pre-Columbian Amazonian settlements than previously believed possible. Many also argue that particularly in the pre-Inka age the Andes themselves were not the barrier to communication and trade that has long been assumed. In short, highlanders and lowlanders were numerous and they knew each others' worlds, sometimes intimately.[9]

To oversimplify: prior to Inka conquest in the late fifteenth century highlanders in what would become the core of the Audiencia, or colonial "Kingdom," of Quito were apparently made up of the following cultural-linguistic groups, north to south: Pasto, Otavalo-Caranqui, Cayambe, Panzaleo, Puruhá, Cañar, Palta, and Chacha. It is not clear whether Quechua, the language of the Inkas, preceded or followed conquest, but local tongues were still in use when the Spanish arrived in the 1530s. North of Pasto, in what would become the vast and unruly Quito sub-

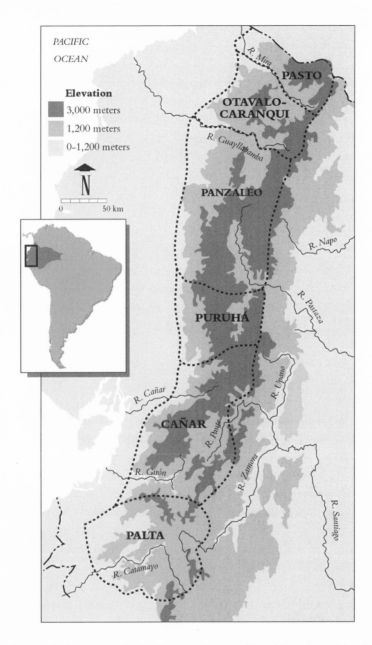

Distribution of ethnic groups in the Sierra on the eve of Spanish conquest. Map drawn from Carol Cooperrider, from Linda Newson, *Life and Death in Early Colonial Ecuador,* (Norman: University of Oklahoma Press, 1995), courtesy of Linda Newson and the University of Oklahoma Press.

district of Popayán, the dozens of indigenous groups never reduced to Inka rule (and barely to Spanish) included the Abad, Quillasinga, Mocoa, Chapanchica, Barbacoas, "Pubense," Páez, Guambiano, and Pijao. Linguistically, some appear to have been isolates, others possible members of an ethnic grab bag called macro-Chibchan.[10] Popayán's pre-Columbian history is in general less known than that of central Quito, but recent archaeological work in the upper Cauca Valley records maize-based chiefdoms near Cali by the second century B.C.E.[11]

Inkas and Spaniards

It was not the descendants of these "proto-Colombians" but rather the Cañaris of the southern Ecuadorian highlands who staved off Inka penetration until shortly before Spanish arrival. Somewhat paradoxically, however, the Cañaris would end up supplying warriors to both Inka and Spanish armies; in 1572, for example, it was a Cañari executioner who rather proudly beheaded the captured rebel Inka Túpac Amaru in Cuzco's central square on the viceroy's order, and a Cañari community appears to have maintained a distinct identity in Cuzco's Barrio Santa Ana throughout colonial times.[12]

Less fortunate were the more southerly Paltas (in Quechua literally "avocados") of Loja and environs. After fierce resistance, their bloody defeat at Inka hands led to a spiraling demographic collapse that only continued under Spanish rule. Their culturally related neighbors, the so-called lowland Jivaroan peoples of the eastern Andean piedmont, remained fiercely independent; after a few harsh lessons in guerrilla warfare the Inkas left them alone. The still more southern Chachas, of Chachapoyas (modern Amazonas Department, Peru), resisted then served Inkas and Spaniards after the manner of the Cañaris. Hints of their pre-Columbian splendor are only now coming to light.[13]

The numerous Puruhá of the high and chilly basins surrounding the extinct volcano Chimborazo (6,310 m), Ecuador's highest and most heavily glaciated peak, appear to have survived the Inka invasion with less dramatic effects. Rather like them were the Panzaleo of the Latacunga and Quito-area basins, nearer the equator. The Panzaleos were said to trace their origins to the five-thousand-meter-high Tungurahua Volcano, which towers over and threatens the modern town of Baños, although its northern neighbor, Cotopaxi (5,897 m), is physically more imposing and historically more destructive.

In traveling between Quito and Latacunga the Panzaleo also paid homage to the volcanically extinct but still very much "alive" Ilinizas, twin peaks over five thousand meters at the edge of the Pacific escarpment to the west. East of the rich Chillos Valley, adjacent to the higher Quito terrace, loomed yet another jagged snowcap, Antisana (5,758 m); its flanks are now among the last Ecuadorian refuges of the Andean condor. Although all these mountains were of deep religious significance to both aboriginal and Inka Quiteños, no evidence of high-altitude human sacrifice comparable to that found in the central and southern Andes has yet been discovered.[14]

Among the Cayambes and Otavalo-Caranquis living north of Quito in the shadow of the extinct Cayambe (5,790 m) and lesser peaks the Inka war machine sputtered, southern invaders quickly becoming embroiled in chiefly feuds followed by open rebellions. Partly as a result of these difficulties, the conquest of the nearby Pastos, not so renowned for their violence, was never completed. Although modern Ecuadorians are generally fond of their nation's association with the former Inka empire and Quito's second city status within it, it is important to remember that it was probably only in the 1460s that Tupa Inka Yupanki (Sapa, or "True" Inka, 1471–93) arrived, and only under his successor, Wayna Kapak (1493–1525), that the northern highlands up to Pasto were subdued—about the time of Columbus's famous voyages. Fierce resistance from the Caranquis and Cayambes ended with a great massacre of rebels at what became known as Yaguarcocha (Quechua "lake of blood"), near modern Ibarra, shortly before the Spanish invasion.[15]

Inka control of the Ecuadorian coast and Amazonian lowlands was minimal, and highland consolidation only partially achieved through population shuffling (the so-called *mitmaq* colonies) and rotational labor requirements *(mit'a,* later hispanicized as *mita).*[16] Traditional Inka *anan/urin,* or upper/lower moiety divisions were rarely applied beyond Quito itself and the Cañar district, and decimal population divisions uncommon north of Tumibamba (modern Cuenca). Significantly, examples of Inka stonemasonry in Ecuador are limited, and virtually

Inka ruins of Ingapirca, Cañar Province, Ecuador

absent in the city of Quito. With Wayna Kapak's death about 1527, apparently from smallpox inadvertently introduced overland from the Caribbean, the governorship of Quito was disputed by his sons, the half-brothers Atawallpa and Waskar. The resulting civil war was won by the native Quiteño Atawallpa, but the still-festering conflict left both empire and victorious Inka dangerously vulnerable when a well-armed and gold-hungry band of Spanish adventurers reached Cajamarca in 1532.

Meanwhile, to the north of Pasto lived numerous, scattered, and reputedly bellicose and even cannibalistic groups of great cultural and linguistic diversity. Almost all were distinguished for their fine goldwork, a lure for European conquistadors already making their way inland from the Caribbean and Venezuela. It was here in the rugged interior of "New Granada," as the Spanish came to call it, that the legend of El Dorado was formed. The regional colonial capital of Popayán, located at a comfortable

altitude almost a thousand meters below that of Quito in the shadow of
Puracé Volcano (4,646 m), was said to have been named for a local
"Pubense" cacique (a moniker derived from Pubén, an earlier lord and
possibly the true indigenous site name for Popayán). A kind of
confederation of chiefdoms may have obtained in the region in late pre-
Columbian times, but no evidence of a dominant state has emerged.

Southward from Popayán flowed the great Patía River, carving a
massive gorge between the western and central Andean cordilleras before
emptying into the Pacific Ocean near modern Tumaco. Northward from
Popayán flowed the mighty Cauca, meandering almost a thousand
kilometers before joining the Magdalena and emptying into the Caribbean
Sea northeast of Cartagena. On either side of the Central Cordillera, in the
shadow of the heavily glaciated Nevado de Huila (5,750 m) and other
peaks, lived the Páez and Pijao, bellicose mountaineers subjected to Spanish
rule only around the turn of the seventeenth century. In general, greater
Popayán's pre-Columbian ethnic diversity, difficult terrain, generalized
political fission, and near-universal wealth in gold set Spanish-indigenous
relations on a crash course. Up to and beyond 1599 they would resemble
the chronic, open violence of the Chilean and north Mexican frontiers
more than the accommodationist colonial regime of highland Quito.

Onto this already crowded north Andean stage circa 1532 came
rumbling and sometimes stumbling hoards of European men, some of the
wealthier among them accompanied by African captives who served as
squires and auxiliaries. A few brought wives and mistresses. The newcomers
also introduced horses, cattle, sheep, wheat, grapes, citrus fruits, smallpox,
measles, and a rather belligerent or at least uncompromising sect of
Christianity to the land. Often against the will of their masters, Africans
also brought many things, among them myriad languages and gendered
political concepts, traditional poetics and methods of recounting the past,
medical and mechanical skills, musical forms, spiritual beliefs, and in some
cases Islam.

The Spanish conquest of the northern highlands, including not only
Inka-dominated Tumibamba and Quito but also Pasto, Popayán, and Cali,
was led by a captain of Francisco Pizarro named Sebastián de Benalcázar
(spelled Belalcázar in Colombia). His most able opponent was the Inka
general Rumiñavi (literally "Stone-face"), and in fact the greatest pitched

Statue of Sebastián de Benalcázar, Quito

battle of the conquest of greater Peru took place in Puruhá country not far from Mount Chimborazo. Rumiñavi was eventually captured, tortured for information regarding a rumored treasure hoard, and executed. (As at Cajamarca, captivity and gold already seemed natural bedfellows.)

The Inka city of Quito was occupied by the Spanish and renamed in honor of St. Francis on 28 August 1534. This is not the place to recite the details of conquest and its aftermath, but it should be kept in mind that for the next three centuries Quito would remain a colony. That is, *for almost twice as long as Ecuador and Colombia have been independent nations, Quito was a colony.*[17]

Most of what came to be called the Kingdom of Quito on late sixteenth-century European maps was claimed by Spain, but in demographic terms the greater part of this vast territory remained indigenous, in some places politically so. Some enclaves, like Guayaquil and many Popayán mining camps, were fast becoming de facto colonies of western Africa. Meanwhile, at the colony's relatively isolated core a surprisingly small number of Europeans, strictly speaking, was charged with containing the universal impulse against subjection (which extended, by the way, to fellow Europeans). This loyalist cadre, formalized as the high court, or *audiencia,* of Quito in 1563, would try to manage various forms of discontent at both center and margins by astutely mixing cajolery, rewards, concessions, and rare but startling acts of state terrorism. As will be seen, the king's servants did not always win, and like all government, ruling Quito, though not quite a gamble, was always an unpredictable game of give and take.

Certainly for greater Quito's native peoples the greatest shock had occurred within a decade of conquest, and that shock took some time to wear off. This was particularly true here given Quito's role in the 1540s Peruvian Civil War and the early conquistadors' numerous and deadly adventures in Amazonia. Nevertheless, the future of the colony had not been fully decided in its heady first years. Nor perhaps would it be settled in these. What is noteworthy is that around 1599 Quiteños of both sexes and all classes and colors seem to have discerned clearly for the first time the full ambiguity of their situation. That is, they now recognized both the potential for gain within and limits of control of the Habsburg colonial system. Now relatively mature, if still groping, that system—that cluster of competing church, state, and local bureaucracies and interests—was understood to be both parasite and host; in short, colonialism had shifted from pillage to symbiosis and negotiation. An example of the potentially strange fruit of this transition is the subject of Sánchez Gallque's 1599 painting.

What follows are six chapters exploring various and related topics intended to highlight the ambiguities and uncertainties of Quito circa 1599. The story begins with a shipwreck in the coastal Province of Esmeraldas, home of the Arobe ambassadors pictured on the cover. The fragmentary but true tale behind the portrait offers a rare window on Quito's evolving relationship with a sector of its cartographic edge. Chapter 2 moves to the highlands to discuss African slavery, first in the context of the capital city, then in the marginal gold mines. Embedded in this discussion are what I believe to be necessary reflections on contemporary attitudes regarding human captivity and its relationship to "sin." Chapter 3 opens up to treat the vast and dynamic urban and agrarian indigenous sectors of Quito's central highlands, emphasizing strategies of adaptation to colonial rule and ending with a summary of recent demographic findings.

Chapter 4 returns to the gold mines, north and south, to discuss their inner workings and overall productivity, but also explores a conflict of cultures at Quito's southeast periphery as startling and revealing as that of contemporary Esmeraldas. Here in a corner of upper Amazonia indigenous peoples of Jivaroan ethnicity defeated and drove out Spanish and mixed-heritage gold-seekers some time around 1599. In part the case begs examination because a people the Spanish called "Jívaros" were said to have risen up in this year (the second inspiration for this book after the Sánchez Gallque painting). As will be seen, however, a more important feature was outcome: the Spanish never again gained a foothold in the region and lowland Jivaroans of several "tribes" remain unconquered today. The case serves as a stark reminder that Spanish conquest was by no means inevitable, even when substantial gold deposits were at stake.

Chapter 5 returns to the highland capital to explore Quito as a gold-fueled marketplace at the turn of the seventeenth century, a city whose dizzyingly diverse material culture betrayed an infectious bonanza mentality. Rapidly shifting patterns of trade and production for foreign exchange are also discussed, a reminder that secondary colonies had to be quite flexible economically in order to remain competitive. Finally, chapter 6 returns to the coastal fringe to revisit the district's resilient martial, or neo-conquest, political economy by way of Quito's soldiers' encounters with pirates and still more bellicose native peoples. As always, Quito, despite its notable glamour, fecundity, and dynamism, was on the defensive, in many ways at war with itself.

These six chapters are not arranged in order of importance, but rather are intended to form a series of narrative journeys or arcs from margins to center and back again. Chapter 1 takes the reader from the Pacific coast to the Quito highlands and also introduces the core themes of human captivity and gold-lust. In the highland interior of chapter 2 these themes are cast into sharper relief in discussing the lives and struggles of African slaves and their descendants—those living at Quito's social and demographic margins, as it were—in both urban and nearby gold-mining contexts. Chapter 3 readjusts the aperture to treat Quito's highland indigenous majority, or demographic core, emphasizing its members' extraordinary diversity, mobility, adaptability, and general wile vis-à-vis Spanish institutions and individuals. Chapter 4 returns to the far reaches, in this case the jungles of upper Amazonia, to highlight a specific indigenous-Spanish encounter. Returning to the city, chapter 5 links the mines of the margins to a dynamic cluster of social and economic sectors at the core. Finally, chapter 6 returns to the Pacific coast to examine Quito's troubles with pirates, socially marginal soldiers, and cannibals.

A LETTER FROM THE KING

President and Judges of my Royal Audiencia of the city of San Francisco de Quito: That city has written me of the good effects that have resulted from the pacification and resettlement of the mulattos [sic] and warlike Indians of the Province of Esmeraldas carried out by Dr. Juan del Barrio de Sepúlveda and that part of it which served Our Lord, [namely] the souls that have been reduced and converted to our Holy Catholic Faith, and the great importance of continuing that discovery, pacification, and [congregated] resettlement for the security of that coast and reception of my subjects' ships that put in there, and so that the fruit of the mines of gold located in that land be enjoyed; and [recognizing] the importance of opening a road from those settlements to the said coast, which could easily be accomplished, and with which commerce and trade would grow; and one could take port there and disembark and go by land to that city [Quito]; and because I desire that that pacification and population begun by Dr. Juan del Barrio de Sepúlveda be finished, I command that you carry out the instructions I have given you, so that the Indians of that province be reduced and made to come to truly know our Evangelical Law, and to enjoy the benefits that their pacification and resettlement would bring; and whatever you do, advise me.

I the King [Philip III]
Valladolid, 17 November 1602.

In Jorge Garcés, ed., *Colección de Cédulas Reales dirigidas a la Audiencia de Quito, 1601–1660* (Quito: Archivo Histórico Municipal, 1946), 32–33.

ONE: Castaways

On 19 December 1599 a ship called *San Felipe and Santiago* left Panama's island port of Perico for Callao. On board were some eighty Spaniards of all ages and both sexes, passengers on their way to join relatives, carry barrels and bundles of merchandise to wholesalers, or take up new posts in Lima and beyond. Also aboard were about a hundred African slaves: women, children, and men on their way to permanent drudgery in Peru's many and scattered cane fields, vineyards, mines, convents, and elite households. Beyond these 180 "souls" the *San Felipe and Santiago* carried almost a million-and-a-half pesos' worth of merchandise, mostly European in origin, but no doubt including substantial East Asian goods: contraband spices, silks, porcelain, and such like. The voyage south was smooth and uneventful until, a few hours before dawn on the Day of Kings, 6 January 1600, the vessel suddenly ran aground, stuck fast off Mangrove Point, very near the border separating the "untamed" provinces of Barbacoas and Esmeraldas on the lowland Pacific fringe of the Audiencia of Quito.[1]

Working quickly in the darkness, the crew evacuated the passengers, both captive and free, filling the ship's boat and rowing to the nearby coast, saving—miraculously—everyone. Attempts to return to the listing vessel were repulsed, however, by darkness and heavy surf. Such a return would have been ill-advised anyway; at daybreak the crew watched the sea cleanly split the *San Felipe and Santiago* in half, the prow sinking and the stern breaking free to float almost ashore, "two or three [harquebus] shots" from where it foundered. Meanwhile all the provisions and the million-and-a-half pesos' worth of merchandise freed from the hold bobbed and twisted momentarily in the swirling sea before floating far away from the luckless castaways, carried off by a powerful current. Perhaps El Niño was to blame.

The survivors preferred to lay the mantle of guilt on the pilot, however, citing his carelessness or inexperience. But there were not to be many survivors in the end. The pilot did know, or rather believed, that they had landed in "an unknown land, inhabited by wild Indians who eat human flesh," and a decision was made, based on his advice, to begin marching southward along the beach toward Portoviejo. He apparently did not realize this Spanish settlement lay more than five hundred kilometers to the south, no easy trek even in the best of circumstances. The bedraggled hoard marched for a week until a stevedore, apparently angered by the inevitable flood of new and irritating demands, decided one night to burn the ship's boat. This done, the 180 castaways found themselves unable to cross the numerous rivers and broad estuaries that lined the coast, and an advance party of nineteen men, both enslaved and free, led by the ship's master, Alonso Sánchez de Cuellar, set off for Portoviejo on a pair of crude rafts. The remaining castaways would suffer thirst, then hunger, and finally fevers, slowly perishing over the course of the next several months.

The rafts were kept out of open ocean for fear of the swift currents that had carried away the merchandise, and Sánchez de Cuellar and his followers spent most of the next several weeks making their way on foot southward toward the beaches of Atacames, just beyond the mouth of the Esmeraldas, Pizarro's legendary River of Emeralds. One day there appeared offshore a raft manned by a small number of Amerindians, perhaps fishermen. Uncertain yet hopeful, the castaways fashioned a white flag and waved it as a sign of peace, but the men turned around and paddled hastily up a nearby river, most likely the Atacames. Not long afterward they returned, however, claiming to be subjects of a Captain don Alonso Sebastián de Yllescas, "mulatto" chieftain of that district; they had gone to warn him of the presence of strangers in his territory. At their head was

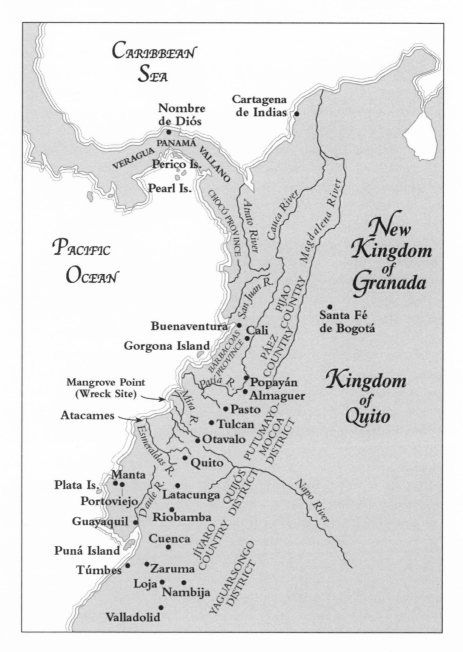

The Kingdom of Quito and the wreck site of the *San Felipe & Santiago*. Map drawn by Carol Cooperrider.

Yllescas's son, don Juan, and he carefully inquired what people these were, and what their intentions. On finding Sánchez de Cuellar and his starving followers to be Spanish subjects cast upon these shores by an accident of nature, assurances of friendship and refreshment flowed more freely.

The next day the elder Yllescas himself appeared in a canoe carrying food and supplies, offering to help the unfortunates along. Seeing their great need he promised to return with yet more victuals in four days. Four days passed, and true to his word the Afro-American chieftain returned to the ample beach of Atacames with two canoes and three rafts spilling over with plantains, fish, fruit, and meat. Yllescas gave generously, asking only for a few knives and metal objects the crew members had managed to retain. After eight days of eating and idling on the beach, these, clearly the luckiest of the castaways of the *San Felipe and Santiago,* decided to follow another ill-informed mariner among them who claimed that Portoviejo lay just around the bend (they had in fact gone far less than halfway, and would have been wise to ask their hosts' opinion). Yllescas appeared saddened by the castaways' decision to leave without his aid, but he bade them farewell and offered the same hospitality if they were forced back, advising them to watch out for certain "mulatto runaways" inhabiting the forests to the south.

As Yllescas no doubt predicted, Sánchez de Cuellar and his company did not get far. Seven days marching exhausted their food supplies and landed them at the foot of a formidable escarpment lapped by crashing waves; they decided to take don Alonso's advice. He had told them of a route connecting Esmeraldas to the highland capital of Quito, and after a second and no doubt embarrassing meeting at Atacames he sent them with food and three Amerindian escorts northward on a raft to the village of his "brother-in-law," don Francisco de Arobe, "mulatto" lord of San Mateo Bay.

Here at the edge of a seemingly impenetrable rain forest they met the first Spaniard they had seen since the shipwreck, a Mercedarian friar who called himself Juan Bautista de Burgos. One can only imagine their conversation. Don Francisco eventually invited the men to dine with him at his own house some days later, after they had refreshed themselves and properly demonstrated the innocence of their intrusion.

Sánchez de Cuellar later described Arobe's house and surrounding buildings as well hidden, located some six leagues upriver from the ocean, strategically tucked into a tiny valley surrounded on all sides by steep hills. Apparently having lost all memory of their 160-odd companions, languishing as they must have been so incredibly nearby (no more than two days downriver by canoe!), Sánchez de Cuellar and his party spent yet another *twenty days* feasting and "idling" among the Afro-indigenous villages of Esmeraldas. It was almost as if they did not care to move on.

At last they set off, making their way up steep creekbeds and along knife-edged ridges into the cloud forest and páramo flanking the great Pichincha Volcano, sentinel and sometimes scourge of Quito. Don Francisco had revealed to his rescued companions several royal proclamations from the city's high court, or audiencia, describing a recently established peace between the Afro-Esmeraldeños and their highland neighbors. Among the provisions was the promise of safe passage to Spanish shipwreck victims who might happen upon that coast.

What luck! What great timing! As per royal edict don Francisco de Arobe and Padre Burgos accompanied the survivors to Quito, and even marched ahead to have extra supplies dispatched by their friend in the audiencia, Dr. Juan del Barrio de Sepúlveda. The previous year, 1599, Dr. Barrio had commissioned an indigenous Quito artist named Andrés Sánchez Gallque to paint a portrait of Francisco de Arobe and his two sons, Pedro and Domingo. The painting was sent as a coronation gift to Philip III, a memento of peace and of the supposed aperture of Esmeraldas Province.[2]

✣   ✣   ✣

In a tour de force of historical detective work, Adam Szászdi in 1986 pieced together a chronological sketch of Esmeraldas up to the time of the 1599 painting. His reconstruction and various primary documents from Seville's Archive of the Indies and Ecuador's National History Archive in Quito form the backbone of the following narrative.[3] Apparently the two "mulatto" clans that hosted Sánchez de Cuellar and his men had been in the region for some time, victims (or descendants of victims) of similar shipwrecks.

Alonso Sebastián de Yllescas was the son of Alonso de Yllescas, a native Cape Verdean who had grown up in Seville. Yllescas (after a town

Don Domingo Arobe, by Sánchez Gallque

near Toledo) was the surname of one of the wealthiest merchant families in that great commercial entrepôt on the Guadalquivir, and the slave baptized Alonso was on his way to the household of a Lima factor when his ship was caught in contrary winds and currents near Atacames. The exhausted crew eventually dropped anchor and went ashore with a number of slaves, seventeen men and six women, to search for food. Shortly thereafter a brisk wind kicked up, driving the poorly anchored vessel onto a reef. Like others who came later, crew and passengers set off down the beach for Portoviejo.[4]

Meanwhile Yllescas and several other African castaways made off into the bush, "without the slightest intention of returning to servitude," where they somehow managed to ally with local indigenous peoples, particularly of the Nigua group—and soon the Cape Verdean baptized Alonso was recognized head of an independent chiefdom. This shipwreck seems to have occurred around 1553, but it was not the first case of its kind.

About 1545 another Lima-bound ship had become stranded on the same stretch of coast, perhaps closer this time to Mangrove Point than Atacames, and surviving slaves made a similar dash to freedom. Among them was the African Andrés Mangache and his Nicaraguan female companion (enslaved in the Spanish conquest of her Central American homeland). There, near San Mateo Bay, they raised two sons, Juan and Francisco. Francisco took the name Arobe, and it is he, an Afro-Amerindian, not a mulatto, who commands the center of Sánchez Gallque's great painting.

Alonso de Yllescas also had children by an indigenous woman, apparently daughter of a Nigua cacique, and the two "neo-tribes," the Yllescases and Mangache-Arobes, joined in the struggle for domination of local waterways, fisheries, and arable flats. Having passed some fourteen years as a captive laborer in Seville, Yllescas was quite familiar with Spanish ways and seems to have been consistently more suspicious than the Mangache-Arobe clan when faced with military or missionary challenges.[5]

Some time around 1570 Yllescas was joined in his independent resolve by a defector of European ancestry named Gonzalo de Ávila, a famed swimmer and harquebusier born on Tenerife, in the Canary Islands. One chronicler who happened to have met him said Ávila had spent time as a youth among mixed-heritage slave-trade middlemen, or *tangomãos*, near Cape Verde, and had there enjoyed "the infamous vice and liberty of Guinea."[6] Subsequent experiences among Spaniards in Hispaniola, Panama, and Peru seem to have left him disillusioned in any case, and Ávila confirmed his change of loyalties by marrying Yllescas's Afro-indigenous daughter, María.

Numerous challenges to the castaways' freedom would come from coast and highlands in the years leading up to 1599, most of them privately organized military expeditions, variously called *jornadas* and *entradas*. As early as 1550, men like Benito Hernández of Portoviejo petitioned for rights to conquer the Esmeraldas maroons and their allies. A sixteen-year Indies veteran, Hernández offered his monarch, then Holy Roman Emperor Charles V, one-third of all wealth recovered, including gold, slaves, and emeralds.[7]

Other failed entradas took place in the mid-1570s under the direction of Andrés Contero (from whose company Gonzalo de Ávila had

The Torre de Oro, or "Tower of Gold," on the Guadalquivir River, Seville

deserted). Contero and many followers did not live to tell the tale.[8] In the same years, however, a Mercedarian friar named Miguel de Cabello Balboa, native of the Andalusian town of Archidona, managed to reach the maroons from Quito, gospel in hand. Cabello Balboa would go on to write a partly imagined (and only recently resurrected) history of the Inkas—"The Antarctic Miscellany"—but the real, firsthand drama of his first meeting with Alonso de Yllescas is revealed in this excerpt from a 1578 letter to the king:

> I left this city of Quito carrying ornaments, a bell, images and altar
> vestments and a supply of food, clothing, and presents to give to the
> blacks, mulattos, and natives of the same province [of Esmeraldas]
> and Sunday, fifteenth of the month of September of the said year
> [1577] the ship outfitted for this proposition put in at the bay and

river they call Tacames, having been informed that there these
people tend to congregate with greatest frequency, and having
touched land the ship departed, leaving me and my three
companions on those unknown beaches, where we passed many days
without encountering or seeing any trace or signal of habitation or
the passing of any person through that land; and God was served that
after much waiting we were sensed by the natives and they gave
notice of us to the blacks, who then came to us from a river below
in a great canoe and three rafts filled with many Indians outfitted for
war and we, viewing this most fearsome spectacle, were greatly
frightened by our risky and dangerous situation, and arriving close
to us the black man who was captain of the rest, called Alonso de
Yllescas, raised in Seville, began to question us, asking what we
wanted or what we were looking for in his land, and I, explaining
the aim of our journey, assured him and persuaded him to step onto
the land, to be more completely informed, [telling him] that I was
priest and vicar of all that land and one of my companions deacon
and the other two peaceful men; and being satisfied with this, and
that there were no more than the four of us present the canoe was
beached along with the other rafts and he came to me with signs of
love and veneration, asking me to extend my hands and one by one
the said Alonso de Yllescas and the Portuguese [*sic*], his son-in-law,
named Gonzalo de Ávila, and all the rest of the mulattos one by one
went embracing my three companions; [and] taking them by the
hand we took them to pray in a small chapel which we ourselves
had constructed, afterwards taking them to our small *rancho,* which
likewise we had made with our own hands, we read to them and
declared to them the provisions and sureties which for their relief we
carried, all which was well received by them with signs and
impressions of much happiness, [and it was] accepted and agreed that
we would live with the necessary order, joining together; and having
approved of this they left us, promising to join us there on the beach
where I was with my companions, to then go together to the Bay of
San Mateo to populate [i.e., form a Spanish-style town] . . .[9]

Alonso de Yllescas must have known from his years in Seville that the surest way to a cleric's heart was an offering of gold, and in addition to the promise to voluntarily resettle with his people at a site amenable to the Mercedarian visitor, he and his son-in-law, Gonzalo de Ávila, donated almost one hundred pesos' worth of gold dust for the adornment of the new chapel. Needless to say, Cabello Balboa was noticeably encouraged by this spontaneous show of piety.

But the settlement was not to be. Perhaps Yllescas had seen a disturbing glimmer in the priest's eyes when the gold-dust-filled kerchief was opened on the altar; we will never know for sure. In any case, Alonso de Yllescas and his followers—and likewise the Mangache-Arobe clan, who had come to Atacames to mingle briefly with their sometime rivals—disappeared on their canoes and rafts after making these promises and offerings. A search for their village sites yielded nothing and Cabello Balboa, having no other source of sustenance than that provided by his future congregation, was forced to return to Quito. A 1578 attempt to reestablish contact via the Yumbo territory of the upper Guayllabamba River, a major tributary of the Esmeraldas flowing down from Quito, was stopped short when indigenous guides found themselves in the middle of the maroons' boar-hunting grounds. The escorts froze, thinking they would be ambushed at any moment and enslaved or killed. One porter who had only recently escaped from such captivity was so worried by this prospect that after fashioning a new canoe oar used to beat a hasty retreat he buried the woodshavings.[10]

Cabello Balboa, who would later write a fabulous *relación* of his failed Esmeraldas mission (in hopes of finding sponsors to support his return), had learned to respect Alonso de Yllescas. Indeed, the odd mix of awe and disgust for this maroon leader that emerges from the Mercedarian's writings was clearly more than a product of acute fear, or respect born of terror. It suggests instead more thoughtful reflection, perhaps on the value of freedom for one who had known slavery so intimately.

Yet true to his order's precepts, the Mercedarian friar ended his 1583 report by beseeching the current Peruvian viceroy, don Martín Enríquez, to expedite "the ransom of [these] bound souls, who, improperly baptized, are in the service of Satan, and your excellency, moved by a most Christian zeal, must sympathize with such an unjust captivity and consider the ransoming of those captive daughters of Zion."[11] For this Andalusian priest, freedom, or rather redemption, was defined by conversion to Christianity and concentrated resettlement, captivity—interestingly described in the feminine—by ignorance or rejection of both Faith and urban lifestyle.

Clearly the maroons had their own definitions of captivity and redemption, and time and again Alonso Yllescas—and later his son Sebastián—would demonstrate not only stubborn pride and confidence in having achieved physical and spiritual independence for themselves and their multiethnic families, but also a keen understanding of what "captivated" European intruders.

For the maroon chief successful resistance would require exploiting the chinks in character of every Spanish priest and soldier that came his way. To each he would apply a confusing blend of tactics: now prodigious generosity, now shrewd negotiation, here offers of future assistance, there hints of unexploited treasure, and constant promises of submission—always followed by an unexpected, unannounced retreat to the interior. As the events of the following decade would testify, Alonso de Yllescas seems to have preferred classic Renaissance dissimulation to the cruder and more risky practice of traditional guerrilla rebellion. Though shared with the Mangache-Arobe clan and several independent indigenous bands, the Province of Esmeraldas was unequivocally his.

Cabello Balboa found little support for another missionary expedition, and the Audiencia of Quito was distracted by other frontier challenges. A major revolt in the upper Amazonian settlements of Quijós Province, just east of Quito, along with the capture—off the unpatrolled coast south of Esmeraldas—of a Spanish bullion vessel by the English pirate Francis Drake, put "reduction" of the green province on hold once again. By 1583, however, a Spanish soldier with support from both Quito and Guayaquil began a series of audiencia-sanctioned expeditions to "punish the blacks" of Esmeraldas. In anticipation of total success, the ambitious captain, Diego López de Zúñiga, was grandly but prematurely named first governor of the Province of Emeralds. López de Zúñiga quickly proved himself no luckier than Andrés Contero and other predecessors, and by the time his fortune and health had jointly dissipated some ten years later, it was clear that Yllescas remained true governor.

The 1580s were marked by a struggle, often exaggerated by participants but always genuine, that pitted López de Zúñiga and his men against the interests of the church, now represented by a mysterious Trinitarian friar named Alonso de Espinosa. Immediately recognizing enemy disunity, Alonso de Yllescas and the other maroon bands of Esmeraldas stood ready to play yet another game of cat and mouse.

Late in 1583 López de Zúñiga entered an encampment near San Mateo Bay occupied by members of the Mangache-Arobe clan. There he found nine or ten thatch-roofed dwellings, a horse, some Castilian chickens, plantings of maize, manioc, beans, and plantains, and a half-dozen or so indigenous captives. Everyone else had evacuated. Eventually, a "very large" mulatto man who appeared to be the local chieftain contacted them and spoke through an interpreter (what language he spoke we do not know). He asked the soldiers, who were quite obviously armed and dangerous, how long they intended to stay. López de Zúñiga informed his looming interlocutor of his intentions to settle for at least ten years, with hopes of founding a town. The terse reply? "Not enough food."[12]

Following the tactic used by Yllescas, this unnamed maroon leader disappeared into the forest with his people. López de Zúñiga spent the next two months searching for traces of them in vain. Exhausted and ill with all manner of fevers, most of his men paddled upriver and climbed through the rugged mountains to Quito. The "governor," meanwhile, along with forty disillusioned volunteers, began to make his way south toward Portoviejo, hoping to catch sight of a promised relief vessel from Guayaquil. Near Atacames, apparently, the retreating soldiers were approached by maroon chieftains Francisco and Juan de Arobe (sons of Andrés Mangache and his Nicaraguan wife), who kindly offered much-needed assistance. Within days the vessel from Guayaquil arrived, but before their "rescue" the intruders had time to note that these "friendly" maroons commanded a substantial number of indigenous subjects, all of them casually adorned with gold pectorals, nose ornaments, earrings, lip plugs, and bracelets.

Using this last memory of Esmeraldas as a lure, López de Zúñiga was back in the green province with twenty-five recruits from Guayaquil in a few months. But this second entrada would end just as badly as the first. It seems the governor was moved to take a more confrontational tack this time, as evidenced by the (apparently intentional) drowning of a black man named Antón in a river near San Mateo Bay (possibly connected to the chieftain who had given them the slip previously). Later, López de Zúñiga would claim this man was a much-feared witch, or spell-caster, who had tyrannized the Mangaches, but other testimony suggested his was a peaceful maroon settlement the "governor" had ordered attacked by surprise, under cover of darkness. Calling "the black" Antón an *hechicero* was an obvious pretext for violence, and it only heightened maroon and indigenous suspicion of the pretentious Spanish governor.[13]

Violence, it turned out, was no more effective against these unpredictable opponents than diplomacy. Thorough reconnaissance yielded nothing until one day, apparently on a hill beside the Río Verde (flowing into the Pacific just north of the great river Esmeraldas), López de Zúñiga's men came upon a wooden cross. Closer inspection revealed an inscription reading: "Juan de Urquizo was here on the last of November of the year 1584, and whoever arrives here will find letters at the base of this cross." In the earth below the soldiers discovered a gourd, and in the gourd a letter addressed to their leader, Governor López de Zúñiga. It had been written by a friar named Alonso de Espinosa, and he claimed to have independently "reduced" the maroons to the service of God and crown.

Needless to say, this was a great blow to the title-holding governor, and in the coming years he would complain bitterly that this misplaced Trinitarian (the order had no house in the Americas) was undermining his mission. For his part, Alonso de Espinosa would just as consistently counter with vitriolic letters to the king condemning the greed and unscrupulous methods of López de Zúñiga and his men. Although we would much rather hear, for example, the opinions of Gonzalo de Ávila's Afro-Amerindian wife, we have only recovered thus far the (often shrill) voices of these Spanish intruders. In any case, it is clear that throughout the 1580s the Esmeraldas maroons and their subjects took advantage of both invading parties. By carefully maneuvering and generally avoiding confrontation they remained largely aloof, and almost entirely independent, for yet another decade.

Still, in the immediate term López de Zúñiga hoped Espinosa's efforts would serve as a spearhead for his own designs. After all, the priest, who had only recently come to Quito from Lima, had been sent to Esmeraldas

by the audiencia at the request of *the governor's own wife,* Mayor de
Bastidas; she had apparently assumed her husband needed some spiritual
guidance during his jungle sojourn. After finding the note beneath the
cross, López de Zúñiga and his men paddled upriver to meet the priest
and his supposedly "reduced" maroon companions. Peace offerings were
made on both sides, celebrated by the Spanish with harquebus shots to
heaven. But the true governor of Esmeraldas, Alonso de Yllescas, was not
present; he had cautiously chosen to stay home, promising to come to the
Mangache-Arobe encampment for a more formal meeting with the
visiting governor-by-title in two weeks.

Like their leader, López de Zúñiga's men were impatient, and they
resented being made to wait by an escaped slave-cum-rebel captain.
Furthermore, this was an armed entrada, and armed entradas were
supposed to yield two things: gold and tribute-paying subjects. With
peaceful submission threatening to eliminate the latter possibility, the
soldiers began dreaming of gold mines. While waiting for Alonso de
Yllescas to make his appearance, some maroons in the encampment
intimated that there existed some days' journey away a "river of gold."
This place was protected by enemy Indians, they were warned, but who
knew what riches might be unearthed? Before the two weeks were up,
the encampment dissolved. Most of López de Zúñiga's men were off to
find their fortunes. As Padre Espinosa put it:

> ten days passed and with only four remaining no one wanted to
> wait due to the greedy desire *(codicia)* to go in search of a river
> where they recover great sums of gold, the same which has been the
> cause of many losses and deaths of governors and captains, and when
> the said don Alonso de Yllescas arrived to comply with that which
> he had promised he found no one to receive the peace offer except
> some Indian women and children we had left there. Asking them
> where the governor and his camp had gone, they said: "to search out
> the river of gold." Embarrassed and insulted at the lack of respect
> they had shown him, being as he is the key to the land, being as it is
> under his hand and dominion; these have been the reasons why they
> [the Yllescas maroons] retracted the obedience they had previously
> offered Your Governor in the name of Your Majesty [and why] we

alone stayed on while the said governor and soldiers decided to
return, as they did, to this city of Quito by way of Portoviejo[.][14]

As Espinosa blamed the soldiers for their greed, the governor would later
claim that Yllescas's people had misled his own with false promises meant
to destroy them (the gold-seekers found only abandoned thatch dwellings
and swollen rivers, and a critical supply raft was upended in the process).[15]

They were probably both right. After all, the glimmer of gold had
stripped the veil of peaceful intentions away before, and if the maroons
were to retain any kind of autonomy in Esmeraldas they would have to
turn the region's legends of untold wealth to their own advantage. In
truth, Esmeraldas had no emeralds, but for one who understood the
Spaniards intimately, flashing gold pectorals could be used to draw the
enemy's gaze, only to blind him. But now the moment had arrived to
change course. Just as López de Zúñiga's second military mission
dissolved, Espinosa wrote up a peaceful offer of submission in exchange
for a measure of autonomy for don Alonso de Yllescas, his subjects, and
allies. The Cape-Verde-born neo-cacique was to be formally called
"governor" for the first time:

> The blacks and mulattos asked Your Majesty to grant them and
> concede to them a general pardon for all and sundry crimes
> committed against your Royal Crown as subjects and vassals and
> along with this a letter of liberty as much for them as for their
> children such that neither now nor ever shall they pay tribute and as
> for the Indians who come out in peace, they should be kept [from
> paying tribute] for ten years, as per your royal decrees and that Your
> Majesty concede to don Alonso de Yllescas—as I have said he holds
> the key to the province—the governorship over your subjects and
> vassals and natives of the said province and as such from now on he
> should be considered their master and if any other person should
> come against his liberty we ask that [neither he nor his people]
> should be imprisoned nor their goods sold nor transferred [to
> others] and having done this, Your Majesty shall be given the land
> calm and pacified.[16]

King Philip II, by Sánchez Coello

Quito's audiencia judges would perhaps have been wise to take Yllescas's offer seriously, but they did not. The historian Szászdi suggests the *oidores*, at the time led by the venal and senile Pedro Venegas de Cañaveral, were under the sway of a powerful merchant, Rodrigo de Ribadeneira, who sought to displace the vanquished López de Zúñiga as governor of Esmeraldas.[17] It was the summer of 1585 and papers were already being prepared in Madrid to back this claim. The audiencia thus received the Espinosa letter and six indigenous captives (said to have been held by the maroons for almost thirty years!) without ceremony. The redeemed were fed and clothed at the audiencia's expense, a copy of the letter dutifully forwarded to Spain to be filed. Meanwhile preparations were under way for a new military expedition to be led not by "Governor" Rodrigo de Ribadeneira, but rather his war-hardened brother, Captain Andrés Díaz de Ribadeneira, veteran of Chilean and numerous European conflicts. Little did this experienced warrior know he would simply join a growing list of world-weary soldiers who met their match in Esmeraldas.

And what of these soldiers? Who were they and what did they hope to gain? One whose story bears recounting was Martín Alonso de Merlo, a veteran of both failed López de Zúñiga entradas. Merlo wrote a letter to the Council of the Indies in 1587 requesting a vacated *encomienda,* hoping his failure to "punish" the Esmeraldeños would be offset by numerous earlier accomplishments. Like many of his companions, Merlo was an old Indies hand, in this case seasoned by participation in the chronic Amerindian wars of interior New Granada. Before this, and much more impressive, perhaps, was his claim of service in Old Granada, during the second Alpujarras Revolt of 1568–70. Apparently Merlo had served as ensign against the rebellious Moriscos, or forced converts of southern Spain, and he had marched under the banner of the Andalusian town of Antequera, his home. Merlo's moment of glory came in the 1570 siege of La Galera—a fortified desert town said to resemble the prow of a sea galley—located in the rugged Sierra de Castril foothills some 120 km northeast of the famed home of the Alhambra. Merlo had entered the fortress through a subterranean passage and captured five "Turks," whom he personally handed over to the expedition's leader (and King Philip's half-brother), don John of Austria.[18]

Many witnesses backed Merlo's claims of extraordinary service, in both Spain and the Americas, but it appears he never gained an encomienda in Quito for his troubles. How much more brilliant those memories of the subalpine Alpujarras hills must have been after two years spent vainly searching equatorial jungles for invisible enemies and golden rivers. To scramble through desert scree toward baldly visible ramparts and sworn enemies could hardly contrast more sharply with the endless trudging, sometimes leaderless, through armpit-deep estuaries, sweating and swatting mosquitoes, hacking through refractory mangroves, never certain even of the enemy's enmity, much less offensive strategy. The campaign against the Moriscos had been more than mildly challenging, to be sure, but Alonso Merlo learned harder lessons in Esmeraldas; this American battlefield was, literally and figuratively, a quagmire.

Another experienced soldier who foundered in Esmeraldas was Cristóbal de Castro, son of another old soldier, Captain Ramos González, former constable of the silver mines of Guadalcanal and Aracena (in the Sierra Morena just north of Seville). The young Castro escaped from the second López de Zúñiga expedition into Esmeraldas so ill he nearly died, yet, like Alonso de Merlo, this was not his first jungle tour; he had spent some eight months with his father and brother thrashing about in the Zamora lowlands, far to the southeast, hunting rebellious bands of Amerindians the Spanish called "Jívaros." The elder Ramos, like Merlo, was an Alpujarras veteran, but he had also fought against the "bellicose and valiant" Vallano maroons of Panama, an exercise more relevant to the task at hand. Taken together, these soldiers who went against the likes of Alonso de Yllescas and Francisco de Arobe were not amateurs or incompetents, but were rather apparently among the best the empire had to offer. Yet in spite of their deep and combined military experience, firsthand and otherwise, the Province of Esmeraldas remained indomitable.

Failed entradas could yield unintended gains for some outsiders, however, as befell Pedro Zama, a cacique's son from the small port of Manta, just west of Portoviejo. Zama, a famed diver and pilot, had steered the balsa raft sent by a local captain to rescue López de Zúñiga at San Mateo Bay in 1584. In compensation for this and other services, most conspicuously his single-handed rescue of a sinking galleon (also in 1584, near Manta), Zama asked for one thousand pesos and rights to work the nearby salt pans of Charapotó with twenty draft laborers. Since Manta was said to be a rather small town, with only about twenty Spanish house-holders and fifty working-age indigenous men, the Council of the Indies recommended instead the office of Indigenous Head Constable (Alguacil Mayor de los Naturales), and an annual rent of two hundred pesos.[19] Insulting as it might have been to men like López de Zúñiga, the often-repeated act of aiding Spaniards vanquished by the maroons of Esmeraldas had itself turned lucrative.

And there would be more chances to capitalize on failure. Rodrigo de Ribadeneira was granted capitulations for the conquest of Esmeraldas on 23 August 1585, and they included the rights to the title of governor of the province for three generations, a two-thousand-gold-peso annual stipend, and licenses to found three Spanish towns. All these perquisites would soon be lost, mostly due to the maroons' ability to continue exploiting divisions among their would-be spiritual and military conquerors, but also due to Ribadeneira's apparent lack of resolve. In any case, the wealth of Ribadeneira was never sufficient to offset the obstinacy of López de Zúñiga, which was itself more than matched by that of the friar Alonso de Espinosa, who would eventually be arrested and sent in chains to Spain.

Before diving into this thicket of conflicting testimonies, however, it should be noted that the Trinitarian did manage to extract another pledge of peace from Alonso de Yllescas and Juan Mangache-Arobe in February of 1586. Yllescas consented only on condition that the Ribadeneira entrada be suspended, and rejected an invitation to Quito to meet with the audiencia. Mangache, on the other hand, did make the trek to the capital, accompanied by twelve male and two female indigenous subjects, and on 14 April 1586 they ceremoniously rendered fealty, symbolized by a bow and quiver of arrows. The items were handed back to them with equal pomp, reluctant recognition of their continued, de facto autonomy.

Like López de Zúñiga, Rodrigo de Ribadeneira seems to have wanted to turn the missionary's apparent success into his own. It was he (in the guise of wealthy merchant-turned-benefactor) who hosted the Mangache ambassadors and lavished over seven thousand pesos' worth of gifts on them, including kettles, machetes, hatchets, scissors, knives, hats, and cotton cloth woven by recently reconquered Quijós tributaries. He also threw in a sword, shoes, and silk outfit for Juan Mangache.[20] Some items were also given to Espinosa for the adornment of his chapels, but the gifting and feasting came to an abrupt end a few days later. The friar suggested that he and the visitors ought to get back to Esmeraldas quickly; several of the indigenous escorts were falling ill.

López de Zúñiga, meanwhile, offered vigorous protests to the audiencia, claiming that any success with the Esmeraldeños should be credited to him, not the priest—but it was too late, he was now just another failed captain. Then trouble struck during the return journey. A soldier accompanying Alonso de Espinosa and the maroon ambassadors somehow died along the trail to the lowlands, apparently murdered. The circumstances of the death remain murky, but the event was used by both would-be governors and the audiencia to undermine the authority Espinosa had gained through his letters to the king and the Council of the Indies. (Szászdi goes so far as to describe the manipulation of testimony and forced recall of the Trinitarian friar "a case of Machiavellian defamation.")[21]

Whatever the truth, the conquest of Esmeraldas was no closer to being accomplished in 1587 than it had been in 1577; Ribadeneira's brother, Andrés Díaz, had arrived in May of 1587 at San Mateo Bay from Panama with forty-five soldiers only to find no evidence of the entrada they were to join, and worse, no evidence of the famed "mulattos and Indians" said to control this corner of King Philip's great backyard. What had happened?

The captain would eventually make his way to Quito to confront his brother, but it made no difference; yet another Esmeraldas campaign was dead on arrival. Rodrigo de Ribadeneira turned his attention back to commerce, and as will be seen in chapter 5, he did rather well, making a fortune in the new woolen textile trade. But just before his death in 1600 he would have trouble being properly recognized as a cavalier in spite of "gracious donations."[22] Like Alonso de Merlo and many others, Ribadeneira had taken active part in the defense of the Spanish Habsburg empire, including that most glorious of sixteenth-century victories, the 1557 defeat of the French at St. Quentin (near the modern Belgian border). But these were distant memories when compared with recent failures in Esmeraldas. There would be no easy titles here, no seigneuries for losers.

Meanwhile Padre Espinosa was captured along with Juan Mangache in the buffer province of Niguas, apparently with some trickery, by two soldiers sent from Quito, Juan Nieto de Torres and Pedro de Arévalo.[23] Mangache was soon released, but Espinosa, on his way to Spain under the apparently concocted charge of buggering native disciples, escaped, returning to Esmeraldas somehow from Panama dressed as a layman. Captured and jailed a second time, he was successfully deported to Spain, but, according to Szászdi, managed yet again to escape and return to Esmeraldas, where he died perhaps in the early 1590s. Like Gonzalo de Ávila and Miguel Cabello Balboa before him, this Spanish missionary seems to have fallen under the spell of life among the maroons of the green province. Something unnamed held him in thrall. But had Espinosa really formed "a confederacy and alliance with the said blacks and mulattos," as the soldier Pedro de Arévalo would later claim?[24]

It is difficult to say, but clear enough that the Yllescas and Mangache-Arobe clans remained aloof as ever and essentially independent for yet another decade, even as both chieftaincies passed on to the next generation. Esmeraldas came to everyone's attention once again with the capture of the Elizabethan corsair Richard Hawkins near Atacames in 1594. The capture of Hawkins and his three vessels was carried out by Spanish naval forces dispatched from Lima, with no help from the maroons.

Whose side were they on? No one knew for sure, but with the added risk of pirates an unsubjected coast seemed increasingly worrisome in a lightly armed colony like Quito. As will be seen in chapter 6, a 1587 skirmish with other corsairs on Guayaquil's Puná Island, though "victorious," had served as an acute reminder of the audiencia's vulnerability. There a "friendly" Amerindian cacique had been easily strong-armed and his house turned into an enemy base. Apparently there was genuine reason to worry about Esmeraldas, as well. According to Hawkins's later account (he was eventually ransomed and returned to England), he met what he called the "molato chief" of Atacames, presumably the younger Yllescas, and was given a more-or-less friendly reception.[25] The last straw came in the form of yet another shipwreck off San Mateo Bay in 1595. The crown's desire for the pacification of Esmeraldas was at last rekindled.

The new Peruvian viceroy, the Marquis of Cañete, soon entrusted an expedition to Captain Francisco Arias de Herrera, *corregidor* (a title similar to governor) of Guayaquil. Arias claimed to have already established contact with "a mulatto captain" on the coast, and to have sent his son and daughter-in-law ahead to settle a town among some indigenous peoples nearby. Despite these promising developments, a military mission in 1597 failed miserably at San Mateo Bay with the usual attrition of greedy soldiers, disappearance of human quarry, and onset of debilitating fevers. Arias not only failed, but was further humiliated by being stripped of his title by the Council of the Indies. Exasperated by so many useless conquistadors, the viceroy, council, and king were open for suggestions.

❋   ❋   ❋

A judge newly appointed to Quito's High Court, Dr. Juan del Barrio de Sepúlveda, was full of ideas for Esmeraldas. Dr. Barrio had arrived in Quito in late 1596 after being transferred from the Audiencia of Panama. There he had had some experience with pirate-friendly maroons and refractory indigenous bands. But whereas the general policy toward runaways and rebels on the isthmus had been less than conciliatory, Dr. Barrio would follow the more peaceful tack pioneered by Cabello Balboa and Espinosa on Quito's Pacific fringe.

Within a year of his arrival the new audiencia judge—taking advantage of his role as interim president—began organizing a multi-pronged "spiritual" conquest of Esmeraldas and neighboring territories. Enlisted in this endeavor were several members of Quito's venerable Mercedarian monastery (established in the same year as the Spanish city, 1534), among them Juan de Salas and Juan Bautista de Burgos, the man who met the Sánchez de Cuellar castaways. In the course of the next five years, the audiencia would expend thousands of pesos on missionary salaries and gifts aimed at drawing Esmeraldeños of all colors into the Christian, if not quite Spanish, imperial fold. By the time Sánchez de Cuellar and his fellow castaways arrived offshore in early 1600 it would have appeared that Dr. Barrio's "conquest" had succeeded. But could it last? Or was it even bona fide?

Both questions would be answered in the negative within a decade or two, but in the meantime Dr. Barrio spared no expense in cementing alliances and parrying the more hawkish thrusts of the old soldier elite of

Main church façade, San Lorenzo del Escorial, Spain (architect Juan de Herrera, finished 1582)

Quito. Indeed, the piles of testimonies that inform this narrative, along with the remarkable portrait of the Arobe ambassadors, bear witness to the sincerity of this late-Renaissance man of letters. Not only were the "mulattos" of Atacames and San Mateo Bay feasted and baptized, but also headmen drawn from among their more than occasional indigenous enemies, the neighboring Cayapas (or Chachi), "Yumbos," and Barbacoans. New villages were established and christened with saints' names upon indigenous ones, and although several were abandoned soon after their inhabitants fell mysteriously and often terminally ill, they sounded much more reassuring to men like Dr. Barrio than so many scattered thatch dwellings in the wilderness. For the Spanish, like the Romans, urbanization was the handmaiden of hegemony.

An optimistic letter to King Philip II written in March of 1598 spelled out the nature of the oidor's plans for the reduction (the term suggests "purification" as much as pacification) of Quito's Pacific northwest. Here Dr. Barrio revealed for the first time the limits of his trust in missionaries. Quito, like Panama, had to deal with its "maroon problem" in order to prosper, ideally by way of a new seaport to displace Guayaquil. A road would be needed, of course, fortified by Spanish towns. It was hoped also that gold discovered along the way would offset the treasury's already lavish expenditures.[26] (It would in fact take several more centuries for these goals to be even partly achieved, and not until the *1990s* would the towns of the Esmeraldas backcountry be directly linked by road to the highland cities of Quito and Ibarra.)

Had the delirious, dying king received this letter in his chilly bedchamber in the vast palace-monastery of San Lorenzo del Escorial he might have chuckled. Here was an audiencia president diverting desperately needed crown monies to fund a potentially disastrous missionary enterprise in a jungle fringe. But by the time the letter reached Madrid the king could not respond, and Dr. Barrio went on paying local merchants hundreds and even thousands of pesos over the next two years to gift and feast the new subjects.

In June of 1598 the storekeeper Miguel de Aldaz was compensated some four hundred pesos for "seventy-eight-and-a-half yards of colored damasks, eight-and-a-half yards of simple taffeta, and five-and-three-quarters ounces of silk, all from China," gifts for visiting Cayapas and Yumbo ambassadors. The fact that all these fabrics, purchased directly by the royal treasury, had been illegally imported from Acapulco seems to have bothered no one.[27] In the following days Santiago de Villalobos was paid two-hundred-odd pesos for "the maize, potatoes, chicha, mutton, salt, bread, capsicum peppers *(ají),* and firewood" consumed by the same visitors at a series of feasts.[28] In September 1598 Juan de Aldaz again took payment for "twenty-six-and-a-quarter yards of colored damasks, three hats, three yards colored taffeta, three embroidered shirts with three [matching] blankets, six knives, thirty-nine strings of beads *(chaquira),* ninety needles, and eighteen trumpets, all from Castile and China." This odd assortment was meant "to clothe the six Indians of the Province of Barbacoas who came to this court in peace."[29] For certain grocers and dry-goods dealers in Quito the business of the "pacification and reduction of the infidels" of the Pacific lowlands had become a business indeed!

Church and Monastery of San Francisco, Quito (architect Fr. Jodoco Rique, 1535–1554)

As men like soldier-cum-merchant Rodrigo de Ribadeneira had apparently learned, the conquest of the Indies was as much about commodity exchange as physical domination and spiritual conversion, and Quito was now the marketplace of the north Andes. As will be seen in later chapters, the city had thrived since conquest on a vibrant internal commerce linking the capital to distant agricultural outposts and gold-mining frontiers. By 1599 it had become clear to everyone, however, that the old mining camps were petering out due to a combination of exhausted deposits and indigenous flight, rebellion, and death from disease. Esmeraldas was one of several fringes that offered hope of revival. Its conquest promised gold (and perhaps emeralds), native subjects, new settlements, new markets, and even a road and port to link up more directly with Panama (and Mexico, and China). But were these grand plans really what Dr. Barrio had in mind?

Not exactly; at least not if the judge's constant references to the spread of the Christian faith can be given any value whatsoever. A letter from early 1601 emphasized the spiritual breakthroughs of the Esmeraldas enterprise, and it reads almost as if Dr. Barrio was writing not to the new king, Philip III, but to the ghost of his father, whose 1590s requests for information on Amerindian "reductions" are copied and underlined and interspersed throughout this bundle of papers. Glowing testimonies from Mercedarians like Juan Bautista de Burgos, curate of the maroon settlement of San Mateo, suggest an almost millenarian energy. Burgos's visit to the Yllescas encampment, which he dubbed San Martín de Campaces (after the day of his arrival, 11 November, and the name of an apparently vanquished or incorporated indigenous band) was marked by feverish church-building and mass baptisms, including that of the wife of don Sebastián de Yllescas.

For Dr. Barrio, the coup de grâce of this spiritual conquest had come with the confirmation in Quito in July of 1600 of the younger Yllescas and his brother, Baltásar Antonio, following the Sánchez de Cuellar rescue. After several days of instruction in the Jesuit compound, a half-block from the audiencia palace, a moving ceremony took place in the parish church of San Blas. With all the prominent citizens and most of the clerics of Quito present, along with "many other people, Spanish and Indian," the maroon caciques—outfitted like their compatriots the Arobes with East Asian and European finery—were blessed by Quito's bishop, Luis López de Solis. Dr. Barrio was named Sebastián Yllescas's godfather, and the Quito corregidor, don Diego de Portugal, his brother's.[30] Two more weeks were spent touring the partially built churches, chapels, and convents of the city, and gifts of tools and garments flowed freely from its numerous shops (the bill picked up, in some cases, by Dr. Barrio himself). There was no precedent for this course of action in the history of Quito, and few comparable ones anywhere, at any time in colonial Spanish America.

The excitement following these landmark events was palpable. Baltásar de Medina, a Quito potter who turned soldier to escort Padre Burgos into Esmeraldas with the returning Yllescas brothers, seems to have been (like several European visitors before him) nearly converted to the lifestyle of the maroons and their indigenous subjects. In a request for money and horses to supply the upper way stations of the new Esmeraldas

Church of San Francisco interior, Quito

Trail, he could not help but add a gushing description of a great fiesta held in the Yllescas village of San Martín de Campaces. It was probably the greatest party the young man had ever witnessed:

> The people here celebrate a fiesta every six years, but with the arrival of the padre [Burgos], they decided to have it early, and all the mulattos and Indians, small and large, came loaded with birds, pheasants, partridges, turkeys, wild chickens *(paujils)*, and fowl of a thousand varieties, and small animals and grubs *(sabandijas)* of many sorts, all which was received with great contentment, and the fiesta lasted ten days[.]

Medina tantalizes us with these bare ethnographic details—and an amazed hunter's precise count of the game killed. He ends with the postscript:

"I counted the Indians present at this feast and there were 157 idlers *(gandules),* a few boys, and a few women."[31] Another soldier and old Esmeraldas hand, Pedro de Arévalo (quartermaster for López de Zúñiga and several failed predecessors), suggested that between the Yllescases and Mangache-Arobes there were some fifty Afro-Amerindians *(mulatos o zambahigos)* to be reckoned with.[32] How incredulous the members of the Council of the Indies must have been upon reading these accounts of Esmeraldas circa 1600. How could the famed quagmire of Quito's Pacific coast be suddenly so harmless? Had all the fuss been over just a few hundred happy idlers clustered here and there, content to celebrate nature's prodigious bounty at six-year intervals?

Dr. Barrio may have imagined Esmeraldas as a Christianized menagerie of sorts, but the idyll was not to last. Kinship in Christ, however sincerely (or naively) offered, could not contain the baser impulses of Quito's many and desperate elite householders, and private disillusionment followed close on the heels of public displays of piety and thanksgiving. In reconnoitering a portion of the Esmeraldas Trail in the latter months of 1600, the old soldier, Pedro de Arévalo, noticed "a sort of island" alongside the lower Santiago-Cayapas estuary,

> where many earthen pots and jars were visible, and asking the said
> Captain don Francisco de Arobe what this was, he said that there
> was formerly a settlement [there] where the Indians of all that land
> subject to the said mulattos and those of the Province of the Cayapa
> and Conboncanos [?] and others of the said coast retrieved and
> continued to retrieve much gold, but not because the land produces
> it, nor the river, but rather it appeared [to me, Arévalo, again
> speaking] to be worked gold, and it was there because it was, as said,
> a former village and shrine *(oratorio),* inhabited by Indian goldsmiths,
> and there exist there many small terra cotta idols with figures of
> lions and evil things, though of fine workmanship[.][33]

This was undoubtedly the site the Spanish would later call La Tolita ("Little Mound"), necropolis and perhaps ceremonial center for indigenous Esmeraldeños whose culture had faded into the forest and mangroves some fifteen hundred years earlier.[34] Here the Arobes and their subjects scavenged for the jewelry that adorned their noses, ears, lips, and chests—the same fabulous, recycled ornaments proudly displayed in Sánchez Gallque's 1599 portrait.

There is no evidence of a gold rush following Arévalo's reconnaissance, but within little more than a decade tensions between Spaniards and Amerindians in this region—especially with a group of Cayapas, or Chachi neighbors called loosely "Malabas"—would reach the point of rupture. By 1611 the Esmeraldas Trail was cut off. Attempts to settle a Spanish town in Malaba country by a certain Captain Miguel Arias de Ugarte had apparently triggered the violence. Afterward a priest and a few soldiers not killed by darts and arrows staggered into Chachi and maroon villages begging for assistance. Aid was "lovingly" offered, the humbled and wounded sent on their way, yet from here forward, the maroons (and likewise the Chachi) would play an ever more ambivalent role in the region, never perfectly allied with church or crown, yet never sworn enemies.

In return for what he liked to call the "bloodless conquest" of Esmeraldas, Dr. Barrio was promoted to the office of alcalde del crimen (roughly district attorney) in the viceregal Audiencia of Lima in July of 1602. He was further promoted to full judge in March 1604, and died in office some years later.[35] Perhaps he lived long enough to hear of the passing of his godson, Alonso Sebastián de Yllescas, who died of fever in 1607 in San Martín de Campaces. Never one to admit captivity, especially that of the spirit, Yllescas frustrated the new resident Mercedarian, Fernando Hincapié, by refusing to confess his sins. Eventually he changed his mind—perhaps wanting to cover all bets, as before with Dr. Barrio—but still the maroon leader remained, in the words of the priest, "rebellious and obstinate" to the end.[36]

A QUITO IMMIGRANT'S LETTER
TO A RELATIVE IN SPAIN

For the love of God, having seen this [letter], I hope you come at last with your wife and mother to where I am, which is in Chimbo, where no more want shall come to pass, God willing. And to ensure your voyage, [I have entrusted] a merchant, Julio Ferrosin, with 700 ducats of eleven reales (less nine reales), which he carries in the form of one gold disk handed off to him by Pedro López de la Hera, as stated in the accompanying letter. Thus, when God is served to carry this money there, come straightaway, as it will bring you great contentment and a fine old age. And I ask Your Mercy [to use this money] to purchase a pair of black slaves, pretty, big girls (*hermosas muchachonas*), to come and serve you, and bring all the white cloth you have in the house, because here it is highly esteemed, and the women go well-dressed in silk, because here it is quite expensive; and bring six pillows covered in velvet of various colors and a good rug, so that these 700 ducats will be well spent on necessary things, with just a little of the remainder for the trip to Nombre de Diós [Caribbean port of Panama], since there I will have monies ready to pay your passage [from Spain] and also to get you here, where I am . . . [and] do me a favor and bring me a half-dozen good halberd and partisan blades and a saddle and a shield for yourself . . . and also bring a half-dozen lance-heads—good ones.

Juan Fuero of Chimbo to Juan Fernández Resio in Cuenca (Spain)
28 February 1587

Translated from Enrique Otte, *Cartas privadas de emigrantes a Indias, 1540–1616* (Mexico City: Fondo de Cultura Económica, 1993), no. 414.

TWO: Captivity and Redemption

Desiring that the conscience be fully discharged and our Lord served, we exhort and call upon in the name of our Lord all masters of slaves and those served by morenos ["brown" individuals of African or part African heritage] and Indians and by other persons, that they be very observant and take particular care, watching over their [whole] family, in particular teaching them each day and reciting the doctrine, and taking them to mass and sermon on Sundays and mandatory feast days, and making them confess and take communion and receive all other sacraments . . .
—Chapter 33 of the 1594 Quito Synods

In mid-July 1594 a notary recorded the last wishes of an elite woman on her deathbed in Quito. Ysabel de Baeza was a native of the old Kingdom of Granada, a four-time widow, owner of some houses in Seville and a modest *estancia* in Ambato, a few days' ride south of Quito. She also claimed five slaves: Magdalena and her four children, Luisa, Felipe, Juan, and Antón. Doña Ysabel's real estate was to go mostly to her children and grandchildren in Quito, but the fate of the slaves was more carefully circumscribed. Magdalena would serve her dying master's daughter for four years, after which she would be freed. Luisa was to serve Baeza's granddaughter and Felipe a great-grandson, both "until the time when they ransom themselves *(se rescaten)* and give each one on their own behalf four hundred pesos of current silver." The younger Juan and Antón were to stay in the household of Baeza's executors until they also freed themselves, each for three hundred pesos. The slaves were not to be sold by these temporary masters, and the fourteen hundred pesos thus collected were to be placed in a chaplaincy fund *(capellanía)* administered by Quito's Augustinians. The masses thus financed by the self-redemption of Ysabel Baeza's slaves would in turn help release her soul from the temporary captivity and untold pain of Purgatory.[1]

Captivity and redemption defined bodies and souls in many contexts in the sixteenth-century Spanish empire: there were the luckless Christians held by "Turkish" corsairs and merchants in the *baños* of the Maghreb, war captives like the rebellious Moriscos taken in the Alpujarras uprisings, and a variety of prisoners jailed for both petty and capital crimes in Spain and the colonies. Then there was the matter of "doing time" for sins in the afterlife, settling accounts with God for venial or worse misdeeds on Earth. Finally there was African slavery, which, although it shared aspects of all these other forms of early modern European captivity and redemption, found mostly unapologetic mercantilist objectives pushed to the fore.

We do not know if elite Quiteños made conscious links between these various forms of captivity and redemption, but it seems safe to say that few were so moved by such associations to free African slaves. Slaveholding was of course not completely dissociated from sin, as evidenced by occasional deathbed manumissions for the "discharge" of the owner's conscience, but with luck, as shown by the example of Ysabel de Baeza above, an owner could have the best of both worlds, mortgaging her or his own soul against the value of a slave or two, or four, in the bargain. We do not know what African slaves thought of this apparent material-capital/spiritual-capital continuum either, but their constant and often wily attempts to secure bodily freedom suggest a far more visceral understanding of captivity and redemption than their masters could ever know.

What follows is a first attempt to tell the story of those women, children, and men of African heritage not so fortunate as the Esmeraldas maroons circa 1599. African slavery in the city and provinces of Quito has

Sepulcher stone of merchant Diego Rodríguez de León and his wife, Leonisia de Figueroa, Franciscan Monastery, Quito

received little attention for two reasons. Firstly, the highland core was home to dense indigenous populations; as will be seen in the next chapter, the conquistadores and their descendants worried mostly about hanging onto encomienda grants in order to work their agricultural holdings, even around the turn of the seventeenth century. Secondly, Quito proper was not like much of New Granada to the north, or coastal Peru to the south; placer gold mines and sugar plantings were scattered, distant, and mostly marginally productive. Vineyards never took root. Still, the city of Quito emerged soon after conquest and civil war as an important center for trade and colonial administration and the city thrived in these years from its connections to a complex network of farms, pasturelands, and gold mines. By the 1590s the mines of Quito's northern sub-district, the Gobernación of Popayán, had become critically important.

More dynamic and adaptive than is often assumed, Quito's early colonial economy would shift dramatically toward textile production by the first decades of the seventeenth century. Before this, however, most merchants traded gold, and to a lesser extent agricultural and livestock products like biscuit and leather, for European clothing, tools, books, wax, olives, oil, wine, East Indian spices, Chinese fabrics and porcelain, and other accouterments of contemporary Mediterranean living. Crown officials collected taxes on this trade and on brute gold production, paying themselves handsome salaries in fine gold pesos, all this in the great silver age of Potosí. The merchants and administrators and high churchmen of the colony were still very much a part of the Atlantic, or as some historians would have it, "Greater Mediterranean" web—there were even a few Portuguese, Italians, and Greeks among them—and such people seem to have felt they needed "black" slaves. Why?

As the late Frederick Bowser noted for contemporary Lima, African slaves served urban elite interests in several ways: they cooked and cleaned, groomed and saddled, ran errands, supplied companionship, and generally did everything "mechanical" that their masters would not.[2] The native peoples of Quito and vicinity in fact served similarly, but the law protected them (at least in theory) from corporal punishment, forced relocation, and, most importantly, sale. African captives were mobile capital, legally reduced to intelligent livestock (Aristotle's "natural slaves"); they could be pledged for debts, rented, donated, or auctioned off in a financial emergency. Lastly,

Elite residence, Quito

the ownership of African slaves, who were individually more expensive than much prime real estate in these years, was, in Andean cities swarming with part-time indigenous servants, a critical badge of prestige. Indeed, the power symbolism of slave ownership was so infectious even native lords took to petitioning the Indies Council for license to "ornament" themselves with armed Africans as early as the 1550s.[3]

A close reading of Quito and Popayán's earliest surviving notary records (for the years 1580–1601), among other documents, yields some patterns of north Andean slavery circa 1599. Some documents also hint at the possibilities and problems faced by free people of color—the "redeemed"— whether of African or mixed descent. In all, some 250 sales are recorded in these twenty-one years, marking the transfer of fewer than 400 slaves—a small sample, to be sure—but other transactions include export licenses issued in Madrid or Seville; wills and codicils; dowries for marriage or convent life; powers of attorney to buy, sell, or recover runaway slaves; apprenticeship agreements; notes of obligation for merchandise transport; liens on slaves; debts owed by or to people of color, slave and free; references to marriages or child-producing unions between people of color and native Andeans or Europeans; and rare letters of freedom. In sum, the record is varied and rich. Select details drawn from these documents are presented below, followed by a discussion of African slavery in Quito's marginal gold mines, real and imaginary. The chapter concludes with a description of slavery in the mines of Popayán in the first years of the seventeenth century drawn from religious records, further evidence of how Africans and their descendants in Quito and its vast hinterland became most intimately linked not only to elite survival, but also salvation.

The City

One interesting feature of the small notarial sample should be noted right away: among adults, roughly the same number of women were sold in the city of Quito as men. Approximately 116 adult women were exchanged between 1580 and 1601, 22 of them with children and 1 pregnant; single men appear in 114 cases. Twenty-one children aged sixteen and under were sold alone, 9 girls and 22 boys, and in sixteen cases men and women were

sold as a couple (marriage was treated as one of the conditions of sale, or
cargas, discussed below).[4] Enslaved men worked in a variety of tasks, serving
as squires, muleteers, cowboys, majordomos, blacksmiths, and so forth, but
on occasion they engaged in more traditional (and more deadly) tasks like
gold mining, pearl diving, and sugar cultivation. Women seem to have been
most often connected to elite, urban households for domestic service—
including that most intimate of servile tasks, wet-nursing—one possible
explanation for the anomalous, near one-to-one sex ratio in the city's sale
records.[5] As in other slave societies, the importance of this female slave presence in the household, the inner sanctum, as it were, of patriarchal society,
cannot be overestimated in Quito. We can only imagine, for example, the
psychological implications of the relationships formed (and severed)
between enslaved wet nurses and creole elite children.

From bills of sale and other documents the following ethnic monikers
(naciones) arise, the number of references for each in parentheses: Angola
(48 plus a company contract to import c. 20 more), Bran (38), Biafara (33),
Congo (16), Bañol (11), Çape (10), Pijao (6), Mandinga (6), Nalú (3), Biojo
(3), Gelofo (or "Wolof," 3), Cape Verde (2), Caçanga (2), Mojango (2),
Moquende (2), Terranova (2), "Ciciliano" (1), Folupe (1), San Tomé (1), Páez
(1), and Engico (1). Aside from the lone Sicilian and native American Pijao
and Páez captives (discussed in the next chapter), the majority of slaves
given ethnic designations—not to be taken too literally, of course—thus
came from the Upper Guinea Coast (roughly Cape Verde to the Sierra
Leone Estuary), the second largest grouping from the vast Angolan hinterland.[6] Sometimes vague or enigmatic terms were used, such as the general
"guinea/o" or "bozal" ("untamed," i.e., not hispanicized), but others include
names like "Juan Savana" and "Alonso Jagan, mulatto."[7] Some, like twenty-
seven-year-old Catalina "of the land of Angola," had brands certifying their
origins.[8] Well over half the slaves sold in Quito were African-born, in any
case, but among those native to the Spanish-Portuguese empire *(criollos),* the
following birthplaces appear (in alphabetical order): Anserma, Buga, Cazalla
(Andalusia), Cali, Cartago, Cuenca (Ecuador), Grand Canary, Guayaquil,
Jérez (Andalusia), Lima, Lisbon, New Spain, Quiebralomo, Quito, Panama,
Pasto, Popayán, Riobamba, Santo Domingo, Seville, Tunja, Veragua
(Panama), and Zamora (southeast Ecuador). General terms were just as
common, for example: "native of this land" *(criolla de esta tierra).*

Manuscript recording sale of Felipa Criolla de Cartago, 3 June 1600
(courtesy of the National History Archive, Quito)

Lest one forget that slavery and color were already closely linked in the minds of most Spanish subjects by the end of the sixteenth century, color descriptions should be noted, such as: "black slave female" *(negra esclava)*, "Juan the black" *(el negro Juan)*, "the secretary's black female" *(la negra del Secretario)*, "of black color" *(de color negra)*, "married blacks" *(negros maridos)*, "Guinea black" *(negro guineo)*, and "a black [girl] ten years old or above" *(una negra de edad de diez años para arriba)*. Other salient examples include: "tiny blacks," "Little Juan the little black," "a dark black slave named Gaspar between wild and Latinized," "a black, tall of body," "of mulatto color," "Magdalena, a little mulatto slave [girl]," "a mulatto the color of cooked quince," "'La Quijota,' mulatto female," "of a brown color," and "Antón of the Nalú Nation, small yet robust, [and] not too dark." Perhaps most revealing of the equivalence of "black" and "slave" was the phrase: "a black, brown in color" *(un negro color moreno)*. Free people of color had to be explicitly called "free" *(libre, horra/o)* or, very rarely, "householder" *(vecino):* "a freedman of brown color," "free brown female," "brown-colored householder of the city of Cali," "Antón Galarza, free brown tailor," and "Pedro Ramón, gray/brown *(pardo)* in color, householder and resident of this city."[9]

Redemption of the temporal sort was not impossible for slaves of African heritage, and although we do not know their exact numbers before 1600, free people of color do appear in a variety of contexts in the Quito documents. Freedom seems to have come from self-purchase in several cases, deathbed manumission in others. María de Villoria, described as "free *mulata*," sued for ownership of a house in Quito left her by a former master, Martín Duque.[10] Freed native Africans were rarer, but an exception was Duarte González, "native of Angola." He was issued a letter of freedom by Audiencia Secretary Diego Suárez de Figueroa in September of 1596.[11]

These so-called letters of liberty *(cartas de libertad* or *alforría)* are extremely rare, and nearly always have a catch. For example, in 1605 a Popayán widow promised freedom to three-month-old Diego, the only son of her slave Francisca. The offer was said to be in recognition of his mother's good service but also her direct aid in canceling the master's debts "and for fifty pesos current gold dust." In truth Francisca, who remained a slave, had purchased her child's freedom—it had not been granted. Similar was a Quito shoemaker's letter freeing baby María Victoria, whose mother,

Manuscript recording sale of Domingo de Nación Angola, 30 June 1600 (courtesy of the National History Archive, Quito)

Catalina Bañol, had died in childbed in September 1600. Good service was again claimed, but it was forty pesos paid by the child's father, a slave in the household of Quito's corregidor, that sealed the deal. It is more than likely the shoemaker realized he had no means of raising the baby himself and that her survival depended on the corregidor's nursemaids.[12]

Once free, people of color pursued a variety of occupations in order to support themselves and their families. In 1585 Antona Bautista, called a "free brown" by the notary, registered for a license to truck and barter in the city.[13] A will was filed in 1596 for Catalina de la Paz, also called "free brown," noting her houses and a small piece of land near Quito's Dominican church; the tile roof on one house suggests above-poverty income.[14] "Free mulata" Juana Çagala purchased a half-*solar* lot in Quito's St. Sebastian neighborhood in 1599, and was said to have hounded the seller for a year to get the ninety-peso exchange properly notarized.[15] Many free women of color worked alongside indigenous and mestiza women selling food and dry goods in Quito's several market squares.

A half-dozen or so free men of color are noted as mule skinners operating along the Royal Road linking Quito to Popayán and Cali in the north and Cuenca and Loja in the south, along with the coastal route to Guayaquil. One such man, Antón de Arenas ("brown in color"), purchased his freedom with five hundred pesos' worth of horses and biscuit in 1595, his pledge backed by another free man of color, Juan de Torres. A major wine and dry goods carrier circa 1600 was Julián Maldonado ("free brown"), owner of 110 mules, a house, a store, and a ranch in Chimbo, near Riobamba.[16] (His signature is reproduced at the end of this chapter.) In 1586 Juan de Larrea, "free brown" and a resident of Quito, obliged himself to a local merchant for thirty-odd pesos' worth of merchandise, including coarse cloth, a skirt for an indigenous woman (possibly his wife), and some iron tools. His debt was paid off fourteen months later. Not so lucky was "brown" tailor Juan Pascual, who barely escaped debtor's prison in 1600 over a loan of eight pesos.[17]

In 1573 an apparently free Afro-Quiteño named Bartolomé was named town crier *(pregonero)* and master of weights and measures *(almotacén)*. The former office was not exceptional, as many native Andeans and even slaves throughout Quito and Popayán performed this job. To have been named master of weights and measures for a growing commercial city like Quito, however, does appear to have been something of an exception. Bartolomé was given "a fat *vara* with the city's insignia on top," the staff indicating his second office and also serving (presumably) as a potent symbol of authority.[18]

Another free "brown" man in early Quito, Bartolomé Hernández (possibly the same man as the pregonero and almotacén above), filed suit against two Spaniards for infringing on his landholding outside the indigenous village of Carangue, near present-day Ibarra. The suit over rights to the lands of Quitubara, lasting from 1596 to 1602, was decided in Hernández's favor. The judges of Quito's audiencia had apparently been moved by his testimony, in which he claimed, "being as I am a poor, old black man of more than eighty years, in charge of a wife and children, I do not have any other capital *(hacienda)* nor means by which to support them except for the aforesaid, my estancia."[19] The audiencia reaffirmed Hernández's title to five *caballerías* (about five hundred acres), which he had purchased some time before for thirty silver pesos. The possibility of holding land and even winning protection from predatory Spaniards in the courts, as this case attests, does not appear to have been withheld from free persons of color in early Quito (though clearly they had to fight tooth and nail for it). In another case from 1593, a free mulata named María de Villorin sold several *solares* of urban property in Quito, mostly to indigenous buyers, as evidenced by sales tax *(alcabala)* records.[20] More common were African-American cowboys and majordomos such as Cristóbal Carmona, a free, married man who worked a wealthy urbanite's estancia for two years in exchange for an eighth share of future herd growth and rations of wheat, maize, salt, and cheese.[21]

Freedom was not without rewards, but apparently one could not be both "brown" and free in sixteenth-century Quito without scribes making a note of both. On the opposite side, slaves were always explicitly referred to as chattels in legal documents, their captivity justified by pat phrases, for example: "three slave units, two males, one female" *(tres piezas de esclavos dos varones y la una hembra)*, "per unit" *(cada pieza)*, "the other unit is female and is called María of Angola country" *(la otra pieza es hembra y se llama María de tierra Angola)*. Examples of this detached and dehumanizing language abound: "a black, untamed Guinea slave woman subject to slavery and servitude, my own, named Micaela, native of the Bran country," or "it is a just and true price and [the slave] is not worth more," or "subject to servitude and free of liens," or "taken in just war and not in peace" (*abida en buena guerra y no de paz,* a phrase thoughtlessly applied to creole as well as African-born slaves). Still more revealing are: "had in a good black woman" (*abidos en buena negra,* the last word crossed out and replaced with the standard "guerra," suggesting either a Freudian slip or cruel jest), and "as bones in a sack" (*por huesos en costal).* This last term, found in bills of sale throughout Spanish America, derived from the slave market at Cartagena; in full it went: "as bones in a sack, soul in mouth" (*como huesos en costal y alma en boca).*[22]

The disclaimer was intended to protect the seller from suit should the slave in question "give up the ghost" upon closure of the sale, but could this phrase not also suggest that both buyer and seller agreed slaves had no souls at all, just weak and debilitated bodies? Perhaps Spaniards of an academic turn of mind pondered such issues, but justifications for African chattel status were never seriously debated in these years. Spanish law protected buyers by demanding disclosure of "defects" *(tachas, defectos)* and other conditions (cargas) that might render a servile captive unproductive or otherwise problematic, for example: "without a single defect" *(sin tacha ninguna),* "with all her or his defects, good [*sic*] or bad," "not contagious," "[sold] as sickly, alcoholic, thieving, prone to running away and gambling, and with other vices customary among bad male and female blacks." Further examples abound, among them: "in particular, as a bad woman and a thief," "I sell him as is, a killer and a fugitive," and "[she] is and has been ruinous in service and of little importance." On the other extreme were phrases like: "not a drunk, nor a runaway, nor a thief, nor sick . . . because she has not had nor fallen to nor felt thus in all the time she has been my slave."[23] In sum, slaves were categorized as either near-perfect or horribly vice-ridden, depraved, violent, thieving, sick, and generally incorrigible. As these phrases and terms suggest, some Quiteños expected such "defects" among the African slave population—even as they traded them at premium prices. Occasionally they went so far as to joke about their poor captives maliciously. Despite the majestic rendering of the Esmeraldas ambassadors on the cover of this book, "blackness" was already deeply stigmatized in the Quito highlands by 1599.

Illness was particularly prevalent among newly arrived African captives, and although slaves received some professional medical care, their lot was little better than that of the more numerous indigenous Andeans felled by waves of epidemic smallpox, measles, and influenza (the mid-1580s were particularly deadly in Quito and throughout Peru). Others suffered from congenital or recurring illnesses, mental instability, or old injuries, as suggested by the following descriptions: "skinny and debilitated," "a cloud [cataract] in the left eye," "sick [and] lame in one hand," "sick with diarrhea and tapeworms," "very sick, and they say she has scabies [or elephantiasis?], and is unable to stand on her feet," "[perpetually] drunken," "old, sick with buboes, deaf, and a runaway," "thin," "much time spent in bed," and "sick in the womb" *(enferma de la madre).*

Statements denying slave illness and "vices" are equally revealing of a given master's preoccupations and prejudices. Twenty-year-old Cartago-born Felipa, for example (see fig. 15, p. 60), was said to be "neither a drunk, nor a runaway, nor does she speak with the Devil, nor does she chew coca [leaves], nor suffer from goiter, heart trouble, *dolor de los tados* [pain in the . . . ?], stomach pains, or illness of the womb."[24] On the reverse side, one woman sold in Quito appears to have been singled out as the receptacle of her master's accumulated disappointment, contempt, and rage: "a captive slave and subject to all servitude, taken in just war and not in peace, which I sell as a drunken, thieving, demon-possessed runaway, crazy and lame, with a sick heart, epilepsy, rashes, hemorrhoids, buboes, leprosy, scabs, [and] a withered arm."[25] Such obvious exaggerations further suggest that bills of sale were not simply "objective" legal documents aimed at limiting liabilities, but may have served on occasion as vehicles of ridicule, pages on which to vent frustration with African insubordination. At worst, they hint at an emerging racist rage.

As Bowser described in the case of Lima, a common "defect" masters claimed of slaves was their (unsurprising) tendency to run away. This form of active resistance was treated in sale documents as just one of several annoying "features" of second-rate slaves. Such individuals were sold at discount, their names followed by these adjectives and phrases: "prone to flee" *(huydor),* "ruinous and feral" *(bellaca y cimarrón),* "[currently] missing, a runaway, [which I purchase] at my risk if already dead," and "I sell with declaration that he is a fugitive *(fugetivo)* but with no other defect." Also: "[no problems] except that the said Francisco absented himself from my power just one time," "missing two or three days," and "married to a slave [belong-ing to another master, and] presently at large for not wanting to accompany me to Spain."[26] In 1599 Catalina "mulata" escaped to Pasto with three hun-dred pesos' worth of her widow-master's silver, gold, and pearls.[27] "Black Juan, by nation Portuguese" ran away so often to visit his wife María that his master, a Quito-area textile mill operator, finally sold him.[28]

As these examples from the notary Protocols illustrate, Quito slaves ran away for good reasons. Some had been separated from marriage partners, others simply disappeared for short periods to annoy their masters and presumably enjoy a few days of freedom. Several could not tolerate captivity. Twenty-year-old Juan Bran, described as "not very black," and with what may have been ritual scars on his face (one cicatrize "in the shape of a star on his forehead") ran away for the first time on sale day, 19 July 1600. The buyer immediately cancelled the contract. Twelve days later Juan was purchased by a Quito couple at discount and with the seller's disclosure that "after only eight days in my custody [Juan] escaped from me on a horse, and after searching for him and locating him I put him in the public jail of this city, from which I just brought him to make this sale." In November of the same year Juan appeared again in a sale contract, this time purchased by city smeltery operator Sebastián Gutiérrez. The exasperated Quito couple claimed: "beginning only a few days after we bought him he began to run away, costing us a great deal to search him out and apprehend him and as a result of this defect (defecto) he is presently in leg irons, and thus we hand him over." In the course of gaining such notoriety, Juan's value had dropped from four hundred pesos hard money to three hundred bags of salt.[29] Age did not dull the urge to run for some; in the same year (1600) fifty-year-old Hernando Mandinga was said to be still at large after a full year and a half of freedom. He was last seen in the vicinity of Pasto.[30]

Physical abuse, although rarely mentioned in notary records, must have also driven some individuals to flee. In 1598 a slave named Juan Congo testified that he had been ordered by Quito's archdeacon to whip an unnamed slave woman for her "ruinous" behavior and chronic marronage; she was now hiding in a cave, nearly dead from hunger.[31] Earlier, in 1580, an enslaved woman belonging to audiencia judge Diego de Ortegón was stabbed to death by the master of another woman in a city plaza for challenging his authority to intervene in an argument.[32] A Popayán master sued to recover the value of Cristóbal Criollo, apparently murdered by an overseer in the mines of Jelima in 1592, and a Quito merchant filed a complaint in 1600 with the audiencia after his slave Ynés was nearly beaten to death by Corregidor Diego de Portugal for alleged housebreaking.[33] Redemption in the form of temporal freedom came hard, it seems, and for most slaves only at death. Some runaways found permanent refuge in the coastal lowlands and parts of Amazonia, but the topography and small numbers of slaves in the highlands rendered *grand marronage,* or permanent flight, and consequent formation of maroon communities less attractive or likely than on the outskirts of Lima, Panama, or Cartagena.[34]

City slaves focused instead on self-purchase and pressuring masters to keep families intact, yet neither objective was easy given their extraordinarily high value. Prices ranged from 100 to 800 pesos current silver per slave, but averaged about 450 pesos for healthy men and women between sixteen and thirty years of age in the 1580s. By the mid-1590s average prices for women were nearer 500 pesos (roughly in line with Bowser's figures for 1590s price rises in Lima), but men's values seem to have remained about the same unless they had a skill.[35] Elites may have preferred women in household settings, enough that they would pay a premium, but stronger demand for able-bodied men in the mining camps and on the coast was also a likely cause for the apparent price disparity and unusual sex ratio in city records. A young mother and nursing-age child might sell for 700 pesos in 1585 in Quito, but closer to 800 or even 900 pesos in 1595; the same was true with pregnant women. Children under sixteen sold for 200 to 400 pesos throughout the period, and similar prices were paid for slaves over forty.

Sales of multiple slaves (i.e., beyond family groups or couples) are quite rare in the notary records, although this was beginning to change in Popayán. An exception was a 1597 sale in Quito of six slaves for 2,200 pesos current silver, an average of 367 pesos each. Tachas, or "defects," reduced prices most of the time, by about 40 or 50 percent in extreme cases, whereas skills seem to have increased prices by about 20 percent. When compared with sale prices, slaves appraised in wills and dowries seem to have been overvalued by about 20 percent, and one self-purchase at 650 pesos (in this case a mature woman) was probably also inflated.[36] To get an idea what this amount of money could buy, a contemporary land sale registered in Quito's Protocols bears comparison. A fairly typical farm—three caballerías (about three hundred acres) of land planted with barley, maize, and potatoes; three yoke of oxen fitted with ploughs, harnesses, and a cart; numerous iron tools, including ten sickles; and thatch-roofed structures of adobe and wood—sold in its entirety for 630 pesos current silver in December 1587.[37] Given the apparently desperate demand for slaves in early Quito, masters appraised them well above going market rates when it served their purposes.

Beyond simple demand, however, slave prices were probably also inflated by a ready supply of gold. As will become evident in later chapters, gold was a major trade item in Quito in these years, and on many occasions slaves were purchased with gold ingots. A large contract drawn up in 1597 to trade for slaves in Angola via Lisbon and Seville merchants involved an investment of over 8,000 pesos of fine gold (worth about twice as much in silver).[38] In another case from 1596 a Potosí merchant asked factors in Quito to send bars and disks totaling some 3,200 pesos fine gold to New Granada to purchase slaves and merchandise.[39] The sale of Ynés Bran (twenty-four) and sons Manuel (four) and Juan (one and a half) for 1,100 pesos "current silver" *(plata corriente)* in 1600 was paid in the form of "a large gold disk" *(tejo de oro grande fundido).*[40] In the same year Beatriz Biafara (twenty-two) and her daughter Juana sold for 900 pesos current silver, paid with two gold disks.[41] Thirty-four-year-old Leonor Bañol was purchased in 1601 by a Quito audiencia attorney with a gold disk worth 700 silver pesos.[42] Sometimes merchants or clerics sent gold ingots with factors to Panama to buy young slaves at prices more attractive than those found in Quito.[43]

About as often slaves were purchased with silver, both in coin and bullion form, and in at least one case slaves were traded along with worked objects, an even more blunt reminder of their chattel status. In 1583 Rodrigo Núñez de Bonilla, a prominent Quito encomendero, signed a 1,400-silver-peso debt in exchange for two African-born women and "a large cross of gold with seven large emeralds and its silver box."[44] In 1601 twenty-six-year-old Francisco Biojo was sold to a Quito physician for 470 pesos plus a year's worth of medical care for the seller and his household.[45] On several occasions no currency was exchanged at all, replaced with

View of Popayán, Colombia

commodities like wool, hides, cloth, and cordage. A 1583 sale of a recent runaway named Catalina, born in New Spain, was concluded with an exchange of 450 *arrobas* of salt (rather like Juan Bran, above) four days after her disappearance. Similarly, a creole boy named Francisco Adán was traded in Popayán for 350 gold pesos' worth of imported fabric and finished garments in 1592. Still more blunt was the March 1600 exchange of twelve-year-old Francisco, "branded with an 'S' on the chest," for 180 iron rods to Quito armorer Antonio de Aguirre; this young boy, whose mother had died in faraway Ibagué, New Granada, was said to be a chronic runaway, "for which reason he is in leg irons."[46] Slaves were also mortgaged, pledged as principal or collateral security for cash loans; as such they were often repossessed and auctioned. In early 1601 Antón Cobó was jailed before bidding started so that his deeply indebted master could not run away with him.[47]

As elsewhere in Spanish America, owners sought means of gaining steady cash rents *(jornales)* from slaves, so they encouraged skilled trades. In 1551 the Quito town council granted a farrier's license to Juan, "brown slave" *(moreno esclavo)* of Captain Rodrigo de Salazar, a prominent encomendero; he was given permission by the cabildo to open a shop "to shoe and bleed *(sangrar)*" horses and perform other blacksmith's tasks, presumably turning over rents to his master. The venture was backed by another prominent Spanish Quiteño, a council member named Lorenzo de Cepeda, who promised to pay any damages "that might come to any animal shoed or bled by fault of the said Juan moreno."[48] Such tasks were still considered appropriate for Africans in 1596, when Padre Luis Suárez Ponce apprenticed his slave, Juan Primero (literally "John No. One"), to become a farrier and veterinarian *(albeitar)*. Suárez had just purchased Juan Primero, a fifteen-year-old native of Biafara, for 450 pesos current silver. A skill would render him more reliable as a producer of rents and more valuable on the market if the need to sell arose.[49]

Some Quito artisans were wealthy enough to own slaves themselves, similarly investing in them by imparting skills prior to resale. In October 1600 hatmaker Antonio Núñez sold his house and five slaves—two of whom, Miguel and Pablo Congo, were described as professional hatmakers *(oficiales sombrereros)*—to a Quito wholesaler for 2,500 pesos. Núñez then turned factor, signing for nearly 4,000 pesos' worth of merchandise to ship to Popayán in exchange for gold dust.[50] In this case skilled slaves served as a bridge to a presumably better future. In 1600 Luis Álvarez, also a hatmaker, purchased an indigenous Pijao captive serving a ten-year sentence for 140 pesos (Núñez had in fact done the same). A year later Álvarez had accumulated sufficient capital to purchase a 500-peso African-American "lifer," Anserma-born Juan, eighteen. Here temporary indigenous slavery served as a bridge to ownership of an African. Skill offset age in the case of Antón Chana (also known as Chanco), a forty-year-old confectioner who sold for 500 pesos in 1601.[51] Such plans did not always work out, however; in 1601 a Quito tailor sold Sebastián, a Cali-born youth of fourteen, to a priest. While in the former's service the boy had suffered a rupture (perhaps a hernia), for which he was bandaged, and he had now run away so many times he was perpetually in leg irons.[52]

People of color also recognized the value of trades, and some were able to use their skills to purchase freedom or at least a better life. In 1601 Agustín de Soto ("free brown") signed on for a year with a master shoemaker on his way to Lima; Soto, a skilled leather-decorator (*argentador*), would receive the substantial sum of 170 silver pesos, free medical care, two new shirts, and suit of local cloth.[53] "Free brown" Pedro Caro signed on for three and a half years as custodian of Quito's Our Lady of the Remedies sodality in 1600. He would receive the modest sum of fifty-one pesos, but also a suit of black cloth and two pairs of shoes per year, along with "good treatment."[54]

Some free people of color invested in the futures of children and other minor relatives. Free creole Juan Moxansa apprenticed his eight-year-old brother, Domingo, to a cobbler for three years.[55] In similar fashion, Duarte de Morales ("free brown") apprenticed his sixteen-year-old son, Gerónimo, to a Quito shoemaker in 1599.[56] "Free black" Juan Bañol apprenticed son Juan, Jr., to a Popayán tailor in 1592; he would serve four years and receive a suit of local cloth upon "graduation."[57] As early as 1581 Afro-native Americans were similarly apprenticed in Quito, as in the case of twelve-year-old Juan "mulato," son of an indigenous Quiteña named Ysabel. Juan was signed on for four years' service to the hosier Fernando Ferrel.[58] Though such trades still qualified as "vile and mechanical" in the eyes of elites, it is clear from these and many other examples that free people of any color in sixteenth-century Quito did all they could to get beyond the sort of hard labor normally associated with slavery.

What emerges, then, from the Quito notary records for the years 1580–1601 is an urban milieu marked by great diversity, both among elites and the working classes. Slaves were slightly more likely to be women than men, with their occupation almost universally domestic service. African-born individuals outnumbered the locally born by a fair margin, evidence that the 1580 unification of Spanish and Portuguese crowns had led to greater penetration of the interior by factors of the transatlantic slave trade.[59] Yet far from being an absolute economic necessity in late sixteenth-century Quito, where indigenous peoples were still numerous and quite available for rotational unpaid labor (the *mita ordinaria*), African slaves seem to have been mostly a conceit of status-conscious elites.

The Mines

There was little opportunity for such conceits in the scattered and mostly transient goldfields of the greater Quito colony. Aside from the shipyards and transport trades in and around the Guayas Estuary, only in the gold mines of the far north and south were Africans considered essential to survival, especially where encomienda abuses had exhausted the indigenous labor pool and attempts at forming mine mitas had failed.[60] As gold production faltered in the 1590s, many elite Quiteños began to write for crown-subsidized imports of enslaved Africans, a common enough call from Potosí to New Spain in these years, but here with some revealing justifications and unexpected results.

Members of Quito's town council, along with audiencia judges, routinely suggested that African slaves be imported in order to relieve native peoples of the burdens of mining and other "deadly" activities. In recommendations to the crown regarding the "vein" *(veta),* or deep-shaft mines of Zamora and Almaguer in 1592, for example, Licenciado Arias Pacheco suggested the nature of the work (excavation, or *desmonte de piedras)* was so strenuous indigenous men could not sustain it, "the blacks being stronger." Second, the mines were so rich that even poor mine owners could buy slaves with day wages *(jornales,* that is, in installments gained from daily produce). Arias Pacheco added, almost casually, that "the climates of these two places are hot, which is a great help to the blacks with respect to the poor climate *(destemple)* of Potosí; blacks do not work well in the recovery of silver."[61]

Arias Pacheco was here conflating altitude and mean temperature, a reasonable enough assumption in the tropical Andes, yet Africans did work in "cold" mines in Quito's hinterland, including the rather high (c. 3,000 m) silver mines of Malal, west of Cuenca (the mines of Zamora and Almaguer ranged from c. 1,800–2,200 m above sea level). And had there been no indigenous persons to work the mines of Potosí, Africans and their descendants would no doubt have been forced to adapt to that extremely high-altitude (over 4,000 m) and cold environment. Indeed, as Peter Bakewell and others have shown, some five thousand slaves lived and worked in Potosí by the turn of the seventeenth century in spite of dire Spanish predictions of climate unsuitability.[62] For their part, highland native Americans proved more than adequately strong in many lowland gold mines.

In 1592 another Quito official recommended the troubled mines of Zamora—then experiencing the twin effects of indigenous rebellion and demographic decline—be repopulated with five hundred crown-subsidized "blacks," a third of them women between fifteen and thirty (for reproductive and "pacifying" purposes), to be purchased by mine owners on five-year liens. The plan, which would include the auctioning of a supply contract *(asiento)* in Seville, would revive the district's glory days of the 1560s, and would not "consume" the newly introduced Africans. Instead, the judge claimed that "the climate of the said mines is very appropriate for the conservation and even increase of the blacks."[63]

The Council of the Indies echoed these sentiments in recommendations to Philip II, citing "the great decline of the natives," and arguing that Africans should be sent north to Popayán and south to Zamora, Jaén, and Yaguarsongo, since "there is no doubt that such lands are perfectly suited to the housing and conservation of the blacks, who survive and even live better, more healthy, robust, and with great strength in very hot countries." The climates of Popayán and the southern gold districts were judged to be quite similar to those of the Africans' home-lands, "which are below the torrid zone in the Kingdoms of Guinea." The climate was so perfect, it was claimed, that "it would provide in abundance the staples that blacks crave *(apetecer),* which are rice, maize, tobacco, fish, squash *(zapallo),* manioc, and other vegetables." This new labor force would not only help to conserve the few remaining native Americans, but would also be preferable for mine work, "their labor being greater *(mayor)* and more graceful and gay *(mas lúcido)."* In sum, the council asked the king to authorize double the shipment of Africans requested, at minimum one thousand slaves per year, a third women, all to provide the Spanish with the metallic staple *they* craved.[64]

As evidenced by numerous sixteenth-century *relaciones,* Africans had already been among the first miners to work under Spanish control in Popayán gold districts like Arma, Anserma, Cartago, and Almaguer, but the poverty of local elites, exhaustive labor practices, and indigenous attacks prevented formation of a stable population. Although Philip II and his successors never seem to have listened, (presumably) cash-starved residents

Façade of Dominican Church, Popayán

were unceasing in their demands for crown-subsidized slaves.[65] A particularly revealing remedy was proposed by Licenciado Francisco de Auncibay. In 1592, this Quito judge penned a bizarre plan, loosely patterned after Thomas More's *Utopia* (1516), to develop the mines of Popayán.[66] In line with the Council of the Indies' own recommendations, Auncibay called upon the monarch to purchase some one thousand Africans, males and females between the ages of seventeen and forty, all to be sent to the northern provinces. Here, as in the Zamora proposal, they were to be purchased by local mine owners who would reimburse the crown in installments, at interest. The money for repayment would come from the slaves themselves, in gold taken from their labors in the region's abundant alluvia. Organized into carefully managed mining camps, or *pueblos,* the Africans would dutifully extract and hand over the subsoil wealth of the province; *et voilà,* cash rents for everyone (except the slaves). For their part, Auncibay claimed, the Africans would "receive no injury," and would gain "civilization."[67]

What of Christian redemption? Auncibay was not finished: The goldfield slaves of Popayán were to be thought of as rescued captives, poor wretches taken from the supposed cannibal hell of Africa and transplanted to a new land, a land without evil, blessed by God. In the judge's own words:

> The blacks would not be harmed; in fact it would be a service to
> them to be taken from Guinea, from that fire and tyranny and
> barbarity and brutality where without law and without God they
> live as savage brutes; but carried to a better land, healthier for them,
> and fertile, they would be happy at their salvation, allowed to live
> with order and religion *(en policía y religión)* and to secure many
> temporal benefits, and what is far more important, many spiritual
> ones[.][68]

For this free, elite Quiteño it was to be the Africans' *privilege* to be captured, banished from their homelands, shipped across the sea, forced to work as permanent chattels, yielding their entire produce to their captors until death. In essence echoing Cabello Balboa on the maroons of Esmeraldas, the judge proposed redemption *through* captivity.

This incredible proposal, for all its optimism, did not overlook the possibility of African unwillingness to see things the same way. Auncibay, himself a slaveowner, understood resistance, and his sixteenth-century coercive tactics will no doubt ring familiar to historians of later Brazilian, North American, and Caribbean slavery. Among his twenty-seven conditions for the smooth working of this scheme we find such rules as: "No. 4, [The slaves] must not be allowed to learn to read nor write, nor to fence (*esgrimir,* i.e., practice swordplay), nor to ride horses, nor are they to bear arms, offensive or defensive, because with this [i.e., these controls] there will be no fear," and "No. 6: See to it that the slaves [miners] are married to black women, because matrimony is the surest means of taming and pacifying the black man."[69] Also familiar is "No. 25: All tools and machetes used by the blacks in their mine work are to be kept at night in the house of the mine overseer or owner, and not in the slaves' quarters." And if one doubts the violence meant to reinforce the system, "No. 15: The punishments administered to the blacks will be lashes and the loss of ears, and for three-time runaways, they shall be stripped *(desgarronarles),* placed in shackles, leg irons, pillories, and the *campanilla* [an iron collar with a hanging bell], but not exile nor the galleys [the usual punishments for Spanish criminals], and if the crime is heinous, death."[70] For Auncibay, there was nothing strange or contradictory about calling for forced mine labor as a means of sustenance for self-consciously pious, Christian elites and simultaneously atonement for African captives.

The business of locating sufficient African "guilt" to justify such arguments would be tackled in the coming decades by Cartagena Jesuit Alonso de Sandoval, but in the meantime Popayán elites strained to accumulate capital from remaining indigenous tributaries to make the (ultimately unsubsidized) transition to a slave-based mining economy.[71] The result might not have pleased Auncibay, but the growth of slavery in Popayán was a distinct departure from the rest of the Audiencia of Quito, where gold mining—with the exception of Zaruma (discussed in chapter 4)—all but disappeared after 1600.[72] However it was produced, Popayán gold was a mainstay of Quito's mercantile economy.

❊   ❊   ❊

Washing gold with the *batea* near Barbacoas, Colombia

In 1614 the convent of nuns of the Encarnación of Popayán was audited after a series of scandals involving fiscal and sexual misconduct.[73] One product of this investigation was an inventory of the convent's gold-mining assets, including a gang, or *cuadrilla* of slaves, a variety of tools, beasts of burden, and mining and associated agricultural properties. The overseer of the captive cuadrilla listed each of the forty-seven members, identifying family units and the *capitán,* or head slave miner among them. About a third retained African ethnic or place names as surnames (Congo, Angola, Bañón, Bran, Folupo); thirty-three were active in mining, the rest either underage or engaged in support tasks. Since this number of active miners exceeds the number of men listed, one must assume women (and probably also children) were doing the work of gold extraction as well. Interestingly, the majordomo referred to the miners themselves as "gold pans" *(bateas),* reducing them to their basic economic function as gold washers.[74] These thirty-three "gold pans," he claimed, produced an average of thirteen hundred to fourteen hundred pesos of gold dust per year, or about thirty-nine to forty-two pesos each. At approximately 4.2 grams per peso, the captive miners yielded, in modern terms, from 164.0 to 176.0 grams per year each, or between 5.5 and 6.0 kilograms total. Even if the gold was of high karat this level of production was quite low; it would have yielded only modest rents against the costs of maintaining so many slaves.[75] The documents contain no hint of the possibility of redemption through self-purchase.

Yet the cuadrilla's production at the convent's mines, called San Onofre and San Lorenzo, was not substandard for the region and period. An annual finance charge totaling some 240 to 260 pesos was subtracted from the gross, and the cuadrilla required about 400 pesos "of the said gold" for its sustenance, not including tools "and other necessary things." Another subtraction was the mine administrator's annual salary of 50 pesos. Other mobile capital, unfortunately not priced, but possibly requiring some maintenance as well, included 4 mules used to haul maize to the miners, 140 head of cattle at a nearby pasture to provide meat and milk, and 20 horses, presumably used to round up these cattle and carry burdens. Tools included the thirty-three actual, wooden bateas, or gold pans, fifteen iron excavation bars, and thirty-three *almocafres* (a specialized hand tool for placering). The mining properties themselves included key

Church of La Hermita, Popayán

fixed capital assets, most importantly "their waters and established buildings." But even with all the necessary deductions, which also included a
9-peso consulting fee *(mineraje)* paid to an experienced miner, probably the
majordomo, the output of the mines exceeded the convent's *censo,* or long-
term loan income in 1613.[76]

Of the forty-two captives of working age, twenty-five were men and
seventeen were women, yielding an effective sex ratio of about 3:2.[77] This
was not quite the proportion called for by Quito's oidores (two-thirds
male), but it was much closer than the figures presented above for the city
of Quito. A total of twenty-two slaves in the group lived in apparently
stable unions, and of these eleven couples, seven had produced offspring. If
this case is at all indicative, slave mining operations at this early date seem
to have been organized in hopes of reproducing the labor force.

The low productivity of this particular group of captives—in terms of
gold pesos registered per slave per year—may have been the result of
calculable factors such as poor-quality deposits, inadequate or inept
supervision, or redirection of mine labor to subsistence activities during
times of necessity or drought (placer mining was, after all, as dependent on
water as agriculture). But early modern Spanish mentalities regarding
captivity and redemption may have also jammed the wheels of rational
commerce from time to time. Masters, even when insulated from the
miners' groans by walls and hired overseers, had to think about their souls'
survival; caught up in scandal, the nuns of the Encarnación may have been
uniquely placed to ponder the tangled relationship between just rents and
"the wages of sin" circa 1614.

It was not by accident that such a large slave gang—large for the
period, at least—belonged to a convent, a corporation made up of the
daughters of local elites. Nuns professed as brides of Christ, their
bridewealth often consisting of little more than one or two African
slaves.[78] These slaves were many things to them: domestic servants, badges
of prestige, companions, insurance against poverty in this world and
perhaps against prolonged captivity in the world to come. Pooled together
and planted in the goldfields they could underwrite hundreds of lifetimes
spent in chaste contemplation, and could literally buy a stairway to heaven
for their masters, if not themselves. In the high Andes far from the
touchstone Mediterranean, in a rent-seeking mercantilist age where gold

still glittered in a sea of silver, in an embattled Catholic world just a generation or two removed from the Council of Trent, here more than elsewhere, perhaps, the line between material and spiritual capital blurred and even disappeared. Here treasure could be dug from the bowels of the earth, traded for status, renown, an unforgettable funeral, and perhaps, though no one would have been so bold as to claim it possible, even eternal life. Slaves produced cash rents, rents sustained elite society. Elites reinvested rents in pious works, a "grace fund" that ensured a speedy release from the hellish captivity of Purgatory.

What do we make of Ysabel de Baeza's apparent twist of the knife in her 1594 will? Or the apparent irony (for us at least) of a nunnery sustained by enslaved gold miners? Certainly it should not be forgotten that indigenous labor was the most important subsidy of the colonial Andean economy, in Quito and elsewhere, but as this brief examination of Quito's cloistered urbanites and scattered gold-seekers has demonstrated, from the beginning African slavery was the reverse of the coin of European freedom in many parts of the Americas—freedom from mechanical drudgery, from social obscurity, from spiritual mendicancy— indeed it was at times the whole coin, the redemption value of white bodies and souls.

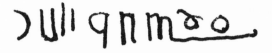

NATIVE LORDS WRITE TO KING PHILIP II

Most Powerful Lord:
We, don Francisco Anaguampla, curaca and cacique principal of the town of Píntag [just southeast of Quito], don Alonso Asanguiango, don Juan Golimba, don Andrés and don Juan Pallacho, Juan Mitima, and don Andrés Inga, *principales* of the town, in our name and in the name of the other Indians in the town of Píntag do declare: In your Royal Name the Indians were ordered to be gathered into towns in order to be taught the elements of the faith and to become experienced in civil life. And so we gathered in and populated the town of Píntag at your command; and at the same time our ancestors were assured by your royal *amparo* or certificate of ownership that the lands we had near Píntag would remain ours. Jerónimo de Cepeda, the official in charge of the resettlement, put up boundary markers and assigned them as our fields and lands for our sustenance, marked them off and also set aside common grazing land for the town of Píntag, all of this done according to these landholdings. However, little by little, day after day, many Spaniards have been encroaching on these lands, and, to our misfortune, they have been occupying land within the markers set up by Jerónimo de Cepeda. They have created so many farms and ranches that they now surround the whole town and we have no place to get firewood or water without asking their permission; so we perish of hunger because we have no lands to sow or grazing land for our cattle. We owe over 2,000 *fanegas* of wheat for tribute because we have no community lands to sow for paying the tribute and even though we do sow something, their cattle eat it; they force us to work on their farms so we lose our own crops. We cannot go to church to religious instruction, and when we do go on Sundays or holy days they grab us, mistreat us, and force us to guard their cattle and work for them as if we were their slaves. We are just so many and cannot do everything. And so we hate to go to religious instruction, and because of excessive labor both men and women flee the town, for even though Your Highness ordered that a fifth

of the Indians do such work and no more, they do not content themselves with this fifth, nor even with half.

In order to remedy this, we plead and ask Your Highness to send a royal order commanding that the boundary markers of our lands and common grazing land be respected and to this effect the markers be placed in their original sites as they were originally set. An official should be named to do this and certify that these are our lands. We ask above all things justice and what is conducive to this. So we ask that the original provision be returned to us, etc.

don Francisco Anaguampla, n.d. [c. 1580]

AGI Escribanía de Cámara 924c, f.757; trans. and repr. in Nicholas Cushner, *Farm and Factory: The Jesuits and the Development of Agrarian Capitalism in Colonial Quito, 1600–1767* (Albany: State University of New York Press, 1982), 181–82.

THREE: Tilling the Center

In 1597 doña Beatriz Ango bequeathed her inheritance, a choice mix of urban and rural properties, to her grandson Carlos. Doña Beatriz, now probably in her late sixties, had retreated to a small room "behind the chimney" of a house located on the lower flanks of the mighty Pichincha Volcano overlooking the capital city of Quito and eastern snow-peaks from the neighborhood of San Roque. Perhaps it was time for doña Beatriz to follow the example of contemporary women of her class: to spend the rest of her days in austere isolation, contemplating past deeds and the fate of her soul. Beatriz Ango was daughter of one of the great caciques, or native lords, of Otavalo, the richest of the highland agricultural provinces north of Quito. She was better known, however, as the widow of a man the Spanish called don Francisco Topatauchi, "El Auqui" (i.e., "The Prince"), dead since 1582.

Shortly after conquest the properties—urban plots and scattered farms and ranches—had been granted by Quito's town council to don Francisco, who by birthright if not universal indigenous assent was arguably Quito's native lord of lords. His father had been, after all, the fearless Atawallpa, last of the independent Inkas, executed in 1533 despite an eye-popping gold-and-silver ransom.[1] But the clash at Cajamarca and subsequent misadventures of the Pizarro brothers were already distant memories in turn-of-the-century Quito. Now the prince's grandson, in the documents "don Carlos Atabalipa," was reduced to petty real estate management in a city crawling with predatory Spaniards of a new kind.

Apparently don Carlos had no knack for this business, and within a dozen years his debts and subsequent sell-offs led to the literal "fall" of the House of Atawallpa. In desperation he at last traded away the carved stone portal of the main dwelling to the builders of San Roque's new parish church. The prized and symbol-laden threshold sold for only 150 pesos. (Oddly enough one of the buyers was a neighbor, Andrés Sánchez Gallque, the indigenous painter of the 1599 portrait of the Esmeraldas ambassadors.) If it was any consolation, masses would still be said for the departed Inka prince; his 1582 will had stipulated a chaplaincy be funded by rents from a rural property not far from the city. As long as his heirs could retain claim to this patch of earth, called Cumbayá, its fruits could be sold to help free his soul.[2]

As don Carlos was losing his shirt and perhaps slowing his grandfather's release from Purgatory, a traveling salesman named Bernardo Más arrived in Quito with a young, unbaptized indigenous captive whom he sold to a hatmaker for 140 silver pesos. Twenty-year-old Xi (pronounced "she") had been seized in March of 1599 in the Central Cordillera of the Colombian Andes northeast of Popayán, victim of a new wave of Spanish attacks on Pijao, Páez, and Utimá "rebels." Rather like the maroons of Esmeraldas, these native mountaineers had come to be regarded as traitors after three generations of successfully driving out or killing every gold prospector or missionary foolish enough to challenge their autonomy. Also like the maroons, they showed no signs of giving up.

As a result, King Philip II had signed a series of proclamations allowing for the enslavement of Pijaos like Xi and various refractory neighbors in the early 1590s. This was a punishment *(castigo)* rarely meted out to indigenous peoples in the Spanish colonies, restricted almost exclusively to nomadic raiders in Chile and New Mexico, and of course professed Muslims in the Philippines. Enslavement in such circumstances—à la Aristotle's "just war"—entailed branding, shackles, and all the humiliations associated with African captivity, yet unlike that slavery this "punishment" was neither permanent nor hereditary. If not resold or felled by disease in the interim, Xi would work for the Quito hatmaker ten years, after which time he was to be released to his own recognizance. Now, in mid-June of 1600, he would join the ever more diverse mix of captives and castaways crowding Quito's bustling market squares.[3]

❊   ❊   ❊

Once again captivity—in both the brutal physical and complex psychological senses—and its inverse, redemption, would form the contours of everyday life, in this case for greater Quito's indigenous majority, high and low. The intermontane core alone had been home to several hundred thousand native Andeans at the city's Spanish refounding in 1534, and for the vanquished the earthquake of military defeat was followed by aftershocks of pestilence, dispossession, forced migration, uncompensated servitude, racialized taxation, abduction, and rape. Whole valleys were allotted to roughly fifty conquistadors in the central highlands, tributes and labor drafts levied through the peculiar institutions of encomienda and mita, youths snatched from their families to serve as domestics and concubines (slavelike) in a new master's townhouse, or as expendable porters on some hare-brained quest for treasure in Amazonia or the Pacific lowlands.

As with African slaves redemption in these harsh circumstances came usually at death, and thus in the first decades of Spanish rule were tens and even hundreds of thousands of native Quiteños redeemed. With few exceptions the colonizer's baser impulses and reflexive self-deception predominated, coarse veils of greed and pity alike obscuring the chaotic splendor of multiple Andean chiefdoms and lowland tropical cultures of astonishing physical, linguistic, political, and artistic range. The new administrative order, Spain's typically tone-deaf late Renaissance bureaucracy, demanded this kaleidoscope be shattered, its varicolored sand-grains separated and sorted, individuals and whole communities alike reduced to quanta called "Indians."

But Spanish colonists and missionaries, however greedy or misguided, never dreamed of genocide. These "Indians" were subjects of God and king, and although many would be brutally exploited across three centuries of colonial rule, subject peoples too had rights. Like the vanquished Moriscos of Al-Andalus they had first of all a right to subsist, the crown an obligation to allot sufficient lands and waters. Second, and critical to any understanding of the Spanish American case, native peoples had been granted legal recourse against mistreatment by both private individuals (usually holders of encomienda grants) and government or church agents. Outcomes would almost always favor the powerful, but the courts were nevertheless obligated by order of the king to hear and document all indigenous grievances. Furthermore, the pope had declared Amerindian souls equivalent (perhaps even superior) to those of Europeans in the eyes of God. The message to all colonists? Mistreat His innocent "children" and risk damnation.

Yet Quito's native peoples did not sit idly by, waiting to be exploited or annihilated. On the contrary, native expressions of willpower flood the colonial record. There was violent resistance, like that of Xi and his fellow Pijaos. There was also wily and creative adaptation, like that of the caciques, market women, and thousands of working men discussed below. Then there was outright collaboration within the new colonial order, as glimpsed in the case of Francisco Atawallpa and his descendants. Even at the core it seemed the conqueror's work was never done, while at the margins the imperial juggernaut, for all its smoke and noise, proved less than invincible. On the other hand, no amount of wile could negate the cumulative effect of Old World epidemic disease, which by 1599 had reduced greater Quito's indigenous population by nearly three quarters. As refugees fled to the cities, Spanish immigrants and their descendants—among them a growing number of mestizos, mulattos, and other crown subjects of mixed heritage—moved quickly to seize the rich lands they left behind.

Native Lords, Merchant Women, and Working Men

The fall of the house of Atawallpa helped ensure that no neo-Inka nobility comparable to that of Cuzco would develop in colonial Quito. Meanwhile, other native lords fared well under the new system, and some even thrived. Best demonstrated thus far by the mixed-heritage Yllescas and Arobe headmen of Esmeraldas, it was the native lords' ability to adapt to a new and dynamic political economy, primarily as intermediaries, that enabled them to remain indispensable. This ability to adapt to and even exploit the changing imperial system was not a chiefly monopoly, however. The record clearly shows indigenous women from all over Quito's vast hinterland simultaneously taking quick advantage of tax exemptions to form a new class of urban retailers. Average indigenous men also found ways to beat the system, some by becoming apprentices and later master artisans, but it is clear that for them the colonial order presented more challenges than opportunities.

Native Lords

Spanish colonialism in the Americas after the turn of the sixteenth century was based on the quasi-feudal institution of encomienda, or "entrusteeship." In this system, conquerors and other prominent colonists enjoyed rents, or tributes, derived from indigenous surplus production and male labor. Tribute collection and other transactions between holders of encomiendas (encomenderos) and indigenous householders were carried out by more-or-less pliant native lords, the original caciques of the Greater Antilles. Brothers, sons, and other heirs could be *principales* (in New Granada called *capitanes*), sometimes lords of smaller, satellite communities responsible for rendering tribute and labor quotas to the recognized "great chief." Where such men and lineages could not be identified the Spanish sought to create them.

Once named, native lords were cajoled and sometimes harshly persecuted by encomenderos and also the crown when tributes came up short, yet they also enjoyed incentives that allowed them to serve as privileged tax farmers. Caciques, principales, and their families were exempt from tribute payment, sales taxes (alcabalas), and rotational labor drafts. Thus, a few managed to combine a knack for land management or trade with access to precious resources and markets to accumulate significant capital. The coastal cacique Diego Tomalá, for example, used tribute in cordage and hides and a prime location near the port of Guayaquil to carve out a personal commercial empire inherited by his son, Francisco. In 1587 the younger Tomalá's Spanish wife was said to be carried around Puná Island by a dozen native subjects on a litter.[4]

In recent years ethnohistorians have examined Quito's early colonial chiefdoms, or *cacicazgos,* in hopes of evoking some sense of pre-Inka politics in the populous central highlands.[5] Frank Salomon has identified several important patterns: 1) from Popayán to Loja the largest political units consisted of petty chiefdoms made up of *llajtakuna* (Quechua singular *llajta*), usually non-nucleated villages centered on maize plantings and headed by male hereditary lords and occasionally sub-lords; 2) commerce in goods and services linked highlands and adjacent lowlands in a manner distinct from the central Andean "archipelago" system, sometimes involving itinerant merchants called *mindaláes* (the city of Quito had apparently been a crossroads for such traffic prior to its development as an Inka fortress and retreat); and 3) Inka impact in the region was both late and shallow, evidenced in part by the quick disintegration of imperial structures upon Spanish arrival.

Native lords more often than not favored the Spanish over the Inkas and they may have even reverted to a pre-Incaic style of politics after conquest. Salomon emphasizes the caciques' regal behavior in the form of "harsh, fiery, and strict" public personae; "institutionalized generosity," specifically ritualized collection and sharing out of food surpluses and maize beer (but minus the hoarding and exchange of cloth products typical of central Andean power play); and emphasis on the lord's house "as a symbolic center, not only of political activity, but of cosmic order."[6] Though certainly evocative of pre-Columbian and even pre-Incaic forms, Salomon's evidence for these structures and patterns of chiefly behavior consists primarily of Spanish documents dated c. 1558–1610 and probably better describes the Quito hinterland at the turn of the seventeenth century than at the turn of the sixteenth.

In moving the argument beyond the question of origins or the essential nature of chiefdoms, Karen Vieira Powers and the late Udo Oberem have documented the colonial careers of several of Quito's most entrepreneurial caciques, among them the resourceful Hachos and Hatis of Latacunga, and the Duchiselas of Riobamba.[7] In these instances local headmen appear to have padded dubious claims of pre-Columbian ancestral importance in order to carve out quasi-principalities scarcely resembling older forms. With the possible exception of the Hachos, these appear to have been truly "neo-cacicazgos," cleverly forged in both senses of the word.

Although pre-Incaic structures and rituals of authority were no doubt revived to some extent by all three families, the Hachos, Hatis, and Duchiselas benefited most under colonial rule by playing off Spanish greed and ignorance. Most encomenderos were no doubt harsh and demanding overlords, but they were few and foreign, and thus more desperate and credulous than is often assumed. When the Spanish overstepped their bounds, self-made neo-caciques could appeal to king or church officials for redress. The crown could easily suppress or ignore the claims of Inka noble heirs like the hapless Atawallpas of Quito, but lesser middlemen were an unfortunate necessity. Like the many far-flung and wily clients of antiquity—and like the Afro-indigenous chieftains of Esmeraldas—the native lord of Quito in the age of the Habsburgs was often a quick study in imperial politics.

We know of one such native lord of Quito, don Diego Collín, through his extraordinarily rich 1598 last will and testament.[8] Collín was an ethnic Panzaleo lord based at Machachi, a cool highland village about a day's ride south of Quito, and he appears to have retained considerable power and wealth under Spanish dominion. We do not know precisely how he did so, but the cultural pastiche that emerges from his will suggests the archetypal betwixt-and-between colonial player. As a sworn Christian Collín commended his soul to God, asked to be buried beneath the great altar of Machachi's church, and donated livestock and luxury vestments (in this case sheets of blue and crimson Chinese taffeta) to an indigenous sodality. A finely wrought Spanish saddle with iron stirrups would be sold to fund his burial and requiem masses.

Collín was also married according to Catholic precepts to an indigenous princess, doña Catalina Chicssi Sanguil, but their union had proved sterile. In order to maintain status as a bona fide native lord in the eyes of his subjects, don Diego had required both wives (plural) and heirs, Christian sacraments notwithstanding. Indeed his will suggests he had successfully revived pre-Columbian patterns of polygamy in spite of his apparently sincere conversion by disguising them as Spanish-style *machista* fornication and adultery. Thus the clever cacique bluntly confessed having fathered three sons and five daughters "in different women who served me," while still making certain to distinguish illegitimate favorites *(hijos naturales)* from "bastards" *(bastardos)* for purposes of succession and inheritance.[9]

Don Diego Collín's probate inventory is equally suggestive of his composite role in the greater Machachi community at the end of the sixteenth century. A significant component of his estate consisted, as Frank Salomon has pointed out, of beadwealth and other locally esteemed Quiteño goods, perhaps most interestingly sufficient spears and feathers to constitute "a virtual Amazonian costume." Yet many other items emphasize Collín's links to the Inkas. Stacks of fine indigenous textiles *(cumbi/qumpi)*, some made from prized and exotic vicuña wool, were carefully redistributed among heirs, along with Inka-style drinking vessels *(keros)* and beaten-silver-and-feather head-dresses ("crowns," or *llautu*).[10] Most explicitly, don Diego mentioned farmlands *(chacras)* "set aside and given me by the Inkas." These were maize fields worked by servile specialists *(camayos/kamayujkuna)* for the cacique's benefit, intended to provide not only sustenance for his household, but also surpluses to be redistributed to the broader Panzaleo "family" on ritual occasions, now identified as the Christian feasts of Nativity and Easter.

Clearly Collín had benefited from collaboration with the earlier, Cuzco-based overlords, yet amazingly he donated these two caballerías of prime bottomland to don Diego Sancho de la Carrera, the encomendero to whom he was now responsible for rendering tributes and laborers. It was a gesture he said he hoped would benefit his soul, but this curious donation also suggests a revival of old patterns of ritualized lord/overlord gifting, full of implied expectations of reciprocity. In similar fashion, houses and other land parcels were left to various individual and corporate heirs, a prized orchard to the Dominicans.

In yet another enigmatic move a half-dozen pewter plates were to be given to two sons and a nephew, but only after they had held "offerings" on the cacique's sepulcher for a year. Later in the document, where sheep were distributed to wife and daughters, Collín requested that "the six [head] remaining be placed in offering on the day of my burial." The attention given to masses suggests don Diego was a sincere Christian, but was animal sacrifice a funerary practice encouraged by the Council of Trent, whose rules had just been proclaimed in the Quito Synod of 1594? In fact, animal *ofrendas* were common to reformed Baroque Spanish mortuary ritual, both in the colonies and on the peninsula.[11] "I name my soul as heir," Collín added, asking that his executors carry out unspecified pious works upon his death. One can only speculate as to why the cacique specifically banned Quito's bishop or any church agent from meddling with or counting up the value of these obsequies.

The remainder of Collín's will was concerned with more hard-nosed succession issues since he had no legitimate heir, at least in the strict legal sense demanded by the new colonial order. Perhaps here the gift of Inka lands to his encomendero served as pledge against further land partition and the potential dismantling of the large and tangled web of relationships that constituted the Panzaleo cacicazgo. Though his will remains in part cryptic, it clearly demonstrates that don Diego Collín had mastered the sort of polyvalence required of Quito's successful native lords under Spanish rule.

The 1606 will of *cacica* Catalina Tuza, heiress of a Pasto-area chiefdom, is similarly ambiguous and rich. Like Collín, Tuza's marriage had produced no legitimate heirs, forcing her to sort out succession in a way acceptable to both Spanish courts and her own indigenous subjects. She had inherited the north-highland cacicazgo as the daughter of a paramount chief *(cacique principal)*. Now, nearing death, she chose a very young nephew to succeed her, then mandated that *his* heir be a daughter.[12] The immediate naming of a male successor satisfied Spanish expectations in lieu of primogeniture, but the call for future reversion to female leadership was a bold challenge, perhaps even a blast from Pasto's prehispanic past.

Like Diego Collín, Catalina Tuza appears to have been a sincere Christian (though very likely on her own, rather than her priest's, terms).[13] In any case, her will called for the auction of certain goods to fund the further indoctrination of her subjects, whose ignorance of basic Catholic principles begged redress. Most notable in the testament, however, is Tuza's devotion of significant property—perhaps half her land and livestock, and nearly all her jewelry and clothing—to the erection and maintenance of a family chapel in her home village, also called Tuza (modern San Gabriel, Ecuador). Her belief that numerous masses financed by the auction of Spanish-style silverware and indigenous garment pins and coral bracelets would aid in releasing her and her parents' (and her dead husband's) soul from temporary captivity in Purgatory was probably genuine.

On the other hand, a conspicuous family sepulcher in Tuza itself would serve as a public reminder of the legitimacy of doña Catalina's lineage (now redefined to suit both natives and Spaniards). The sepulcher was not just a cold architectural conceit, but rather a "living" shrine that would employ a priest and sufficient subalterns to change vestments and light candles continuously for years to come. However economically (or spiritually) questionable from a modern perspective, Catalina Tuza's last wishes were absolutely typical of her class; elite contemporaries, both indigenous and Spanish, saw such pious theatrics as the clearest means of expressing status, and with it power. The cacica apparently wanted everyone to know she, like her Habsburg overlord in Spain, was royalty, and like him she and her ancestors were moving closer to godhead.

As these cases suggest, new religious and legal precepts could be both sincerely embraced and sharply modified by indigenous leaders, often to the befuddlement and annoyance of Spanish priests and seigneurial elites. At times this was the simple, expected result of what historian James Lockhart has called "double mistaken identity," the idea that colonial indigenes and Europeans, formed as they were by very old and resilient structures of thought, tended to speak past one another.[14] One need only study a little Quechua (not to mention less widely spoken tongues like Shuar, Tsáchela, Kamsá, or Páez) to understand the likelihood of this scenario and the potential of its effects in old Quito; in short, local language and worldview, or more accurately, cosmovision, are practically inseparable. At other times, however, and not infrequently if one reads between the lines of the mature colonial record (specifically including the frequent complaints of the colonizer), it appears native Andeans understood Spanish assumptions well enough but still boldly chose to lay down their own willful counterpoint.

Perhaps average indigenous folk only rarely had to fathom whole new mentalities vis-à-vis their own, but cacicas and caciques could not afford such blinkers. Most quickly learned it was alliances with powerful Spaniards, the lavish embrace of Catholic ideals, if not ideas, and manipulation of the courts that defined the postconquest shuffle, a kind of Machiavellian chess game played with a mix of local and European rules. Indeed, up to at least 1599 the colonial Andean world, filled as it was with recalcitrant and mobile Quechua speakers, rife with rumors of treasure, and bordered on all sides by hostile forest dwellers, offered numerous possibilities for enterprising native elites. Though their actions as recorded

Highland Quichua House, La Rinconada, Ecuador

often bring to mind stories of wartime collaboration they were very much active makers of Quito's history at every level. In this context of constant negotiation, the African-born neo-cacique Alonso de Yllescas of Esmeraldas was no anomaly for exploiting his interstice to the hilt.

Merchant Women

There were other interstices to exploit in 1599 Quito, and indigenous women of all ranks and ethnicities were especially quick to carve out profitable niches. Under intense pressure from reformist clerics, the crown had by the late sixteenth century exempted all persons identified as Amerindian from sales taxes as a means of easing the head-tax, or tribute burdens of non-noble indigenous men. Following the law of unintended consequences, the crown's assumption that men were the only economically significant members of the indigenous American family effectively freed many native women from all direct tax burdens. Certainly married women were forced to share their husbands' tribute obligations indirectly, but a number of enterprising "Indian" *solteras* took up (or, in some cases, continued practicing) commerce, and like certain business-minded caciques, a few grew rich.

A sampling of the wills of Quito's women traders suggests most had migrated to the city from the hinterland; some had probably been abducted by Spanish soldiers. Once settled, they spent the better part of their lives in the several open-air "flea-markets," or *tiangueces,* of the highland capital, the benign climate freeing them from any absolute need to rent shop space. In spite of their usually humble beginnings, these women soon began trading more than the vegetables and cheap pottery authorized by the town council. The 1598 probate inventory of Catalina Cañar, widow of a Latacunga sub-chief, reveals a web of connections to not only local but also interoceanic trade circuits. Her possessions included skirts and shawls from Cañar (near Cuenca), Cajamarca, "Huancavelica," Bogotá, New Spain, and China (a blue taffeta), along with a variety of gold and silver garment pins *(topos/tupus).* She seems also to have invested a small amount of cash in the highly lucrative Panama trade.[15]

Another indigenous retailer in Quito was doña Ynés Enríquez, a native of Panzaleo and technically a subject of don Diego Collín. Her will, filed in late 1599, lists debts owed her for jugs of maize beer *(chicha/aswa)* and indigenous-style garments, some made with Andean fabrics (Huancavelica, Cajamarca, Quijós), others from imported ones (Castile, Portugal). In the course of her trading activities, doña Ynés had managed to accumulate a small amount of livestock and a house in the St. Sebastian neighborhood. Her liquid capital was in the form of silver and gold topos and "coral" (perhaps native Spondylus shell) necklaces and bracelets, some of them held in hock.[16]

Similar was Ysabel Angay, native of the Cuenca-area village of Tutiexi. She filed a will in Quito in 1599, noting various debts for jugs of chicha and baskets of maize, and though her own wealth consisted largely of indigenous-style skirts, she must have managed to put together a substantial dowry since her daughter married a cacique from the important textile-producing village of Sigchos.[17] To the chagrin of local clergy, many indigenous and mixed-heritage women in contemporary Quito chose differently, avoiding marriage while openly engaging in temporary relationships. Meanwhile, married women managed to secure divorces with alarming frequency. This state of affairs outraged Bishop Luis López de Solis, who informed the Indies Council in a 1597 letter that he had established a "house of correction" dedicated to Saint Martha. Here "lost" and "scandalous" indigenous and mestiza women were stripped of what the bishop called their "free sensuality" and made to repent. He boasted of an already evident "great reformation," claiming that Quito's women now shared what he thought was a healthy "fear of entering there."[18]

Women of mixed heritage were technically required to pay sales taxes since they fell legally outside the Indian sphere, but some masqueraded as indigenous when questioned by Spanish officials. Such an apparently mestiza trader of local birth was María Rodríguez, daughter of a Captain Zamora, killed in the 1546 battle of Añaquito. By the time she filed her will in 1589 Rodríguez had had four children by a man who repeatedly promised marriage but never followed through. Perhaps it was just as well, since her will suggests she had no need of a husband. Rodríguez was owed mostly small debts by indigenous customers living in and around Quito, but apparently also employed indigenous men as factors in Quijós Province and beyond. Diego Tiguiz, for example, had gone to Amazonia to sell beads *(chaquira),* varicolored garments *(murupachas),* and other items on her behalf.[19]

Rodríguez had also dealt in oxen, hardware, and jugs of chicha, and served as something of a banker, holding a fifty-peso dowry for a young mestiza (like herself), and loaning coin to an indigenous man from Guayllabamba to cure his child's wounded leg. A plebeian version of Quito's high-profile merchants and moneylenders, María Rodríguez seems to have invested her profits in two ways: first, she accumulated wealth in compact form (beads, garments, cash, and topos—all willed to her daughter, Ysabel); second, she bequeathed substantial sums to various sodalities to say masses for her departed soul and for those of her dead relatives.[20]

Indigenous Quiteñas likewise extended credit to plebeian customers. María de Amores's will was drawn up in August of 1596. According to the document, she was owed five pesos by "Ana mulata" for an *anaco,* or indigenous-style skirt, and her belongings included a large Chinese porcelain jar and garments made from indigenous, Spanish, and East Asian fabrics.[21] Also likely engaged in the indigenous-goods-and-credit business was Francisca Vilcacabra, a native of Pomasque whose 1596 inventory listed 250 silver pesos *(tostones),* a variety of fine garments, and what were described as "large" topos; she had also arranged to be buried in the "Chapel of the Natives," a portion of the Dominican complex run by an indigenous confraternity dedicated to Our Lady of the Rosary. She left 100 pesos to augment dowries of female friends, but her principal heir was a two-and-a-half-year-old boy named Francisco, to be cared for by his father, "Luis Serrano, my master." Serrano, apparently a Spaniard, was also named executor.[22] It remains unclear to what degree this was a symbiotic or sexually exploitative relationship, but clearly no one had managed to stop Francisca Vilcacabra from accumulating substantial wealth in her own name.

Sometimes Quito market women's links to wholesalers are explicitly revealed, as in a 1598 obligation letter between two Spaniards for 116 pesos' worth of textiles, consigned to an indigenous retailer named Marta Pasña.[23] A clearer example was Ynés Cufichaguan, born in the Otavalo-area town of Tontaqui but a longtime Quito resident when she had a will drawn up in early 1597. Cufichaguan was owed numerous small debts for merchandise and livestock purchased by indigenous folk and people of African descent, some of them slaves. Thus, alongside copper pots and iron tools, one finds debts like the following in her probate inventory: thirteen pesos owed by "the *curaca* of Pimampiro, named Chumasquina"; "the black woman of the Fleming's house, one *tostón";* nine pesos from "the free black woman Guiomar, who used to belong to Captain Salazar," and so forth.[24] Just like Quito's big wholesalers, women like Ynés Cufichaguan and María Rodríguez knew how to weigh risks and opportunities in the course of pursuing economic security for themselves, their children, and their souls.[25] Likewise, their generous extension of credit to cash-starved consumers in the popular sector helped sustain the flow of goods and services.

As historian Kimberly Gauderman has recently shown, Quito's indigenous market women would form a powerful commercial bloc by the middle of the seventeenth century, a serious challenge to small-scale Spanish and mestizo male retailers, or *pulperos.* These men, subject as they were to rising urban rents and a variety of taxes, would complain bitterly to local and crown authorities over the advantages enjoyed by the so-called

Agricultural plots, La Rinconada, Ecuador

gateras crowding the city's plazas. But with their accustomed mix of tenac-
ity and wile these female entrepreneurs would go on trading freely despite
legislative attempts to control them, and their customers would go on supporting them, voting for "duty-free" goods with their feet and pocket-
books. Seen here in embryonic form circa 1599, the so-called informal
commercial economy is still in the hands of modern Ecuadorian and
southern Colombian women.

Working Men

Non-noble indigenous men, however cunning, faced a colonial net with
fewer holes. Only a tiny minority wound up enslaved like Xi and his
fellow Pijaos, but the Spanish had other ways of punishing a man for
being an "Indian." Worst among these was the encomienda, which,

especially in marginal districts with significant gold deposits, could be a lot like slavery for the average tributary.

In 1589, for example, native (presumably Palta) gold miners working near Loyola, a tiny and remote town in the highlands south of Loja, charged their encomendero, Pedro de Bañuelos, with multiple counts of assault, rape, and other crimes against family members. Angered by work slowdowns, Bañuelos hung three individuals upside down over a fire, forcing them to inhale smoke before rubbing their eyes with a mixture of urine and capsicum peppers.[26] The charges against Bañuelos in fact extended to murder, since one victim apparently died of torture wounds, but Quito's audiencia sentenced the sadistic encomendero to only two years service in the South Sea galleys and a small fine. In his absence, the state attorney noted, the crown would administer the encomienda and collect its revenues.[27]

A similar case from Loyola dating to the late 1570s suggests these abuses were not unique. In fact, Bañuelos may have learned his outrageous behavior from the encomendero Juan de Estrada, who was charged with torture, mutilation, and murder of indigenous wards by dog attack.[28] Encomienda abuses were equally rife in gold-rich Popayán, where miners openly flaunted the law by renting laborers to one another as if they were slaves.[29]

These are extreme cases, to be sure, but virtually everywhere it was applied the encomienda was extraordinarily punishing for men and disruptive of indigenous lifeways more generally. It entailed concentrated resettlement, periodic labor drafts, twice-yearly tribute payment in cash and kind, and indoctrination in the Catholic faith (usually limited to rote participation in the sacraments and forced church attendance). Assessments were periodically adjusted when tributaries, men aged eighteen to fifty, were identified and counted by a roving magistrate. Though on the wane by 1599 since inheritance was limited to two generations and native populations were plummeting from disease, in Quito several prime encomienda holdings remained in private hands until the second half of the seventeenth century.[30]

Even as encomienda rents were reverting to the crown all over the highlands, indigenous labor was made available to private citizens and corporate entities through a new institution after about 1570. This was the

mita, an hispanicized revival of the Inka corvée, or *mit'a* (literally "turn").
The timing of the labor subsidy changeover was critical, since Quito's
economy was undergoing a major transition from mineral production to
textile manufacture in precisely these years (c. 1580 to 1605). At the base of
both industries, however, lay Quito's agricultural and demographic core,
the fertile lands and ample hands that had attracted both Inka and Spanish
conquistadors.

In a pioneering 1947 study, Ecuadorian historian Aquiles Pérez
identified no less than sixteen forms of mita labor in late sixteenth-
century Quito. There were mitas for domestic service, for gathering
firewood, fodder, and household food items, for herding livestock, working
on farms, tending orchards, pressing cane, gristmilling, construction, tile-
making, weaving, and mining. These were just the mitas allotted to private
citizens. For the city, church, and realm there were drafts for both sacred
and profane building construction, roadwork, sewage repair, mail delivery,
way-station hospitality service, and finally and perhaps most physically
punishing, long-distance porterage.[31]

Indeed, well before the encomienda faded indigenous men were
mustered by caciques and handed over to regional crown representatives—
the *corregidores de indios*—for periodic repartition. Whereas the infamous
silver-mine mita of Potosí took away one-seventh of highland Peru and
Bolivia's male indigenous laborers at any given time, Quito's "ordinary
mita" siphoned away a fifth (or, as the caciques of Píntag testified in the
letter preceding this chapter, more than half). By 1599 perhaps five
thousand to ten thousand men were engaged in mita projects at any given
moment in the immediate vicinity of Quito.[32]

Compensation for *mitayos,* often withheld in exchange for advanced
food, clothing, and overpriced merchandise, was little more than an
accountant's shell game. After numerous complaints the audiencia
mandated wages more than sufficient to compensate tribute demands in
1591, but even this minimum, about four to six silver pesos per year
(roughly half the cost of the cheapest jug of Peruvian wine) was rarely
met. The use of mitayos in so-called personal service tasks was limited by
viceregal order after 1600, but "slave wages" continued to be the norm in
recalcitrant and isolated Quito, even in state-run enterprises. As late as
1605 mita laborers at the crown-run Latacunga gunpowder factory

Threshing barley, Peguche, Ecuador

received less than two pesos for a dangerous two-month stint mixing nitrates, charcoal, and sulfur.[33] By contrast, African slaves were rented to contemporary shippers and shopowners for about a peso a day.

Perhaps reduced time in Purgatory was promised to the many mita laborers responsible for constructing Quito's fantastic Baroque churches, most of which were begun in precisely these years. Even these projects could take mitayos far afield. In 1598 thirty workers were drafted to the lime kilns at Nono, a hamlet on the northwest outskirts of town; the product of their labors would be distributed to the expanding San Diego monastery near the crumbling house of Atawallpa in Barrio San Roque. Their work, "for the cutting of stone and necessary firewood," was desperately needed to meet an order for one thousand *fanegas* (about fifteen hundred bushels) of lime within four months.[34]

Large-scale gold-mining mitas, discussed in further detail in the next chapter, entailed long-term relocation to distant and unhealthy sites. Crown officials tried to establish such corvées in the Cuenca, Loja, and Pasto areas in the 1570s and 1580s, but indigenous draftees quickly fled, prompting waves of permanent outmigration.[35] Mita rotations in the emerging sweatshops of the central highlands, though perhaps less deadly than the mines, were nearly as unpopular, driving many indigenous men to look for other means to gain a wage (inevitable given tribute demands).

One alternative was to move to the city and either learn a trade or indenture oneself to an elite householder. Like free youths of African descent, young indigenous men were frequently apprenticed among the many artisans of late sixteenth-century Quito. Some became early masters of low-status trades like tanning, blacksmithing, barbering, and dyeing, but by the turn of the seventeenth century high-status indigenous artisans like master painter Andrés Sánchez Gallque were not unusual. In June of 1601 Luis Satig passed the required peer examination to become a master hatmaker. The testpiece was a large and elaborate friar's sombrero. Soon afterward indigenous shoemakers Baltásar Autay and Hernando Díaz demonstrated mastery of their trade in similar, peer-certified tests.[36]

Simpler indenture agreements, or *asientos,* appear frequently in the notary records of 1590s Popayán, where gold dust was common currency and labor quite dear. Here mostly indigenous men from well beyond the city, but also women and occasionally individuals of African or mixed heritage, found a kind of medium existence. As in early colonial North America, indenture was part refuge, part captivity, but here in South America virtually no "white" servants could be found. Labor-hungry masters promised indigenous migrant workers shelter from labor drafts and paid their tributes, deducting all such nuisances from the subject's salary. These deductions could eat deeply and quickly into the servant's pay, however, since the almost universal wage listed in the Popayán agreements was only twelve pesos' worth of low-karat gold dust per year, the going price for a jug of cheap Peruvian wine or only *one yard* of fine Spanish broadcloth.

In 1592 alone a Popayán scribe recorded over one hundred indenture contracts—this in a city with few more than that number of Spanish householders.[37] It is not clear to what extent these were voluntary or coercive arrangements, but most individuals came from outside the city, especially the rural and mineral-rich near north—places like Timaná,

Cartago, Arma, Anserma, Buga, Cali, and Guambía. The second largest group came from Pasto and its hinterland, including the villages of Túquerres, Mocoa, Abades, and Almaguer. Finally there were farther-flung individuals—from Otavalo, Quito, Chimbo, even Cuenca, not to mention Bogotá and various parts of the New Granadan core, far to the northeast. It is more than probable that the majority of these migrants soon found themselves enmeshed in debt traps, but many just as likely hit the road again when squeezed too hard.

Displacement and Demographic Decline

Indigenous peoples migrated not only in response to labor and tribute pressures, but also massive land expropriation and waves of epidemic disease. The consequences are particularly well documented in Quito's fertile central highlands, where most Spanish colonists quickly attempted to re-create peninsular lifeways. They did so in part by introducing a wide array of Old World crops and livestock, essentially ignoring whatever foods and techniques of cultivation indigenous Andeans had developed over the course of their several millennia of stewardship. Europeans also added an alien system of landholding. With the disappearance of the encomienda, particularly, there was less incentive than ever to respect native peoples' right to subsist. In the 1590s Spanish land seizures, many of which dated to the first years after conquest, were for the first time legalized in a process called *composición,* an ill-conceived crown attempt to raise emergency funds that left hard-pressed indigenous villagers throughout the Americas in the lurch.

Displacement

The well-documented experience of Uyumbicho, a *llajta,* or native village just south of Quito, may serve as an example of the changes wrought by shifting colonial policy from conquest to 1599. In 1596, following Spanish complaints of indigenous deforestation and land degradation, the Quito town council assigned new, corporate lands to the residents of Uyumbicho, apparently placing some villagers in wetland areas and on undesirable parcels divided by gorges. Though the documentary record claims that indigenous farmers were destroying valuable timber reserves on the slopes of nearby Atacazo (4,457 m), an extinct volcano, the truth, as Karen Vieira Powers has suggested, was not so simple.

The Uyumbicho land crisis dated to at least the 1550s, its source early postconquest grants that favored Spanish farmers and ranchers, among them conquistador Hernando de la Parra. In spite of (or perhaps because of) demographic decline, Uyumbicho's residents had been continuously squeezed out by their better-connected neighbors, ultimately forced to practice swidden agriculture on ecologically fragile mountain slopes just to get by.[38] The displacement was no surprise given Uyumbicho's nearness to Quito and prime bottomlands reputedly capable of maize yields of 1:60 and 1:70, equal to modern seed-to-harvest ratios.[39] Uyumbicho's native residents fought tenaciously to hold onto remaining lands for another century, but it was clear by 1599 that Quito's elites, with their shrill and disingenuous claims of indigenous environmental degradation, had won the war.

In 1599 the native lords of Píntag, whose letter introduced this chapter, again petitioned the king, echoing Uyumbicho's predicament:

Don Francisco Amaguampla *cacique principal* of the town of Píntag, don Juan Gualumba, don Alonso Asanguiango, don Juan Paillacho, don Juan Ynbalaço, and don Juan Mitima *principales* of the said pueblo of Píntag on the outskirts of the city of Quito, for ourselves and on behalf of our subject Indians, we being altogether three thousand souls: we state that at the time when Your Highness mandated our congregation and resettlement [1573] we were given a royal provision that outlined lands marked and given us for household and communal tillage *[ejidos]*, also mandating that the town council of Quito not redistribute the said lands, nor declare them clear and free of possession, and with respect to this we were assessed in wheat, maize, potatoes, swine, money, and other things to pay as tribute; and as we were making use of the said lands members of the Quito town council to our damage and detriment, going against mandate, took for themselves and redistributed and sold our lands to such an extent that up to the doors of our houses we are surrounded by the lands, farms, and livestock of Spaniards, mestizos, mulattos, and blacks in such a degree that the said livestock enter the church; and the above-said [Spaniards, etc.] do not allow us passage to collect firewood, water, straw, and other necessary things, and as they are so close to our houses they take that which we have in them, and they kill our oxen and horses, claiming they trespass on their lands and damage them, when the real damage has been done to us; and not only do they harass us in these ways, but they also make us work excessively in their fields and in building fences around lands they took from us and also in constructing their houses, all this to such an extent that we have no time to tend our own fields, nor to make the clothing we need to cover ourselves, nor even to pay our tributes. As a result many Indians have died and others have fled, absenting themselves from the said town, and we village headmen are routinely jailed for not being able to pay tributes nor give as many Indians as requested for farm labor, livestock herding, and construction.[40]

"Blacks" and people of so-called mixed heritage may have indeed begun to displace indigenous villagers in some instances, but the native lords' claims in this matter should be approached with caution. Whereas their 1580 letter noted only "Spanish" usurpers, by 1599 it had become standard practice in colonial legal discourse to blame unnamed "black" and "mixed" persons for various and sundry crimes and misdeeds in hopes of appealing to the king's presumed sense of outrage. When such persons were involved in land takeovers, it was more often as majordomos doing an absentee Spanish master's bidding.

Was Spanish rule any more onerous than that of the Inkas? Although it seems to have been far from obvious to Quito's native lords at first, within a generation of conquest Spanish demands had clearly far outstripped those of their predecessors. Again, Uyumbicho may serve as an example. Headed by the Zumba family of caciques, the llajta of Uyumbicho had been unusually well integrated into the Inka system by the time of Spanish arrival, evidenced by its fiercely loyal resistance in the early 1530s. The Inkas had drawn surpluses from Uyumbicho's residents in the form of vegetable produce, straw, and cotton cloth, the latter an exotic product brought by outliers in hotter Tungurahua. Labor requirements under the mit'a seem to have been limited to firewood collection, tending of royal camelid herds, and serving important travelers at the nearby way station *(tampu/tambo)* on the Inka Trail.[41]

Village land use was apparently not altered significantly under Inka rule, although some maize fields may have been redistributed in the manner noted for Panzaleo, above. Other chacras, or hand-tilled fields, may have been set aside for the royal cult as per Cuzco tradition. Most significantly, the Inkas had resettled a number of *mitmajkuna* from the refractory north-Peruvian provinces of Chachapoyas and Huancabamba *in* Uyumbicho itself c. 1500. The exact nature of these newcomers' relationship with the aboriginal residents and the Zumba family remains unclear, but the lack of evidence of competition for resources or other conflict may suggest accommodation.[42] Surrounding native lords may have viewed Uyumbicho's situation as subservient in the extreme at the height of Inka power, but when measured against life under the Spanish circa 1599, it must have appeared almost utopian.

As early as the 1570s a certain nostalgia for Inka times was in fact expressed by some of Quito's native lords, but idealizing the past would have little direct effect on the grating realities of the present. With the exception of a brief and abortive tumult in seventeenth-century Otavalo, no messianic Inka revival movement ever materialized in the audiencia kingdom of Quito. Perhaps this was in part because unity in Inka times had been a mirage, and fully integrated "imperial" llajtas like Uyumbicho and Machachi had been the exception rather than the rule.[43] By 1599 Quito's indigenous majority—exemplified here by the native lords of Píntag—turned instead to face head-on the more legalistic and avaricious imperialism of the Spanish, occasionally burrowing through chinks in its thick, amoral armor to clutch at Catholic heartstrings.

Demographic Decline

Historian Karen Vieira Powers has used the term *demographic chaos* to describe the indigenous population history of Quito and its hinterland at the end of the sixteenth century. Clearly post- and even pre-conquest epidemics (documented ones occurred in 1525, 1531, 1546, 1558, and

1587–89) had greatly diminished native Andean communities by 1599, but tribute lists suggest the runa majority remained highly mobile despite Spanish efforts at control. In part because of this early assertion of free agency, accurate assessment of disease impacts in early colonial Quito has been quite difficult for modern demographers. Powers and others have offered tentative answers to the following questions: 1) How many people occupied colonial Ecuador at the height of Inka power, and how steeply did their numbers decline after Spanish contact?; 2) How did coastal and eastern lowland populations fare by comparison with highlanders?; and 3) What happened to the many and scattered native peoples of Popayán?

Although precise numbers are chimerical, indigenous demographic decline was nevertheless a punishing reality brought on mostly by unwittingly introduced diseases such as smallpox, measles, and influenza. At right is a summary of geographer Linda Newson's recent survey of greater Quito's demographic history from conquest to circa 1599.

Newson admits that numbers for Guayaquil and Portoviejo at contact are sketchily documented and as presented here might be too high. Still, she is right to point out the far more catastrophic decline of coastal populations when compared with the highlands. Guayaquil's location in a hot, disease-prone floodplain and its function as conduit for animals and people and hence disease from both highlands and abroad could easily have decimated its vast estuarine hinterland on more than one occasion before 1599. Yellow fever and deadlier forms of malaria (e.g., *Plasmodium falciparum*) are suggested only in the seventeenth-century record, but earlier, unrecorded incidences should not be ruled out.[44]

Esmeraldas, on the other hand, may well have been more seriously affected than Newson claims, especially given its constant heat, humidity, and frequent contact with sickly shipwreck victims fresh from Europe and Africa. Newson's figures for Pasto are also somewhat hypothetical, and must be compared with those compiled by geographer Luis Calero; Calero's study of highland *visitas* of Colombian Pasto up to 1616 suggests something like a 68 percent decline, from c. twenty-two thousand to seven thousand, or a depopulation ratio of about 3.1:1.[45] Figures for the rest of Popayán are lacking, but letters from governors and other anecdotal sources suggest dramatic overall declines on the order of southern Quito's Paltas (c. 90 percent/ 10:1).

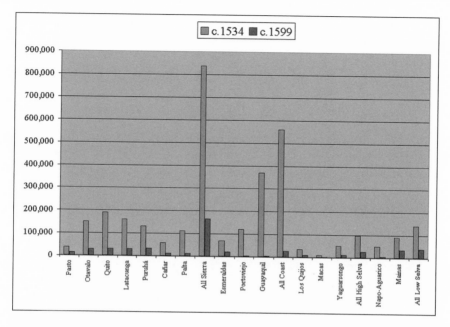

Graph 1. Estimated indigenous population decline from contact to c. 1599 (based on figures in Linda Newson, *Life and Death in Early Colonial Ecuador* [Norman: University of Oklahoma Press, 1995], 341).

Already in 1564 a *visitador* and Quito audiencia judge named García de Valverde claimed in a letter to the Indies Council that native populations in Popayán and its immediate hinterland had fallen from c. 70,000 at contact to only 8,000–9,000 total; the mining camp of Anserma alone had witnessed a stunning crash, from c. 20,000 to 800 in less than three decades. Encomenderos were said to call their native charges "dogs who do not believe in God."[46] As in Popayán, population decline in the highlands south of Cuenca appears to have resulted as much from human as microbial agency. The same waves of smallpox, measles, influenza, and other ills struck here as in central Quito, but an additional pestilence came in the form of gold-hungry "macro-parasites," prospector-encomenderos like Pedro de Bañuelos.

Contemporary observers were not unaware of these patterns. In 1593 Quito householder Antonio Freire made a list of pressing concerns in his home region that he hoped would interest old King Philip during a visit to Madrid. Along with concern over deforestation and overgrazing in the central highlands, Freire noted:

> Of course it is already well-known to Your Highness the great diminution of the natives where there are mines of gold by which cause the Governorships of Popayán and Yaguarsongo and their cities are like deserts, now poor and destroyed, and likewise those of Cuenca, Jaén, Zamora, and the Gold Hill of Zaruma, and other towns in the District of Quito; each day everything diminishes. It would serve Your Highness to give order that [African] slaves be carried there. After all, it is an accepted truth that without natives there can be no Indies, and thus no sustaining those kingdoms nor these (nor enjoying their wealth) if there is no one to remove and refine it [i.e., the gold].[47]

Echoing the "utopian" scheme of fellow Quiteño Francisco de Auncibay, Freire unabashedly acknowledged that his freedom, like that of the entire Spanish empire, was purchased through "Indian" captivity in the goldfields at America's margins. Since exhaustion of that labor force now presented a future of ghost towns, new "Indians," new captives, had to be sought posthaste in Africa.

Just as Freire filed his observations and recommendations in Madrid, the king pondered the enslavement of some of highland Popayán's last autonomous native peoples, the Pijao, Páez, and Utimá of the Central Cordillera. Two months later, in June 1593, Philip II signed a proclamation in the convent-palace of the Escorial authorizing total war, specifically "the punishment and pacification of these warlike Indians." Campaigns set out as early as May of the following year from Spanish towns on both sides of the mountains, troops made up in part of hard-core criminals suddenly freed from prison, now ordered to redeem themselves on the battlefield.[48]

Not only presumed adult warriors like the Pijao Xi were to be enslaved, but all "rebel" males between the ages of ten and a half and fifty, and all females aged nine and a half to fifty. The standard sentence was ten years, though some later captives, like thirty-year-old Calaeche, traded for

hats and cash to a Quito artisan in October 1600, received twenty.
Likewise sentenced to twenty years' service was twelve-year-old Ganzul,
"taken in the just war on the Pijaos." He sold for sixty pesos in Quito in
February 1601.[49]

Captivity with time limits put such individuals in a liminal category,
leading scribes to suggest it was their "service" that was for sale rather than
their persons. Their prices, roughly one-fifth that of African slaves of
similar age and sex, reflected this ambivalence.[50] Nevertheless all Pijao and
Páez captives were branded on the face, a capital "B" on the right cheek
and a capital "T" on the left. What these letters symbolized remains
unclear, but their captors may have had in mind contemporary terms like
bellaco ("ruinous") and *traidor* ("traitor"). In September 1600 a Quito
clergyman purchased a twelve-year-old Pijao boy named Francisco,
"branded on the face" and said to have been "taken in just war and thus
imprisoned."[51]

As an example of what this supposedly just war entailed, an April
1596 raid on a Pijao village yielded twenty-six individuals, at least fifteen
of whom were children under sixteen. Four Pijao women aged sixteen to
twenty-four ("according to their appearance") were also taken, along with
four female indigenous "allies" said to be war captives already, some of
them snatched from Spanish encomiendas by Pijao warriors. Only three
such warriors *(guerreros),* men with painted faces and pierced noses aged
twenty-five to forty, were in fact captured in the 1596 engagement. The
"ally" women and underage children were placed as wards in Spanish
households until further notice; all others were duly branded before being
sold away to unknown fates. Perhaps some, like Xi and Calaeche, taken in
1599 and 1600, would end up in the city of Quito, that great, labor-
hungry marketplace of the north Andes.

❋   ❋   ❋

In a letter dated 14 April 1606 doña Mencia Coya (in Quechua, "Queen")
and her brother, "don Carlos Ynga Atabalpa" (the same, unlucky "don
Carlos Atabalipa" mentioned above, now trying to add more "Inka" clout
to his name) pleaded with young Philip III for mercy. The Inka's heirs
pulled no punches, immediately evoking the spirit of the king's dead

father, "who," they said, "by the greatness of his Christianity, must now be in heaven."[52] Philip II had granted their grandfather, don Francisco Topatauchi, a literal golden parachute. "The Prince," followed by his son, don Alonso, had enjoyed a substantial pension in gold pesos and the service of indigenous subalterns. Unfortunately, like so many encomiendas these days, the grant's dos vidas had been used up. Don Alonso had in fact died in debtor's prison in Madrid in 1588 while pleading at court for an extension.[53] Now the descendants of "the natural lord of all these Kingdoms of Peru" faced penury. Quito's audiencia ignored their petitions for an extension, as did the viceroy in Lima. "It is not just," doña Mencia and don Carlos said, "given the great and notable services of our grandfather, that his descendants should be left without refuge." This letter, too, would go unanswered.

If the early colonial system in Quito's fertile center had followed to some extent Inka patterns of negotiation and exploitation, the Spanish second wave entailed an altogether different approach, one that seemed driven by an even more insatiable demand for land, labor, and gold. Many native lords did better than Atawallpa's descendants, but in hanging on to lands and perquisites all had their work cut out for them. At the other extreme, as the Pijao/Páez case demonstrates, even at the turn of the seventeenth century the crown was not above authorizing armed deviants to liquidate native peoples who stood in the way of expansion, a reminder that the conquest of the Inkas had not been a fluke. For most, however, the game had grown more subtle. As indigenous peoples throughout Spain's colonies had learned by this time, dissimulation, not violence, was the order of the day.

A MINER-ENCOMENDERO'S LAST LETTER HOME

Alonso de Sosa to his father, Juan de Sosa,
Santiago Parish, Toledo (Spain):

I have already written Your Mercy of the reason for my coming to this land from New Spain, namely the perdition of that place due to the inability of men [i.e., Spaniards] to sustain themselves either with or without charges [i.e., indigenous servants], and having had news of some rich gold mines in this land, and having . . . some Indians who if they did not die . . . might have [made me] very fortunate, [but] with their death all fell apart, though I had and still have some small mines that give me ten and twelve pesos each day, which is more than fifteen ducats, and if supplies were not so expensive, I would soon go to serve Your Mercy . . .

In the hour of my writing this I am filled with doubt, for they plead with me more than a little to go as captain in charge of others to populate a town called Santiago, and the province Masquisinango, very near this city, where much gold has been seen, and many domesticated Indians that, upon our arrival, will serve. If I go I will have means to eat, and very well, and could, with the passing of time, serve Your Mercy well, and aid my brothers and sisters, and if I do not go, I shall go as soon as I can to Spain, Our Lord giving me health, to fulfill this, the greatest desire that any man, I believe, has ever had. . . . To my sister doña Isabel I do not write because I cannot send, as I have said, anything, and though one may amuse oneself with a gold nugget such as one finds here, one would rather a hundred thousand letters than a hundred pesos. With my desire that Our Lord watch over thee for many years, and with as much happiness as I wish for my own soul.

From Zamora, September first, 1560.
I kiss the hands of Your Mercy, your son, Alonso de Sosa

ACCOMPANYING LETTER BY DIEGO DE SOSA FROM LIMA TO JUAN DE SOSA, IN CHOZAS DE CANALES (SPAIN):

Very magnificent sir:

A letter of Your Mercy's that came directed by Pedro Gómez de Cáceres, who went to that land from New Spain, but had also been in this land of Peru, it came into my hands, and I guarded it for some days until I could direct it to Mr. Alonso de Sosa, and within the two months that it was in my power news arrived in this city that he was killed with eight other Spaniards, killed by the Indians where they had recently populated and had been at peace and fully calmed, and having gone those whom I mentioned to see certain Indians of theirs, given to them in that province, among them Mr. Alonso de Sosa, befallen by luck his *repartimiento* there, and there he went to end his life. I did not want to write Your Mercy for the sorrow with which I know my Lady doña Francisca will receive this, but as there are things not to be remedied by the hands of men, I thought I should let Your Mercy know what is happening here so that Your Mercies may order that which you deem best, and that the remainder of his wealth may be disposed of properly.

Translated from Enrique Otte, *Cartas privadas de emigrantes a Indias*, nos. 418, 419.

FOUR: Mining the Margins

Going to visit Vulture in his house,
I am like Vulture

I go, blowing like the wind

So how could anyone harm me?

Those who are my enemies
I shall kill forthwith. . . .

I go bringing war

I go bringing speech that cannot be shaken off

I am going to kill my enemies

And whatever they say,
nobody can harm me. . . .

Being a carnivorous jaguar,
tracking from hill to hill

Little brother! I too leapt upon him
to bite him!

—Achuar Jívaro men's war song

The spear of twilight is coming son,
my son

Quick, dodge it!

The hollow spear is coming, son, my
son

My son, Sun, the spear of twilight is
coming for you

Quick, dodge it!

The emesak, as it is called

Let it not lie in wait for you, son, my son

Let it not behold you with the clear
vision of natem trances

As they gradually bear you away

Let each of your steps be disguised as
chonta palm.

—Achuar Jívaro women's war song[1]

Michael Harner's classic 1972 ethnography *The Jívaro: People of the Sacred Waterfalls* introduced a generation of North American anthropology students to organic hallucinogens and shamanic "journeys" in the jungles of southeastern Ecuador. Harner's vivid descriptions of the Untsuri Shuar shaman's "hidden world"—not to mention detailed analysis of the practice of head shrinking—still compel, but there was also history in *The Jívaro*. The introduction begins as follows:

> Only one tribe of American Indians is known ever to have successfully revolted against the empire of Spain and to have thwarted all subsequent attempts by the Spaniards to reconquer them: the Jívaro . . . of eastern Ecuador. From 1599 onward they remained unconquered in their forest fastness east of the Andes, despite the fact that they were known to occupy one of the richest placer gold deposit regions in all of South America.[2]

This is an amazing assertion, but why the emphasis on 1599? In short, Harner's understanding of early colonial history was based entirely on a late eighteenth-century Jesuit historian's account of what has come to be known as "the Great Jívaro Revolt of 1599." This, in summary, is what Padre Juan de Velasco had to say about early European relations with the Jívaro: 1) in 1599 the corrupt governor of Macas, a small Spanish settlement in the rain forest east of Cuenca, set out to tax his subjects, claiming gold was needed to celebrate young Philip III's coronation; 2) though recognizing the injustice, the governor's Spanish subjects and most of their indigenous subalterns submitted; 3) the Jívaro alone balked, but wisely followed instructions given by one Quirruba, a cacique who advised them to dampen suspicion by enthusiastically collecting gold "for the new king"; 4) when the governor visited the isolated mining town of Logroño, south of Macas, the Jívaros struck, massacring all but the women, who were taken as prizes, and the unlucky governor.[3] His fate is what most readers of Harner (or rather, Harner's translation of Velasco) remember most vividly:

> They stripped him completely naked, tied his hands and feet; and while some amused themselves with him, delivering a thousand

The Hunger for Gold Satisfied? Theodor de Bry, *Historia Americae* (Frankfurt: 1594).

castigations and jests, the others set up a large forge in the courtyard,
where they melted the gold. When it was ready in the crucibles,
they opened his mouth with a bone, saying that they wanted to see
if for once he had enough gold. They poured it little by little, and
then forced it down with another bone; and bursting his bowels
with the torture, all raised a clamor and laughter.[4]

Having taken their revenge on the greedy governor, the Jívaros then
moved on to attack the neighboring gold camp of Sevilla de Oro. On the
point of repeating their success at Logroño, Quirruba and his followers
suddenly withdrew, apparently due to some disagreement with temporary
allies. According to Velasco, the few survivors of this and a series of related
attacks retreated to the highlands, never to return to the golden land of
the Jívaro.

Desperately searching for an indigenous counterpoint to the Jesuit's
tale, Harner questioned a Shuar Jívaro elder about past encounters with
Europeans and their descendants, hoping for a breakthrough. Only the
following enigmatic fragment was proffered:

A very long time ago there were the *ai apaci* [*"ai"* white men]. They
were many. They were all of bone to their elbows and to their
knees. They could move their arms and legs only beyond their
elbows and knees. They had shirts and pants. They were fierce and
tall. There were many, many of them, and they had women and
children. All were the same in not being able to move except for
their forearms and lower legs. They didn't have hats but wore
something like the helmets of the [present-day Ecuadorian] soldiers.
These men had machetes of iron that they used for killing. They
carried their machetes on the left hip. The machetes were somewhat
yellow. These machetes had handles of human bone. They said that
they had killed many whites with their machetes. They also had
shoes. These whites had *machu* . . . they rode on top of these. I think
these must have been horses. The Shuar were scared of them. These
whites also had *mua*. I do not know what they were.[5]

Harner plausibly suggests the bonelike articulations that so fascinated his Shuar informant were pieces of body armor (he was further told they resembled turtle shell), the left-hip-borne "yellow" machetes, swords, and the *machus* and *muas,* he-mules *(machos)* and she-mules *(mulas)*. All these details seem to echo early colonial Spanish entradas, but even when pressed the old man made no mention of fighting between whites and Jívaros, much less memorable acts like pouring molten gold down a governor's throat. Had the 1599 uprising been entirely forgotten by the Jívaros in the near four-century interim, or had it perhaps not happened in the way described by Padre Velasco? Or both?

✳   ✳   ✳

The Spanish gold-hunt in the Americas may seem by now a tired cliché, but the topic is unavoidable if one is to understand the dynamics of Quito, city and colony, circa 1599. More than anything else, the early hope of finding precious metals in the Quito backcountry sped immigration and exploration, and its quick discovery stimulated trade and permanent settlement. Substantial gold was discovered in the central highlands within a few years of conquest, particularly at the northern and southern extremes of Quito's jurisdiction, but by 1599 the most promising deposits—both new and known-but-not-fully-exploited—fell only in the most rugged terrain, areas inhabited by some of the Americas' most fiercely independent peoples.

Such was the case in the Jívaro heartland of the Upper Amazonian southeast, the Barbacoan and Chocoan Pacific lowlands of the northwest, and the Pijao and Páez-dominated Central Cordillera of the Colombian Andes; ecologically, politically, and culturally these last gold frontiers defined the very margins of empire. The supposed cannibals of Barbacoas and the Chocó raided roads and even highland settlements circa 1599, and the Afro-indigenous maroons of neighboring Esmeraldas, as has been seen, remained semiautonomous despite the shift in tactics tried by Quito's highest colonial officials. Meanwhile, Spanish relations with the native peoples of the Popayán hill country had devolved to slave-raiding by the late 1590s, emblematic of Bogotá's more belligerent approach. What would be the fate of the Shuar and neighboring Jivaroans? The answer, it turns out, does not quite jibe with that offered by Velasco and Harner, but the riddle of the great rebellion of 1599 must first be placed in the context of Quito's greater gold-mining economy, a subject virtually absent from the historiography until now.

The Gold Cycle in Early Quito

When the Spanish arrived in the equatorial Andes in the 1530s, gold mining was widely practiced and goldsmithing developed to a high art. The Inkas, their neighbors, and numerous predecessors back to La Tolita and before seem to have greatly valued gold for its luster and other "divine" qualities, a view shared by many peoples the world over. The yellow metal's profane utility as money may also have been realized by some north Andeans in the form of beads, or chaquira, traded widely by Quito's roving mindalá merchants.[6] Despite these pre-Columbian parallels, gold certainly became a new sort of commodity under Spanish rule—less a mirror of the sacred and more the means to worldly ends. The native peoples of Quito, like their fellows throughout the Americas, found the European newcomers' insatiable appetite for gold positively baffling. Some, like the Jívaros, may have tried to satisfy it in a literal way.

Quito's first town-council minutes record native Andeans washing gold along the Guayllabamba and other nearby rivers shortly after the formal founding of the city in 1534. The first *libros de fundición,* or royal smeltery ledgers, begin with royal severance taxes paid by the conqueror Sebastián de Benalcázar in 1535. A portion of this first gold taxed in Quito had been mined, but most was melted-down ritual paraphernalia (in the documents *oro de huaca* or *chafalonia*). Plunder of indigenous tombs continued throughout colonial times, but most treasure hunters soon turned their attention to natural sources, first rich placers, or alluvial gold deposits, then vast lodes encased in solid rock. For a time only gold, or rather the genuine hope of finding great quantities of it, fueled exploration, trade, and settlement at Quito's margins.

Gold ingots and buttons of varying karat, Zaruma, Ecuador

Table 4.1. Gold Registered in Quito, 1535–1541 (in pesos of buen oro of 450 maravedis)

YEAR	PLUNDERED GOLD	MINED GOLD	TOTAL REGISTERED
1535	17,352		17,352
1536	12,545		12,545
1537	10,297	1,097	11,394
1538 *(office closed)*	—	—	—
1539	24,308	12,000	36,308
1540	11,106	11,360	22,466
1541 *(to Sept.)*	113	13,780	13,893
TOTAL *(7 years)*	75,721	38,237	113,958

*source AGI Contaduría 1536[7]

Santa Bárbara

The first significant gold strike in the Quito region occurred in a highland canyon called Sangurima, upriver from the villages of Gualaceo and Sigsig east of Inka Tumibamba (modern Cuenca). It lay about a week's hard journey south of Quito following the old Inka Trail. The Spanish renamed the site Santa Bárbara and began exploiting its gold-bearing gravels immediately after conquest in the mid-1530s. Sangurima had been mined in precolonial times, and Cañari tombs from the Gualaceo area were routinely found to contain gold and gold-copper alloy ornaments.[8] By 1538 several Quito-based encomenderos had marched their Andean charges and a small number of African slaves all the way to the mines of the Santa Bárbara district, and in June 1540 the town council of Quito named an *alcalde de minas,* or mining magistrate. Ideally this official would help solve disputes between claimants, hear and investigate abuse charges, and, most importantly, oversee the proper collection of the crown severance tax, or *quinto real.*[9]

Mining at Santa Bárbara consisted of basic placering techniques—making use of gravity and water to separate dense gold particles from stream gravels in the batea, or wooden gold pan.[10] However simple, to be profitable panning required great dexterity and attentiveness, and wise Spanish overlords made every effort to locate and employ skilled indigenous "gold specialists" *(curicamayos)* as work-gang captains and instructors. As seen in chapter 2 the same held true for African capitanes, some of whom must have had experience among the several great placer districts of West Africa. As rudimentary as it was technically, stoop labor in a cold, fast-running river was dangerous; a misstep by a tired panner could quickly end in drowning. According to early sources, however, more deaths at Santa Bárbara were the result of landslides during excavation of steep riverbanks.

Though perhaps exaggerating, the chronicler Pedro de Cieza de León claimed the mines of Santa Bárbara had produced some 800,000 gold pesos (of c. 4.2 g each) by 1544. In a 1576 relación two royal treasury officials in Quito gave credence to this figure, claiming that in 1544 alone eighteen to twenty indigenous work gangs (cuadrillas) of fifty to eighty miners had washed over 300,000 pesos' worth of gold dust.[11]

Output must have declined subsequently, since it was also in 1544 that Peru's first viceroy, Blasco Núñez Vela, sought to forcibly implement the so-called New Laws. Proclaimed in 1542–43, this series of edicts constituted Charles I's attempt to end rampant encomienda abuses and generally rein in the conquerors. Though Núñez Vela was captured and executed by Gonzalo Pizarro's forces outside Quito in 1546, the rebellion known as the Peruvian Civil War fizzled by 1548. The younger Pizarro was captured and executed by order of Lima's first audiencia president, Pedro de la Gasca, and though La Gasca was mostly successful in implementing a watered-down version of the New Laws, a sticking point all over Peru was his call for an end to forced indigenous mine labor.

Quiteños perhaps felt obliged to reaffirm their loyalty to the king by mitigating some abuses associated with the Santa Bárbara bonanza, but the town council (the acting regional government until creation of the Quito Audiencia in 1563) openly ignored La Gasca's ban when it issued the district's first mining ordinances in 1549. Council members dutifully observed that indigenous miners held in encomienda were overworked, underfed, forced to carry heavy burdens well beyond the mines themselves, and cruelly punished for minor infractions. Though they mandated shorter hours, weight limits on shoulder-borne loads, minimum shelter, food, and clothing rations, and limits on the size of work gangs, for Quito's loyal conquistadors the prospect of ending encomienda mine labor altogether was simply unthinkable. Meanwhile, the routine mistreatment of African slaves and their descendants was considered beneath concern at both local and imperial levels.[12]

Zaruma

Placer mines tended to play out quickly, and Santa Bárbara was on the wane by the 1550s. Meanwhile, a new gold rush was on in the coastal mountains northwest of Loja at a site called Zaruma, roughly two weeks' hard journey southwest of Quito.[13] Still actively mined today, San Antonio de Zaruma is almost certainly the oldest continuously running gold camp in the Americas. Unlike Santa Bárbara, Zaruma's deposits dove straightaway into solid rock. A complex and interlaced system of quartz veins scattered across a few low hills presented colonial miners with many points of access to abundant but generally low-grade ores. Here gold came extremely fine-grained, often invisible to the naked eye, and along with it came silver, copper, zinc, and other less-desirable metals.

More technically challenging than the Santa Bárbara placers by far, Zaruma's deposits required skilled overseers, massive labor inputs, and imported tools and chemicals. The first mines were open-topped *(tajo abierto),* or quarrylike operations. In some cases indigenous and slave laborers were made to build long canals to these open works, where they engaged in a kind of hydraulicking, or rudimentary strip mining.[14] By the early 1590s a Quito judge and prospector claimed that substantial holding tanks or reservoirs *(albercas)* had been constructed in Zaruma, apparently so as to continue the excavation process through dry spells.[15]

In 1592 a curious visitor who also happened to be ex-bishop of Nicaragua complained of Zaruma's refractory, polymetallic ores, an annoyance mitigated only by the fact that silver-rich veins tended to be wider and more extensive than gold-rich ones.[16] Another commentator, an encomendero based in Quito, stressed quantity and other positives, claiming Zaruma had as many veins as one could supply with workers and

View of Zaruma, Ecuador

mills. "The veins," he continued, "although not very rich on the surface, still produce much wealth; often they are more promising as they go deeper."[17] Another, anonymous observer gushed with boomtown enthusiasm, claiming:

> The site of these gold mines is one of the best and richest pieces of ground until one reaches Potosí; its veins are extremely rich in gold and they run four to six leagues, some more, some less, and they cross and criss-cross one another, from which may be taken *for millions of years* immense riches in gold, and in each year for some time they have taken more than 200,000 pesos, and the value of Your Majesty's *quintos* alone has surpassed 40,000 pesos.[18]

Clearly the deposits were both extensive and deep, but profitable exploitation would always be braked by technical limitations and labor shortages.

Landslide caused by mining excavation, Zaruma

However poor in quality, these veins were soon followed underground, often at inclines of seventy degrees or more. Here in pits and shafts of rapidly increasing depth workers chopped out and pried loose chunks of ore, pounding against native stone with heavy, tempered iron bars and sharpened steel rods, or gads. Porters and muckers followed close behind, using shovels and more often bare hands to fill hide and agave-fiber bags with huge loads of ore, sometimes over 60 kg (5–6 arrobas). Shouldering these bags, they exited through wet, constricted passages often on the verge of collapse from saturation and telluric slippage. Fear of death by earthquake must have been constant.

Daylight was often reached only by way of hanging ladders and shaky notched logs. At the surface, carriers dumped their cargoes to be sorted by other draftees, refuse cast downslope and gold-bearing rock taken to a nearby mill on the backs of mules or porters.[19] Choppers and muckers were allowed outside only at lunchtime and twilight, their molelike existence otherwise defined by near-total darkness, relentless, Sisyphean exertion against the mountain, and a damp, musty atmosphere filled with quartz-rich dust. For them, in time, breathing itself would become a struggle.

Once sorted, Zaruma's ores were ground to the consistency of beach sand by numerous water-driven stamp mills, or *ingenios de agua*. These enormous, loud, and expensive machines, built on-site by European specialists of several nationalities, represented the pinnacle of technical achievement in the Spanish colonies. By mid-century Zarumeños understood that profit making required massive capital investment.[20] Small fry—those without access to labor or credit—were soon edged out.

As in the contemporary silver districts of New Spain and Peru (not to mention the sugar coast of Brazil), alongside the milling machines themselves there developed a new and exclusive class of colonists, the so-called lords of the engines, or *dueños de ingenios*. Like the encomenderos of Santa Bárbara, their expensive tastes and ready gold fueled luxury trade to the Quito backcountry. Crown control over the gold trade was generally weak, and merchants, like mill lords, knew a gold mill at the margins was akin to a private mint. The Peruvian viceroy Toledo, who established the infamous Potosí mita and rewrote Spanish American mining law in the mid-1570s, claimed in a 1579 letter to the crown that twenty-two ingenios were crushing ore in Zaruma, many of them around the clock.[21]

Milled sands were subsequently "panned" in the batea by slaves and other skilled workers, often with the aid of mercury. Mercury's toxicity was well known, but amalgamation, or the process of bonding this liquid metal to minute gold particles, was considered the most efficient means of capitalizing on the ingenio's crushing power.[22] Blobs of amalgam were subjected to various hand "washings" with salts and other solvents in order to further separate fine gold particles from silver and base metals. Finally, excess mercury was squeezed through a porous cloth, and the resulting silver-gray ball of amalgam heated over a flame to vaporize the rest. Needless to say, workers engaged in this stage of the refining process were at greatest risk for poisoning. The result was a small gold sponge, yellow at last, to be melted down with many others into bars and disks of similar hue and karat.

In spite of these relatively sophisticated refining techniques, Zaruma faced crisis by the early 1590s. Certainly some initially rich veins had begun to play out and drainage was becoming a growing concern, but the core problem was labor. Encomiendas had been sparse in the southern highlands to begin with, and those remaining were held mostly by agricultural elites in Loja and Cuenca. Understandably, these distant encomenderos did not want to lose their precious and already vulnerable workers to cave-ins, poisonings, and other hazards at the hands of Zaruma's miners and refiners.

Viceroy Toledo nevertheless mandated a mita muster in 1579, drawing six hundred men from among four ethnic groups, the Ambocas, Garrochambas, Paltas, and Malacatos of the southern highlands.[23] The draft was soon extended to another hundred or so workers from the Cuenca-hinterland districts of Cañaribamba and Pacaibamba, but indigenous men, who almost universally saw the call to Zaruma as a death sentence, fled in droves. Attempts in the early 1590s to form a mita with a Potosí-like conscription zone, reaching all the way to Pasto, and in one scheme, Popayán, failed miserably. In short, competition for indigenous labor was as fierce in the northern highlands as it was in the south, and many of Quito's so-called vagabonds were not about to return to the mining districts they had just fled.[24]

Some wealthy Zarumeños purchased African slaves, but never on the scale needed to spark a revival. It remains unclear why, but even during the labor crisis of the 1590s only a handful of mine and mill owners appear to have had the means or will to risk such investment.[25] As Ecuadorian historian Galo Ramón notes, the enslaved portion of Zaruma's workforce probably never exceeded 20 percent, a figure reached in 1609 when sixty "blacks" were counted among a much-diminished total of three hundred laborers.[26] Petitions for state-subsidized slaves, as proposed for Popayán, were generally met with some enthusiasm from Spain's Indies Council, then cold indifference from the king. A crisis-induced sell-off of mine slaves in 1611 sealed Zaruma's decadent fate. The half-dozen or so mill lords who stuck it out from here forward faced the horrifying alternative of paying wages in order to keep producing the gold they loved so much.[27]

Popayán

Long before Zaruma began to fade, and in some places as early as the heyday of Santa Bárbara (c. the 1540s), gold in various forms was extracted from the graves and rivers and mountains of the vast hinterland of Popayán. First to be exploited were placer deposits along various Cauca River tributaries well to the north of Popayán city. Mines near the villages of Arma, Cartago, Caramanta, and Anserma were in production by the 1540s. Vein mines followed at nearby Marmato and Quiebralomo, hand-hewn shafts soon reaching fifty meters' depth or more. Indigenous workers were said to have died by the thousands due to epidemics and abuse in Anserma alone, but since the district was virtually cut off from Bogotá and not fully subject to Quito, Popayán's northern encomenderos were left to do their damage unhindered. By 1578 some eight hundred to one thousand African replacements filled Anserma's mines.[28] Relative proximity to the Atlantic ports of Nombre de Diós (Panama) and Cartagena appears to have encouraged the transition, in part by lowering slave prices.

Rich placers were also discovered soon after conquest in the Jelima-La Teta district, roughly midway between Popayán city and Cali. However, these mines, like those above Cartago, were frequently abandoned in the late sixteenth century following attacks from Páez and Pijao warriors. The colonists' desire for gold could not be extinguished, however, and in spite of incessant raids Jelima-La Teta mine owners registered production of some seventy-five thousand pesos annually between 1564 and 1597.[29]

Mine entrance, Chisquío, Colombia

Mill stamps, Chisquío, Colombia

Just west of Popayán itself were the lode and associated placer mines of Chisquío, in many ways the city's lifeblood until the mid-seventeenth century. Rather like Zaruma, Chisquío's gold deposits consisted of weathered quartz veins concentrated in a few wet hills of medium altitude. Both streambed and underground claims proliferated around the circumference of Mt. Munchique, the most prominent peak on the western skyline. The ravines that carved through its ample flanks soon sprouted overshot stamp mills of varying size. Also like Zaruma, laborers included a mix of slaves and indigenous men drawn from private and crown-held encomiendas. Mine and mill owners, meanwhile, preferred to live in the nearby city rather than on-site. According to notary records low-karat *"oro de Chisquío"* served as common currency in Popayán well into the seventeenth century.[30]

Farther south, encomenderos and slave owners forced their charges to exploit placer deposits along various tributaries of the Patía River, a "hot" zone considered a feverish graveyard by nearly everyone who passed through it. Some slaves escaped these isolated mines to form the earliest documented maroon stronghold in the Quito highlands, a site called Matarredonda, said to have been destroyed by Pasto-based encomenderos about 1590.[31]

More significant and longer lived were the vein mines of Almaguer, in the highlands midway between Popayán and Pasto. The Almaguer mines were discovered around 1551 and continued to produce into the early years of the seventeenth century.[32] In the district's heyday, the 1550s and 1560s, some two thousand African and indigenous workers produced thirty thousand gold pesos annually.[33] Notary records show strong commercial links between Almaguer's mine owners and the merchants of both Quito and Popayán.[34]

Still more gold camps were scattered east of Pasto in the barely con-trolled upper Putumayo and Caquetá drainages, and gold produced around Sibundoy, Mocoa, Écija de Sucumbios, and other sites was in high demand in 1599 Quito. Most of these appear to have been small-scale placer opera-tions. As would happen in the more southern reaches of Upper Amazonia, however, consistently violent indigenous resistance braked Spanish penetra-tion into this little-known gold frontier.[35] In sum, there were so many gold sources feeding into Quito from Popayán in the last quarter of the sixteenth century it is nearly impossible to treat them all.

Production estimates

Historians since Padre Velasco's day have implied that gold mining must have been central to the economic formation of early colonial Quito, but until now no one has tried to estimate output or track bullion flows.[36] The task is daunting in part because of the scattered and transient nature of Quito's goldfields; they were the very opposite of the generally concentrated and durable silver districts of Mexico and Peru. As a result of this impermanence, fragmentary smeltery ledgers have come to be scattered among Ecuadorian, Colombian, Peruvian, and Spanish archives. In piecing together totals from these records, as has been attempted in tables 4.2 and 4.3 (combined in graph 2), the peak of a gold cycle of significant proportions becomes apparent.

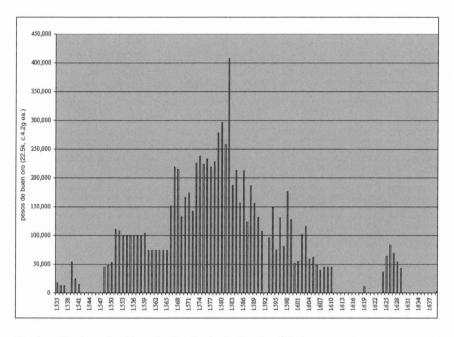

Graph 2. Registered gold production in the Audiencia of Quito, 1535–1640

Table 4.2. Gold Registered in the Audiencia of Quito, 1548–1599 (not including Cali, Cartago, or Anserma smelteries), in pesos of buen oro (c. 4.2 g, 22.5 k Au each)

YEAR	TOTAL	YEAR	TOTAL	YEAR	TOTAL	YEAR	TOTAL
1548	45,100	1561	74,511	1574	237,280	1587	123,730
1549	48,768	1562	74,511	1575	223,430	1588	186,530
1550	53,420	1563	74,511	1576	233,500	1589	156,190
1551	110,640	1564	74,511	1577	219,000	1590	131,280
1552	108,410	1565	74,511	1578	227,950	1591	107,170
1553	99,255*	1566	151,460	1579	278,270	1592	NO RECORD
1554	99,255	1567	218,980	1580	296,330	1593	95,590
1555	99,255	1568	214,860	1581	257,900	1594	150,310
1556	99,255	1569	132,820	1582	406,790	1595	74,720
1557	99,255	1570	166,520	1583	187,650	1596	130,710
1558	99,255	1571	174,280	1584	212,980	1597	80,720
1559	104,201	1572	142,550	1585	156,770	1598	176,830
1560	74,511*	1573	225,920	1586	212,170	1599	127,680

TOTAL (all years): 7,632,005

*averages based on multi-year, unitemized totals; sources for all totals include AGI Contaduría 1538, 1540, 1468, 1469, 1470, and ANHQ Real Hacienda, Cajas 1-37.

Clearly some allowance should be made for contraband, perhaps an additional 20 percent of gross production or more (the same could be said for missing records, since these figures represent totals derived from surviving ledgers), but overall the numbers trace a century of boom and bust in the Quito mines that produced at least ten million pesos, or something like forty-two thousand kilograms of fine gold. The trend depicted in graph 2, which also includes the numbers from table 4.1, bears a striking resemblance to the arc of Seville's contemporary bullion imports as recorded many years ago by economic historian Earl Hamilton. It is clear from notary records that merchants and crown officials in Quito and Popayán were exporting substantial gold to Seville in precisely these years, fueling a voluminous and lucrative transatlantic trade. Though it pales against the volume of silver coming from the Americas in the same period, rather amazingly the gold volume here suggested amounts to almost 23 percent of all gold registered in Seville between 1503 and 1660.[37] Though some of Hamilton's findings have lately been challenged by European economic historians, none of the revisions (mostly having to do with the later seventeenth century) dampen the obvious importance, both locally and abroad, of the Quito gold cycle.

Table 4.3. Gold Registered in the Audiencia of Quito (excluding Cali, Popayán, and Cartago smelteries), 1600–1639 (in pesos de buen oro)

YEAR	TOTAL	YEAR	TOTAL
1600	51,370	1610	45,260*
1601	55,130	1619	11,588
1602	101,360	1624	37,089
1603	115,950	1625	64,267
1604	58,800	1626	83,139
1605	62,600	1627	69,549
1606	48,200	1628	53,880
1607	40,200	1629	43,178
1608	45,260*	1639	2,855
1609	45,260*		

Total (all years): 1,034,935

*averages based on multi-year, unitemized totals; source AGI Contaduría 1540, 1862, ANHQ Real Hacienda, Cajas 1–37.

The Great Jívaro Revolt of 1599

However fantastic their sixteenth-century performance, nearly all of Quito's goldfields were struggling by the turn of the seventeenth century. Three causes were shared: declining ore quality, minimal technical innovation, and chronic shortage of hands. This last factor was by far most critical. As has been seen, the native peoples of the equatorial Andes had suffered tremendously from disease epidemics across the second half of the sixteenth century, and mining districts seem to have been especially deadly. Only in a few instances, as in parts of Popayán, were African slaves deemed affordable substitutes.

Demographic decline hardly explained everything, however, as native (and in some cases African) resistance likewise eroded mining output and blocked potential development. Everywhere draftees fled mine labor in droves and in many marginal districts, such as Esmeraldas and Colombia's Central Cordillera, an unpredictable blend of wily negotiation and guerrilla-style violence kept gold-seekers out, often for decades. The example of the so-called Jívaros of upper Amazonia is most salient, however, since they alone managed to fully reconquer their gold-rich homeland some time around 1599.

The Jívaro heartland is today divided by the Ecuador-Peru border, but the peoples ethnographers collectively call "Jivaroans" remain relatively unified by language and other cultural traits. One of these is their fierce insistence on independence, both from modern nation-states and from one another. Modern Jivaroans consist of four "tribes," or dialect groups: the Shuar (studied by Harner), Achuar, Huambisa, and Aguaruna.[38] Each unit is said to number in the tens of thousands, but estimates remain vague since as in colonial times most families today live scattered across hundreds of thousands of square kilometers of essentially virgin forest, often more than a day's march from the nearest neighbor. It is unclear to what extent modern dialect divisions represent colonial groupings, but enough quasi-ethnographic evidence has survived to confirm that it was indeed the modern Jivaroans' ancestors who rejected the colonial yoke some four hundred years ago.

Spanish explorers entered Jívaro country as early as 1535 while reconnoitering the course of the Marañón River, major affluent of the

Crossing the Zamora River, Ecuador

Amazon. Only following the Peruvian Civil War, however, did they
establish a permanent townsite there as a base for mining gold. Inspired by
the Santa Bárbara bonanza, perhaps, conquistador Alonso de Mercadillo
founded the little jungle hamlet of Zamora de los Alcaides in 1549 along a
great river that now bears the same name. The several-week journey to
Quito was calculated as something like one hundred leagues (c. 550–600
km).[39]

Gold was subsequently discovered in streams all along the Andean
piedmont to the north, south, and east of Zamora, and in such prodigious
quantities that a frenzy of exploration and settlement quickly ensued. In
the 1550s and 1560s Macas, Logroño, and Sevilla de Oro, the towns mentioned by Velasco and Harner, sprang up along the banks of the Upano
River east of Cuenca. Farther south came Valladolid, Loyola, Santa María
de Nieva, and Santiago de las Montañas. It was in the founding of this last

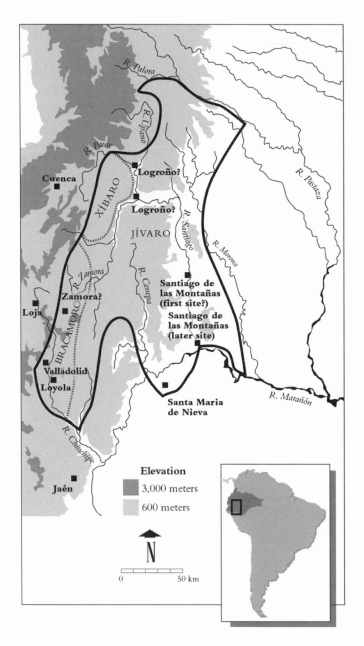

Spanish incursions into Jívaro country before 1599. Map drawn from Carol Cooperrider, from Linda Newson, *Life and Death in Early Colonial Ecuador,* (Norman: University of Oklahoma Press, 1995), courtesy of Linda Newson and the University of Oklahoma Press.

gold camp that Alonso de Sosa, writer of the first letter in interlude 4, was killed.[40] The entire Jívaro region was renamed by the Spanish the Province of Yaguarsongo and Pacamoros in 1557, and a relative of Ignatius Loyola was named first governor. Governor Loyola reported to Quito.

It appears Harner was not far wrong in calling this "one of the richest placer gold deposit regions in all of South America." By the early 1560s Zamora-based miners had encountered some of the largest gold nuggets *(puntas)* ever found in the Indies; one weighed eighteen pounds (c. 8 kg), and others weighing four to eight pounds (1.5–3.5 kg) routinely turned up in streams and among the roots of trees.[41] As mandated by royal edict, the largest nuggets were not melted down, but rather purchased by the royal treasury to be sent to King Philip as curiosities.[42] The abundance of large nuggets suggests a previously unmined district, and the sixteenth-century chronicles generally agree that interior Yaguarsongo had never been subjected to Inka control.[43] Whatever its past, the new invaders had hit paydirt. According to a surviving fragment of Zamora's royal smeltery ledgers, some 167 local and transient miners, encomenderos, and even priests registered nearly 210,000 pesos (c. 875 kg) of high-karat gold in the five and a half years between September 1561 and April 1567; one of them was Alonso de Sosa.[44]

Contrary to Harner, however, much of the gold registered in Zamora by this time was taken not from rivers but from vein deposits located high in the Tzunantza and Cóndor Cordilleras east of the Zamora River. This fact greatly multiplied the hardships of indigenous encomienda and enslaved African workers. The most significant vein deposits were found at Nambija, a site named in the smeltery ledgers but not mentioned by Velasco or Harner. This extraordinarily isolated mountain gold camp, only rediscovered in 1979, required several days' hard, zigzagging journey on foot from Zamora. Here at eighteen hundred meters altitude in some of the wettest and most rugged terrain on the continent, European gold-seekers forced captive workers deep underground. As at Zaruma and similar districts in Popayán, their job consisted of sinking shafts into solid rock with crude hand tools by candlelight.

Nambija, in a word, must have been hell, the kind of place engraver Theodor de Bry had in mind when illustrating the Black Legend at the turn of the seventeenth century. The site's peculiar geology (skarn-type

View of Nambija, Ecuador

deposits in very hard igneous and metamorphic rock) led miners to follow quartz stringers into either huge pockets of high-grade ore (today called *bolsonadas*) or nothing at all. Thus months of punishing labor and heavy investment in iron tools could turn up nothing, enraging mine owners and overseer-administrators. Meanwhile, near-constant rain produced daily landslides and cave-ins. Nambija's altitude kept mosquitoes to a minimum, but nighttime temperatures could plunge to the single digits centigrade, challenging the immune systems of wet and weakened miners. As at Zaruma, huge water-powered stamp mills crashed through the night.[45]

How did the Jívaros respond to this nightmarish invasion? Based on early explorer accounts and modern settlement patterns historian Anne Christine Taylor estimates some twenty thousand Jivaroans populated the Zamora hinterland circa 1535 (including the districts of Macas and Santiago de las Montañas).[46] By 1567, Zamora alone was said to have

Saraguro miner, Pozo del Pueblo, Nambija, Ecuador

twenty-seven Spanish householders (vecinos) who held some eight thousand indigenous subjects in encomienda. However, many of these latter were not "Jívaros" at all but rather resettled highlanders, mostly from around Cuenca.[47] By 1572 a census showed some thirty-two Spanish vecinos in Zamora, but complaints of rapid indigenous population decline were on the rise.[48] By 1580 Zamora miners were calling for tax cuts so they could afford African slaves.[49] Mustering all accounts, geographer Linda Newson has argued that the indigenous peoples of the Zamora area suffered the most dramatic demographic collapse in the Audiencia of Quito outside Guayaquil, a decline of some 97 percent by about 1599.[50]

Reducing Taylor's contact-era population estimate of twenty thousand by 97 percent would seem to yield only six hundred living Jívaros at the turn of the seventeenth century, an appallingly small number that, if true, would make Velasco's story of the great revolt of 1599 all the more compelling. But there is much room for error here since Newson's figures are based on very intermittent head-counts of individuals held fast in encomienda. Trust in the figures assumes total Spanish control, conquest accomplished.

In truth it was the Jívaros who had the run of the land, as much in 1599 as they had in 1535. Because of the district's vastness, inaccessibility, and reputed hostility the fifty years of frenzied activity following the founding of Zamora had in fact brought in at most a few thousand Spaniards, mestizos, slaves, and Andean highlanders. (Another factor was the great draw of Potosí and other contemporary silver boomtowns open to prospector-immigrants.)

Though these several thousand invaders managed to unearth a lot of gold in a short time, they still had only skirted the edges of this enormous jungle territory roughly half the size of Spain. The majority of its hills and waterways remained in the hands of the Jívaros, who for the most part seem to have avoided "reduction" into encomiendas and forced labor in the mines. Dispersed in the interior according to their customary patterns of settlement, they not only could have proved more resistant to epidemic disease than Newson's congregated mine workers, but were also perfectly situated to attack isolated gold camps like Nambija and Santiago de las Montañas. As a result of such sporadic guerrilla raids and mine-worker deaths by disease, both sites were all but abandoned by 1599.

High-karat gold, Nambija, Ecuador

In the colonial record there is in fact no direct evidence to support the 1599 rebellion described by Velasco and Harner, but there are several tantalizing fragments. A document now in the National Library of Spain describes a 1572 "mutiny" in the town of Logroño, site of Velasco's great skirmish, but here it was only two mestizo soldiers, Francisco Hernández Barreto and Juan de Landa, who rebelled.[51] Their story bears brief recounting, since a version of it may have inspired Velasco.

The small military expedition of which these men were a part had been entrusted with the task of rebuilding a town called Nuestra Señora del Rosario, the original site of Macas (mentioned by Velasco). What had happened in the decade or so since Rosario's 1563 founding is not mentioned, but one may assume Jívaro attacks were involved.[52] In any case Landa and Barreto, whom the narrator and apparent expedition leader Juan de Vargas Escalona calls "tyrants" (à la royalist protocol), were said to have planned to overrun not only the administrative center of Zamora and surrounding mining camps, but also Cuenca and Loja.

Barreto would be crowned prince alongside his indigenous mistress, Catalina, who would thenceforth be called "Señora." Upon her accession, "Lady Catalina" was to be adorned with jewels taken from the few Spanish women then living in Zamora. Reminiscent of the madness that had gripped the Basque adventurer Lope de Aguirre not far downstream from here on the Marañón (and only about a decade before), Barreto and Landa promised reluctant soldiers ten thousand gold pesos each if they would only join in forging this new, indigenous-mestizo empire.[53] Few apparently did, and soon the mutineers fell to guerrilla-style attacks on their former companions, hoping to at least assassinate the captain.

Rather like the rebel Aguirre, however, Barreto and Landa had more pluck than luck, and the fort they had built to defend themselves was soon captured by Vargas and his faithful followers. Fighting continued inside and according to the narrator as the rebels fell they not only denounced their adversaries as "vile sodomites" *(putos bellacos)* but also denied the sovereignty of the king. Worse, they died "like heretics," never asking forgiveness or uttering a word about God or Mary, their faces down, eyes open. The fate of Lady Catalina is not mentioned.

It is difficult to make sense of this incident, obviously not an earlier Great Jívaro Rebellion, but nevertheless an event in the southeast gold country likely to be remembered for its sheer strangeness. The 1572 mutiny was later referred to by Quito's bishop, Juan de la Peña, in a 1580 letter to the Council of the Indies, for example. Peña preferred to cast the incident in a more sympathetic light than Vargas Escalona, claiming these "rebellious mestizos" were simply "old soldiers" who should have been "given [means] to eat" (i.e., an encomienda or pension). As the bishop well knew, there was a glut of such individuals in Quito, and they would help incite yet another rebellion, the Alcabala Revolt of 1592–93. In the case of Barreto and Landa, however, "the Devil and Passion took them and they allied with the Indians of that land and killed many Spaniards."[54]

Where were the Jívaros? Another incident, described in a letter now housed in the Archive of the Indies, perhaps rings truer in terms of the details given by Velasco. In 1584 a crown accountant in Cuenca wrote Madrid requesting a raise. Miguel Sánchez de la Parra did not claim to be a particularly hard or efficient worker, but rather (in keeping with the times) stressed distinguished military service. In particular, he had participated in an expedition two and a half years earlier (c. 1581) against presumably Jívaro rebels in Logroño (again Velasco's preferred site). According to Sánchez de la Parra, indigenous subalterns there had risen up and killed sixty Spaniards, then burnt the town.

A small number of survivors had managed to hole up in a fortified house, where they expected to be either starved to death or slain. Somehow word of their predicament reached Cuenca, probably by way of an escaped indigenous highlander, and Sánchez de la Parra and his brother-in-law were the first to respond. They quickly mustered thirty "Spanish" soldiers (several of whom were probably mestizos like Landa and Barreto) and three hundred native auxiliaries before marching down the Paute River gorge and across the jungle to Logroño. Though little fighting seems to have ensued, in the end the Cuencanos were successful, and supporting testimony credited Sánchez de la Parra with "freeing [the captive] Christians."[55]

It is likely that Spanish records and memories of these and similar incidents inspired Velasco, but they fall well short of solving the puzzle of 1599. There are other inconsistencies. For one thing, the "molten-gold-down-the-throat" incident appears to have been directly borrowed from stock images of the conquests of Chile and Nicaragua, a sort of moralist trope picked up and illustrated by Theodor de Bry (whose work Velasco may have consulted).

The image is indeed an indelible one, and it must have resonated as well with Velasco's enlightened late eighteenth-century readers as among sixteenth-century humanists and enemies of Spain. But there is no colonial record to substantiate such a memorable incident, and there is no mention of a cacique named Quirruba, either. Even the idea of celebrating Philip III's accession in the jungle backcountry seems unlikely given that news of Philip II's death in September 1598 had only just reached the city of Quito in the middle of 1599 (Spain was, after all, very far away).[56]

✳   ✳   ✳

As for the ethnographic record, no further information regarding "turtle-shelled whites" like those remembered by Harner's Shuar elder has since been discovered. In fact several ethnologists working among modern Jivaroan groups describe them as a people truly "without history"; that is, they place virtually no collective value on remembrance of things past beyond a generation or two.

According to Philippe Descola, who has worked among the remote Achuar Jívaro (neighbors of the Shuar) since the 1970s, this "spontaneous forgetfulness," or "amnesia," as he calls it, is due in part to the Jivaroan rejection of lineage as a significant social marker. The dead, however powerful or loved in their day, are quickly and intentionally erased from memory so as not to attract their wandering spirits, or souls. Not unlike the *emesak,* or vengeful souls of slain enemies mentioned in the women's war chant at the start of this chapter, the spirits of even the most respected dead ancestors have little in mind beyond the torment of the living.[57] Such a view of death and the soul may be at the root of the Jívaros' exceptional indifference to genealogy, oral recounting of past exploits, and even foundation myths.

The riddle of the 1599 revolt may thus be insoluble from either side, at least in its specifics. By taking a less direct tack, however, it may still be possible to locate keys to the Jívaros' unequivocal success against sixteenth-century Spanish colonialism. What have ethnographers discovered in the broader patterns of culture of these ancient warriors' descendants? For one thing, the Jívaros' emphasis on the present tense just described is closely tied to another trait that may well have aided in fending off would-be captors of past times: an almost anarchistic individualism.

This anarchistic tendency is particularly cultivated among Jívaro men, who strike out on their own shortly after adolescence to prove themselves through mastery of hallucinogenic journeys, hunting, fishing, warfare, stylized speech, and wife-winning. Despite the high frequency of polygyny, however, Jívaro women are hardly powerless; indeed they create, maintain, and exert substantial control over this unusually atomistic society's only unequivocal center, the house and its adjacent garden. Women are regarded by nobody as less than fully formed individuals who, especially after marriage, are as driven as men to prove themselves in the pursuits deemed proper for their sex, namely agriculture, household management, and beer-brewing. Spousal abuse and misogyny are thus seen as signs of male cowardice or deviancy, not deserved punishment of female willfulness.

With individual independence so highly prized and genealogy all but ignored, Jívaro houses are built in near-total physical (and historical) isolation from one another. Each family's "territory," really the extent of its hunting grounds, is neither fixed nor visibly marked, and house sites are frequently abandoned after only a few years for ecological or spiritual reasons, to be replaced by others built perhaps ten to twenty kilometers distant. For the Spanish, like the Inkas before them, meeting up with Jívaros in the first place must never have been easy, since house structures are not only isolated, usually reached by paddling for several days up log-choked, winding tributaries or hacking through jungle over near-invisible footpaths, but also heavily fortified with wooden stockades. Furthermore, constant vigilance, and conversely stealth in stalking human enemies, is learned from a very early age, rendering nearly all Jívaro males above the age of sixteen first-rate guerrilla warriors, perpetually on guard against attackers of any kind.

This exceptional dispersion and militarism, and likewise the highly decentralized and factional politics that gives rise to it, would have made the Jívaro extraordinarily resistant to the usual Spanish (and Inka) methods of domination, namely co-optation of indigenous headmen and forced congregation. Corroborating colonial evidence is occasionally available. For example, a 1587 series of documents regarding disputed encomiendas in the mining town of Sevilla de Oro (another of Velasco's "lost" settlements) center on the inability of both local indigenous wards and Spanish officials to identify a real, undisputed cacique among a group of "conquered" Jivaroans.[58] Among the modern Shuar and Achuar there are no cacique analogues, only shamans and *juunt,* or rare charismatic warriors capable of mustering a dozen or so junior male relatives.[59]

Indeed, the only reason Jívaro men ever band together nowadays, as presumably in the past, is to wage war, usually against neighboring Jívaros deemed responsible for the deaths or injuries of next of kin. For example, a woman beaten to death by her husband might be avenged by a war party made up of a brother or father and select male kin, with the culprit usually shot dead in ambush. The wifebeater's kin, for their part, may regard this punishment as excessive and return the favor by sending out a war party to annihilate someone in the opposing camp. Jívaro blood feuds are thus easily spawned, unleashing a tense mix of centrifugal and centripetal social forces, forces that all but prohibit formation of anything resembling a "tribal" confederation.

Responsibility for beatings and murders is more or less easily ascribed, but even common illnesses and injuries presumed accidental by most Westerners are seen by the Jívaro as the obvious results of shamanic machinations, specific *maleficia* demanding retribution. Thus a death in the family, even of old age, is likely to be followed by a murderous raid against some distant neighbor presumed to be responsible.

Most important to this inquiry into potential causes of sixteenth-century Jívaro attacks, however, is the fact that the secret knowledge considered necessary to cast and discover deadly spells is not assumed to be the exclusive domain of Jívaro shamans. On the contrary, such knowledge is believed to be *greater and more common* among well-traveled and technically proficient outsiders, the flying Protestant missionaries and soldiers of today, and perhaps the gun-toting and gold-milling Spaniards of centuries past. Here is a potential scenario: a Jívaro child falls ill and dies soon after contact with an outsider, something that must have happened repeatedly in the epidemic-stricken late sixteenth century. That outsider, despite protestations of innocence and even ignorance of all matters magical, is immediately assumed to have cast the fatal spell and is marked for liquidation, the sooner the better.

With these ethnographic insights we may tentatively imagine naïve Spaniards like Alonso de Sosa and their highland auxiliaries unwittingly falling victim to vengeance cycles after only a few encounters with small numbers of Jivaroans, no matter how well or ill they treated them. Sosa's Santiago de las Montañas, the cruel mines of Nambija, even Velasco's Logroño are all amply described in the colonial record, but there is no mention of a Great Jívaro Revolt of 1572, or 1581, or 1599. History, as Washington Irving once said, tends often to fade to fable. And good fables tend to come back around as truth. At the same time we know from subsequent documents that the Jívaros did in fact win, or rather confirm, their total independence some time around 1599. It appears they did so in a manner consistent with their culture, slowly pecking away at outside adversaries through small-scale retributive raids followed by retreat to their isolated forest homes.[60]

With time even unstable and ambitious old soldiers of the likes of Landa and Barreto lost interest in this deadly game of hide-and-seek, and Spanish fortune hunters retreated piecemeal to the highland cities of Loja and Cuenca, turning their attention to safer pursuits such as livestock raising and textile production. Survivors' tales spurred a few gold-hungry highlanders to organize Amazonian military expeditions in the mid-seventeenth century, but none relocated the old mines and most failed even to contact the mysterious Jívaros.

From the Western historical perspective we may conclude that the story of the lost goldfields of Quito's vast southeast margins simply passed from the realm of memory to that of legend, only to be recycled as moralist fantasy. From the perspective of the Jívaros, however, the "Great Revolt of 1599," whatever form it may have actually taken on the ground, was apparently viewed as something not worth remembering, perhaps even something to be willfully repressed so as not to haunt the living. Rather than dwell on the dates and details required of myth-debunking, it may indeed be more worthwhile to try to imagine such a fundamentally disorienting encounter through the eyes of the sixteenth-century Jívaros, a people content to exploit the prodigious fecundity of the rain forest while ignoring the gold beneath their feet.

PROSPEROUS SETTLERS WRITE HOME

To my lady, doña Mariana de Monzón, I kiss her hands many times, and also those of my children, whom I have entrusted to Your Mercy [the writer's brother]. Two daughters and one son I have, and two have been carried away from me to heaven. If what I have [here] in livestock and properties I had [there] in Tordesillas, to benefit them and also your [family], it would be more than a little. Even here, where the land is so rich, it is not a little, as I have a quantity of more than 12,000 head of sheep, 2,000 swine, 400 cattle, and 120 horses, not to mention much land under cultivation, houses, and a garden with many citrus trees (although they tell me your garden is very fine, allow me to amuse myself). [But I hope] your suavity (bondad) does not occupy you such that it impedes your engaging in business; do not be slothful in writing to those who engage in commerce, for that is what is most desired and wanting here. . . .

—Alonso Martín de Amores to his brother in Madrid, Indies Council
Procurador Alonso de Herrera
from Quito, 8 Jan. 1580

❊   ❊   ❊

I have not done this before now since I had no way to give you an account of my life. Now I want to give it to Your Mercy, though briefly, in this [letter], and it is that God Our Lord has been served to give me condition, although it has been without license of Your Mercy, or of milady, Mother. And it is that the day before San Juan '77 I got married and veiled with the daughter of a man of good standing and endowments, which is what most gladdened me— and rich, his estate being worth more than 12,000 *castellanos*, and along with his daughter he gave me twelve pounds of gold, which would be 3,000 ducats. And he is named, my father-in-law, Juan de Aranda, and the same name belongs to his daughter, who is my woman, called Juana de Aranda. It is a thing that gives me great contentment, although being so far from you all it is a mixed contentment, but I have hope in God that I shall soon go to see Your Mercies.

I had news from Troche's son, a fellow from that land [Spain] who had just recently arrived, and it delighted me to see someone from there. He informed me that my brother Juan Rodríguez was about to come here. Your Mercies should not be pained at his leaving, because he would arrive at a very good conjuncture. I shall do everything for him that a father would do for his son, [and] here a man of standing has offered, my having informed him of [Juan's] coming, and he responded that it delighted him greatly, because if [Juan] is a diligent man, his estate will soon be worth 5,000 ducats, [that is] if he is as he was when I cared for him, knowing how to read, write, and count, and diligent in the trading of merchandise. Because he here who does not understand these things does not gain to eat, and indeed there are many lost people; he who has not a little money to start out will never have even a *real*, nor shall he make one.

—*Alonso Rodríguez to his father, Alonso Rodríguez de Cuellar, in the Puebla de Montalván (Spain)*
from Popayán, 4 Feb. 1578

Translated from Enrique Otte, *Cartas privadas de emigrantes a Indias,* nos. 345, 402.

FIVE: Adventures in Trade

There is no mountain high enough that
an ass loaded with gold cannot climb it.
(old Spanish proverb)

In early 1564 a traveling salesman named Pedro de
Harrona drowned in the Zamora River east of Loja. He
was accompanied by a mestizo helper and an African
slave named Hilario, but neither managed to save him—
assuming they tried—when he fell and was swept away
by the current. Apparently one of Harrona's packhorses
had become stuck among river boulders and in trying to free the animal
the merchant had lost his balance. Perhaps the horse fell on him and
knocked him unconscious. In any case, the survivors continued the long
climb to Loja with the salvaged goods and a quantity of gold dust, and
there a series of inventories and testimonies was written up by a
professional scribe.[1]

That a river had taken a traveler's life was hardly unusual in the
perpetually rainy Quito backcountry, and Pedro de Harrona might well
have been soon forgotten save for certain circumstances. Simply put, he
died both wealthy and intestate, a guarantee that various Spanish officials

would get involved in sorting out his estate. For posterity, they would leave a trail of paper. The Audiencia of Quito, established only a year before the fatal accident (1563), was charged with settling such dead men's affairs. Quito's high court would unwittingly make Pedro de Harrona an important player in the city's economy for several decades after his death, even after 1599. This is the story in summary, but the Harrona case raises a number of questions.

First of all, what did this traveling salesman hope to gain by tramping through the wild fringes of empire? According to a posthumous inventory and other documents, Harrona was exchanging Spanish imports for gold among the many and rich mining camps of the Zamora district, places like Nambija and Guaysimi. Though apparently never attacked by Jívaro warriors, he traded with men like Diego de Sosa, doomed writer of the first letter in interlude 4. Unsurprisingly, along with numerous bundles of Spanish textiles Harrona carried mining tools: eight almocafres and four *barretas*. More such tools, and perhaps the crushing "feet" of the region's numerous stamp mills, could be made by local blacksmiths from another two hundredweight of "old iron," or from some eighty-five pounds of raw, presumably Basque-made steel *(acero)*. Sosa and his fellow miners in the jungle backlands needed many things besides tools and clothes, of course, and Harrona and others like him supplied them with soap, wax, pepper, wine, vinegar, rice, olives, oil, arms and armor, and slaves. These were the items the merchant carried or was owed money for.

This was not a complex business, really. Miners from Anserma to Nambija produced gold, merchants trucked and bartered for it, usually remitting profits to senior partners in Quito, Panama, and ultimately Seville. Often the trade was conducted on credit, and while most debtors promised future mining yields, one placed an emerald-encrusted gold medal in Harrona's charge as surety. Still others paid directly in gold bullion. One of the merchant's last documented acts was to pay the "royal ninth" in Zamora's smeltery on a 122-peso gold pancake *(tejo de oro)* given him by a miner.[2]

Sorting out the dead man's estate, however, was made difficult by the fact that—like many itinerant merchants—Pedro de Harrona had never married. Less normally, perhaps, he left few living relatives either in the Indies or back home. A Basque, Harrona had emigrated from the small

Gipuzkoan village of Zestoa (actually his name suggests Arroa, a nearby hamlet). Only one close relation remained alive, a sister named María de Goyenequea of the town of Deba.

Although he left no will, Harrona had apparently named as executor his business partner, a fellow Basque named Diego de Guetaria. As if to complicate matters further, however, Guetaria fell ill and died in the midst of the settlement. There was talk of a company between them (and a few other merchants) worth seventeen thousand gold pesos, essentially a pooling of liquid capital to import vast quantities of "Castilian" (really pan-European) merchandise to Quito via Panama and Guayaquil. Others would soon take their place; the Andes were in fact crawling with immigrants trading imported goods for gold.

The Audiencia of Quito, true to its duty with regard to intestate deaths, took over the Harrona estate, first auctioning off the slave Hilario; he was sold to a Cuenca merchant for 230 gold pesos. Debts to the dead salesman were called in quickly and the court set about plotting investments. Some sense of Harrona's spiritual concerns must have also been known, since 1,000 pesos were spent on masses for his departed soul. A substantial portion of remaining monies was apparently entrusted to the bishop of Quito to help clothe and feed "young orphan girls, daughters of the conquistadors."[3]

Thus, by getting himself killed in a jungle river, this obscure, unmarried trader was unwittingly transformed into a sort of spiritual knight, significant benefactor of Quito's growing population of distressed and largely mestiza damsels. But this was not the end of the story. Eventually word of the Audiencia of Quito's decisions reached Gipuzkoa and a Basque clergyman filed a letter of protest claiming that Harrona's sister, a nun, had been unfairly cut out of the deal. Apparently María de Goyenequea wanted to donate her windfall, if there was to be one, to local religious establishments. With a pot of American gold at stake, she had had no trouble finding literate advocates in Deba and neighboring Basque country towns.

But her brother's treasure was in Quito, and it would not easily leave. As the Council of the Indies sent conflicting messages to litigants on both sides of the Atlantic, Pedro de Harrona's accidental donation to the city grew. By the early 1580s the fund, largely managed by Quito's bishop,

Pedro de la Peña, had more than doubled in value, to nearly fifteen thousand pesos. Gains came mostly from censo, or low-interest mortgage returns. Some of the profits were being used to organize a new parish called Santa Bárbara.[4]

As tended to happen with unclaimed cash, the "Harrona fund" seemed to bring out the best and worst in all who came near it. In 1585 Quito's state attorney complained to the king that Bishop Peña was now diverting Harrona's "public" censo proceeds into a private chaplaincy in Lima—solely for the benefit of the bishop's soul. In all, the fund was now said to be worth over twenty thousand ducats (about twenty-five thousand pesos), prompting the attorney to propose the monies be removed from the bishop's control and spent founding a university.[5] This idea seems not to have gained much support, in part because the university-building Jesuit Order had not yet established a firm foothold in Quito. Other contenders quickly emerged.

In 1588 the merchant-led Confraternity of the True Cross requested one thousand gold pesos from the Harrona estate to establish a branch for indigenous devotees, already famous for "disciplining" themselves during processions to the great church of San Francisco.[6] This bid on behalf of native flagellants seems also to have been rejected, but Harrona's gold went on living, essentially serving as the bishopric's core savings-and-loan kitty up to and after 1599. Harrona's private loss at the margins in the early gold-rush days of the colony had thus been absorbed and transformed by the corporate center, becoming, in effect, a pillar of Quito's "central bank."

The story of Pedro de Harrona's money serves as a reminder that early accumulation of liquid capital, particularly in gold, could reverberate for decades in an economy the size of Quito's. His untimely death also points out the dangers faced by roving factors, particularly those who trekked to backcountry mining camps. Harrona's 1564 accident in fact became legendary, a commonly cited example of the dangers of such travel.[7] This chapter examines key features of Quito's gold-fueled commercial economy, among them: 1) urban consumerism, or how gold was spent in the capital; 2) the rise and fall of backcountry trade networks, most notably the shift in merchant focus from southern gold camps to those of greater Popayán; and 3) the major transformations already underway in the region's export-import economy by 1599. Most critical in this last category was the transition from gold to locally manufactured textiles as the major source of outside exchange.

The Urban Bazaar

The colorful silks and starched ruffs given the Esmeraldas ambassadors were not all Quito had to offer in 1599. Merchants large and small and of European, indigenous, or mixed heritage had by this time transformed the city into a consumer's paradise. Amidst the dozens of shops and warehouses lining streets and plazas one could select from a dizzying array of fabrics, finished garments, and accessories from around the world. Here were assorted bolts of Cantonese damask, there piles of Gascony capes, rolls of Indian muslin, kid gloves from Ciudad Real, Rouen and Holland linens by the ton, huge spools of Portuguese and Milanese thread. Exotic and mundane imports crowded every shelf: allspice, cumin, cloves, pepper, cinnamon, saffron; wine, capers, olives, olive oil, almonds, hazelnuts; wax, candles, soap, perfume. Then books, diaries, medical instruments, drugs, reading glasses, trade beads, chemicals, vegetable and insect dyes, and reams upon reams of paper. Elsewhere metal goods: sheepshears, butcher knives, razors, wool-cards, sewing needles, lance-heads, swords, crowbars, horseshoes, nails, padlocks, hinges, stirrups.

Local goods also proliferated: colorful Quito woolens coarse and fine, embroidered Quijós cotton tablecloths, hemp-soled sandals, hardwood furniture, jewelry, hats, saddles, boots; comestibles like sugar, peanuts, candied fruits, pastries, cheeses, hams; barrels of flour, biscuits, garbanzos; rolls of tobacco. Quito's voluminous sales records strongly suggest that homesick Spaniards equated the good life with a daily ration of quince marmalade; they bought it (literally) by the ton. In 1599 an indigenous market woman might still sell more maize beer than muscatel from her spot on the main plaza, but her traditional *anaku,* or wrap-around skirt, was now more likely Chinese taffeta than homespun cotton. The city was rich, or so it appeared. But how exactly did one "keep up appearances" in 1599 Quito?

In September 1598 an encomendero and his wife went to Diego Rodríguez de León's Quito shop to purchase a suit of clothes for their

Merchant Exchange Building, Seville, architect Juan de Herrera, finished in 1599. It now houses the General Archive of the Indies.

son, Martín. The 230-odd-peso price tag—about half the value of an adult African slave and more than twenty times the value of an average indigenous man's outfit—marked them as conspicuous consumers. A tailor had yet to be chosen, but soon young Martín would sport garments of Chinese satin, silk, and taffeta, the finest Segovian broadcloth, a measure of Mexican grogram, all black (save five yards of green velvet) and trimmed with the best Italian and Portuguese embroidering threads. A tailor would add eight dozen black silk buttons, and a (presumably black) felt hat was thrown in to top off the ensemble. Perhaps most important in Quito, land of the shoeless poor, the privileged youth would strut the streets in finely detailed, laced leather half-boots *(borcequis de lazo)*. Like all his vestments, expensive yet austere, the footwear was properly reflective of contemporary peninsular (i.e., Habsburg Court) fashions. Not only was head-to-toe black "in," but by chance the purchase was registered just days after the long-anticipated death of Philip II.[8]

As this and thousands of similar sale records reveal, clothes "made" men and women in philippine Quito. Luxury merchants and haberdashers like Diego Rodríguez de León made it their business to supply the necessary accouterments of personal adornment. In short, gold, both in hand and promised, had enabled the formation of a material culture of astonishing range within two generations of conquest. Such consumption was driven also by contemporary metropolitan standards so powerful even poorer individuals routinely went into debt to clothe themselves according to their perceived station.[9] Knowing how important couture was to the colonial drama, Quito's merchant-clothiers imagined themselves agents of civilization helping to sew together a precarious but hugely promising new world society. Consumption of their specialized wares aided formation of a diverse neo-European social hierarchy while also fostering employment among a growing and similarly diverse class of manual workers.

Sales to local landed elites could be substantial, and they reveal in part how Quito's early credit market functioned. In summer 1597, for example, the encomendero Juan de la Puente and sons signed for over fourteen thousand pesos' worth of merchandise from two traders with close family ties in Lima. Such money could have purchased an entire slave gang or a small ocean-going vessel. The Puente family, descendants of an original Quito conquistador, were uniquely placed to take on such debt. They enjoyed rents from almost nine hundred indigenous tributaries around the village of Sigchos, where they ran a textile mill. It is likely some of the merchandise here purchased was intended for resale among these quasi-captive workers. In any case, the Puentes pledged to repay the sum piecemeal with encomienda proceeds: six hundred pesos cash per annum, surplus chickens and swine rendered at six-month intervals, and textiles from their *obraje*. Merchants would take the truck goods at wholesale, then market them in the city. Put simply, the Puentes financed the high life the old-fashioned way, by "mining Indians" directly.

Encomendero and kin took home several bales of fine European, Mexican, and Asian fabrics. There were also mantles from India, European stockings and kid gloves, women's shirts and gauze veils, fine felt hats; a variety of Asian spices; ten dozen combs; strings of blue glass beads from France, copper implements and vessels of unknown provenance, two large crock pots, numerous iron bars, grates, and pickaxes, and more than a ton of raw iron ingots and sheets. Add a full caparison in velvet and one may imagine how gallant Juan de la Puente must have looked as he bounded across the Iliniza moorlands to Sigchos on his fully clothed horse, himself decked out in shimmering Nanking satin togs, high leather boots, flowing Valladolid cape, and a supple, imported, wide-brimmed felt hat. In his saddlebags one would perhaps find, among other local and exotic treasures, a crinkly new copy of *The Mirror of Christian Living,* a colonial best-seller.[10]

More common were smaller but still substantial obligations like that signed by Quito encomendero Cristóbal Moreno Mazo in February 1598. He purchased three thousand pesos' worth of merchandise, including cloth from India and four copies of the same *Mirror of Christian Living.* The encomendero mortgaged a parcel of land and pledged repayment with tribute proceeds from scattered encomiendas in Ambato, Pusili, Los Cañares, and Cotocollao.[11] Similar was doña Constantina Silvera's purchase of seventeen hundred pesos' worth of merchandise in early 1598; she too picked up multiple copies of *The Mirror of Christian Living,* and pledged to repay the loan within three years. In her case liens were placed on a townhouse near Quito's Augustinian church and on half the value of a sugar mill at a site called "Uli," including two African slaves ("Diego, master sugar maker" and "Pedro Yaia, miller").[12] Like encomienda chickens, eggs, and swine, slave-produced sugar found a ready market in highland cities like Quito. Likewise, it could be trucked to wholesalers for comforting imports—like the self-help manuals everyone else seemed to be reading.

Another shopkeeper with many obligated customers was the apparently French-born Gabriel de Granobles (i.e., Grenoble), who in early 1599 was owed some 116 debts worth 33,000 pesos for merchandise purchased on credit, nearly all of it on short terms. Debts ranged in size from 3 pesos to 2,200, owed by almost as many types of people. His rare account book, or *libro de tienda,* lists artisans like pastry chef Marcos Pérez and silversmith Juan Sánchez, along with the prioress of the Santa Catalina nunnery and several Jesuit administrators.[13] In fact, the tens of thousands of pages of Quito's notary Protocols for the years around 1599 burst with these numbingly repetitive promissory notes, testament to the colonists' general hope for the future. Based on their extraordinary willingness to borrow, they apparently believed both in themselves and in the colony. To keep up such credit-dependent consumption without crashing, however, the city desperately needed both lending institutions and far-sighted financial advisers.

As witnessed in the case of the Harrona fund, church organizations served as vital sources of credit in the early colony. As in the rest of Spanish America, their influence would grow enormously in coming centuries. Nevertheless, cathedral chapters, parish churches, convents, and sodalities had limitations as financial institutions, particularly in incipient, "boom" economies like early Quito's. For one thing, most were not yet significantly endowed, in part because many first-generation colonists managed (unlike Pedro de Harrona) to will liquid funds to home churches and convents in Spain. Secondly, church borrowers generally had to have real estate to pledge, an impossibility for many rootless newcomers. Most importantly, however, church lenders were highly conservative, openly averse to the risks associated with mining and trade. In such circumstances one had little choice but to seek commercial credit. Quito's wholesale merchants alone had the cash required of such enterprises, but according to contemporary testimony and their own commercial paper they rented money only at extraordinarily high and in fact technically illegal rates. Some said they lacked compassion, or at least a modicum of Christian charity.

Sepulcher stone of Cristóbal Martín, Franciscan Monastery, Quito

Enter Cristóbal Martín, Quito's first (and apparently only) colonial banker, a genuine rarity outside continental Europe.[14] A native of Antwerp, site of furious Spanish repression in exactly these years, Martín arrived a penniless tradesman in Quito around 1579 in the retinue of a newly appointed audiencia secretary. An early switch from tailoring to retail sales paid off, and the young Fleming, who remained a bachelor throughout his long life (he appears to have died around 1640), set about building his fortune and forgetting his past. By the first years of the seventeenth century Martín's liquid assets amounted to well over 100,000 pesos. Outstanding private debts to him alone amounted to over 50,000 pesos. The rich Fleming apparently averted suspicion in this xenophobic era, when practically every Spanish sermon was punctuated by venomous denunciations of Low Country heretics and rebels, by proving himself a devout and generous Catholic; he also paid naturalization fees in one of several 1590s "foreigner" round-ups without complaint. How did he make his money?

By 1600 Cristóbal Martín appears in Quito's notary Protocols as the city's largest wholesale wine merchant, and his many links to backcountry gold camps are evident in smeltery ledgers.[15] Gold received in payment for wine and other goods (carried to the margins by others) was reinvested in luxury imports and even sold for silver in Europe via overseas factors. Fueled in part by gold's quickly rising value against silver in these years of the Potosí bonanza, Martín's rates of return were phenomenal, inciting the city's richest and most powerful players to put whatever cash they could spare in his hands.[16] More numerous, those who borrowed from him praised his leniency, his low rates, and his trustworthiness; he was "fidelity" incarnate. By the time Cristóbal Martín was audited during a renewed Dutch scare in 1607 nearly every elite individual in Quito, including the bishop and numerous audiencia officials, was in one way or another dependent on this single merchant-investor.[17]

Cultural Imports

Gold and lenient creditors allowed many Quiteños to spend lavishly on contemporary European symbols of sophistication; their fondness for economically superfluous slaves has already been noted. Shop inventories unwittingly provide glimpses also of Quito's intellectual and "cultured" life around the turn of the seventeenth century. Alongside imported copper kettles and manzanilla olives, well-heeled Quiteños could examine a *mapamundi* ("of the new ones") and thumb through numerous books. Most were religious and didactic, ranging from the Renaissance humanist Juan Luis Vives's famous moral tract, *Instruction of the Christian Woman* (1524), to Francisco Ortiz Lucio's "action" hagiology, *Flos Sanctorum.* Foreigners like Cristóbal Martín may have consulted copies of Antonio Nebrija's great Castilian grammar from time to time. Several Quito merchants carried it. For reading of a lighter but still spiritual sort there was the anonymous *Voyage to Jerusalem*.[18]

It is around 1599 that book lists in Quito's merchant inventories reach for the first time beyond religious themes. Now amidst titles like *The Miseries of Mankind, Universal Redeemer,* and *The Life of St. Catherine* one finds secular works. There were the classical verses of Ovid and Marcus Annaeus Lucan, but also more contemporary ones by Camoens *(Lusiads),*

Garcilaso de la Vega *(Mexicana),* and the Mexican-born Francisco de Terrazas *(Conquista y Nuevo Mundo).*[19] Dramatic pieces were the next wave; Juan de la Cueva's *Comedias y Tragedias* arrived in January 1601, for example. Soon shelves were crowded also with songbooks, astrological charts, legal glosses, and technical manuals treating everything from architecture to armament manufacture. Cristóbal Martín may have winced at military histories like *Against the Walloon* and *The Wars of Flanders,* but he could suggest alternatives, perhaps *The Wars of the Turks and Persians* or *The History of Scotland.* A banned title might have sneaked in between the covers of a multivolume *cuerpo de libros* collectively called *The Crown of Spain.* A reader curious about the other side of the Pacific may have found something intriguing if not altogether true in *The History of the Kingdoms of the Orient.*[20]

It is impossible to say how many of these books were read and by whom, but they appear to have circulated primarily among Quito's upper crust (they do not appear in popular-sector wills, for example). Most titles sold for three to five silver pesos, small change for a person of means, but well out of reach for the vast majority of working-class (and overwhelmingly illiterate) Quiteños. Members of the regular and secular clergy could probably afford *The Tridentine Councils, Against the Koran, The Garden of Holy Love,* and similar titles, but other religious works, like Gabriel Mata's 1587 *Caballero Asisio* (Knight Assisi) were aimed directly at "popular" lay readers tempted by *Amadis of Gaul* and other "fluff" chivalry tales. An unhappy husband, meanwhile, might have admonished a strong-willed spouse while thumping a copy of Fray Luis de León's *The Perfect Wife.*

What can one say about this eclectic blend of titles entering Quito at the turn of the seventeenth century? As literary historian Carlos Alberto González Sánchez has suggested for Peru, the mix of books heading for the colonies in this era reveals a marked polarity between secular "escapist" and pious literature; the Quito titles listed in notary records are obviously no exception.[21] Urban sophisticates could ponder *The English Schism,* then relax with *La Galatea* (Cervantes's 1585 bestseller), brush up on Catholic *Spiritual Concepts,* then pagan *Roman Ceremonies.* Wealthy illiterates—who, judging from their crabbed or obviously templated signatures, were not rare in 1599 Quito—could meanwhile clutch a gilt breviary on the way to mass as a show of piety or accessorize their Alberti-inspired homes with rows of handsome leather-bound histories.

In this, Quito's golden age, city dwellers of various ethnicities felt they could afford to purchase or copy almost any element or accouterment of late Renaissance culture. For them colonial life from bottom to top ought to mimic Mediterranean, or more precisely Habsburg-imperial standards. Along with imported songbooks came musical instruments: clavichords, bagpipes, flutes, *vihuelas,* and guitars. Following the secular/pious split in literature, town troubadours might alternate between numerous military-historical ballads (recited from imported *romanceros*) and more somber, religious ones, like *Burdens of the Conscience.* Meanwhile, indigenous villagers outside Quito commissioned expensive pipe organs for their modest churches.[22] In general, public consumption of high culture was a prerequisite for all ranking players in the early colonial drama. On the other hand, it should be remembered that African and indigenous musicians quickly adopted and explored new realms of sound with instruments like the guitar and vihuela. These and other currents of Quito's plebeian subculture, though all but absent from notarial records, were remarked on by contemporary observers.

Carved religious images, paintings, and tapestries were also imported, but these were already being replaced by local copies in the years around 1599. Indeed, commission agreements between painters, sculptors, architects, and churchmen show this era to have been the seedtime of the famous "Quito School" of Baroque art. Certainly the many surviving works of Andrés Sánchez Gallque imply wholesale embrace (and mastery) of contemporary European painterly technique and form. An Italian master painter, Angelino Medoro, appears in the notary books around 1600, as does a professional European dance instructor.[23]

With few exceptions (like the portrait on the cover of this book) Quito's plastic arts specialists stuck mostly to religious themes. Specialists in profane arts, however, knew more than the latest jig. Games of chance like cards, dice, and dominoes had been present in Quito since conquest (the Inkas had their own dicelike game, which has survived among some modern Quechua speakers), but flourished as never before in the trade boom. An example: in 1601 a Quito merchant and compulsive gambler named Francisco Claros de Valencia was forced to sign a public renunciation of his habit or face exile to Chile. Perhaps he could be described as the inverse image of Cristóbal Martín.[24]

Another high culture import was Renaissance medicine, still very much an art rather than a science. In Quito European-style medical therapy was practiced by both educated Spaniards and indigenous barber-surgeons, all of whom did their best to balance bodily humors with purgatives like senna *(cañafístola)* and frequent applications of the lancet. Fee schedules differed according to education, but success rates were (presumably) equally dismal.[25] More than a few ailing individuals, including the vast majority of indigenous plebeians and many slaves, but also perhaps some members of the creole upper crust, must have preferred the less invasive and more psychologically reassuring methods of traditional native and African therapeutics.

In sickness and in health, the capital city by this time had become not only the colony's style center, but also its religious and political heart. In truth, as in most parts of the world at the time, religion and politics were not easily distinguishable. The point was driven home in Quito on two watershed occasions. One was the solemn processions marking the death of Philip II in May of 1599, the other was the subsequent "gifting," feasting, and baptism of the maroon chieftains of Esmeraldas. We have seen how the Esmeraldas overtures and expenditures reiterated Quito's (ultimately unfulfilled) desire to bind its wayward periphery to the core with ties of Christian love. What about the king's funeral?

Here Quito, itself on the periphery of Spain's world empire, pledged allegiance to its own distant religious-political heart, its own style center. The Habsburg Court and the city of Madrid were in fact only parts, or elements of a greater, "central" cultural ideal current in Spain's colonies. Like fellow urbanites in Mexico, Lima, or Bogotá, Quiteños of varying heritage dreamed also of Rome and the pope, of Jerusalem, and of the rich historical legacy and current conflicts reflected in the shimmering waters of the Mediterranean. In 1599 Quito's city council voted to purchase eight hundred yards of black Chinese buckram and several hundred pounds of candles and wax blocks from two local merchants. These rather expensive items were then used to drape and illuminate the beloved monarch's catafalque (itself an expensive, specially commissioned wooden structure) in the cathedral church. As Carlos Eire has shown for contemporary Spain, Philip II's funeral celebrations were so extravagant "back home" they drove up fabric prices from Burgos to Seville.[26]

Quito, a distant beacon, a tiny neo-Iberian satellite on the other side of the world, had likewise to show itself pious. In this remarkable act of Baroque imperial drama the great lengths of black cloth—significantly of Chinese manufacture—symbolized Philip's ultimate acknowledgement of a Catholic world monarch's greatest sin: pride, or the folly of trying to fathom God's will. After a half-century of unprecedented expansion the Spanish empire was besieged on more fronts than could have been imagined at Philip's accession in 1556. In a way, Quito's own experience was but the empire's in miniature. The candles' white light symbolized not only the weary king's, but rather the entire realm's—all his subjects'—faint hope for divine mercy. In this period conspicuous royal obsequies asserted not only a city's place in the empire, but also its nearness to God. If with enough gold Quiteños could collapse oceans, why could they not also use liquid wealth to bridge heaven?

Women & Wealth

As seen in chapter 2, some elite slave owners resolved such pressing concerns by tying their bondservants to the career of their own burdened souls. Other elite women in Quito, based on inventories in wills and dowries, were similarly confronted with an embarrassment of riches at key life junctures. A more systematic study of these documents remains to be done, but a sample reading suggests that at least two material wealth-related issues (besides salvation) were deemed vitally important by elite Quito women circa 1599. One was the amount of gold in cash one brought to a marriage; second was how much gold jewelry one could marshal for personal adornment. Like dying well, marrying well and looking good (i.e., rich) were issues of fundamental concern for many elite Quiteñas. On the other hand, the frequent appearance of wealthy widows in the Protocols suggests that financial independence—both within and beyond marriage—was also being negotiated.

In June 1598 Quito's budding banker Cristóbal Martín appeared before a notary to assess the value of clothing and furniture brought to a marriage by Beatriz de Águilar. In addition to four disks of gold worth two thousand pesos, the well-endowed doña Beatriz claimed over one thousand pesos' worth of personal items, including a canopied bed with imported linens and silk pillows, finely embroidered shirts, kerchiefs, a "Spring doublet," a scarlet outer-skirt trimmed with velvet, and a large lace mantilla. Doña Beatriz's dowry also included gold-and-pearl jewelry, a brass mortar and pestle, a mirror, a syringe, and a fine men's linen shirt with lace collar (in the Flemish style). This last item, and perhaps also the syringe, may have been intended for the new husband, but the rest was the bride's to have and hold.

Beatriz de Águilar's parents, natives of the Extremaduran town of Ribera del Fresno, were deceased. It was her brother, a Quito merchant, who had made certain that his sister was properly supplied with the adornments appropriate to her class and enough cash to maintain her in this lifestyle.[27] Cristóbal Martín, the trusted Fleming, simply helped ensure that doña Beatriz's dowry had been accurately appraised and registered for her legal protection should a gambling or otherwise wayward husband squander all or part of it.

Gold adornments made up a substantial portion of the financial holdings of nearly all elite Quito women. A relatively modest dowry from 1596, for example, included about a twelfth portion of gold jewelry encrusted with New Granadan emeralds and pearls. The remainder consisted of real estate.[28] One of the largest dowries recorded in 1590s Quito, worth some fifteen thousand pesos total, included (along with two African slaves, substantial landholdings, and piles of clothing and furniture) seventy gold-pearl-and-emerald buttons, two chokers and a belt of the same materials, a heavy gold chain, and an assortment of rings, earrings, bracelets, crosses, and other pendants consisting mostly of fine gold and valued at some two thousand (gold) pesos. As if this did not render the bride sufficiently resplendent, many of her finest garments were embroidered with imported gold-filled thread *(oro de florencia)*.[29]

All that glittered in the standard elite Quiteña costume circa 1599 was not gold, but much of what did was. In another case from 1593, gold jewelry made up more than a third the value of a more modest dowry of a little over one thousand pesos.[30] Similar was a 1597 dowry worth over seven thousand pesos. Here slaves made up more than a fifth of the total, but the majority of the balance consisted of debts to be collected in Almaguer gold dust and jewelry. Thus Tomasina de Figueroa Ponce de León would enter marriage adorned with essential symbols: two female

African servants (each with a small boy), a gold eagle with a large emerald in its breast, a gold crucifix, three gold rings, and a pair of gold filigree earrings. Added to this human/metallic treasure were several pieces of worked silver, including a gilt cup, and also a gilt walnut writing desk.[31]

If these documents are to be believed, then, elite women of marriage age in late sixteenth-century Quito almost rivaled the ancient Inka for pure shimmering glory. More importantly, as noted in chapter 2, gold, whether worn as jewelry or amassed in raw form, was, after a human captive or two, the best insurance a woman had against penury, in this life and the next.

In sum, by 1599 merchants like Cristóbal Martín had made Quito the marketplace and style center of the north Andes, a city whose commercial reach extended beyond regional political boundaries. The colony's special combination of scattered goldfields, concentrated indigenous tributaries, and generous credit terms afforded elites not only superfluous African slaves but also exotic fabrics and accessories, the latest European books and maps, wine from Peru or Spain, and countless other luxuries. Just as American treasure transformed monetary systems abroad, in the colonies it helped create a new and voracious consumer class. Early colonial life entailed not only the prodigious production of crude wealth for export, but also exuberant consumption of the trappings of contemporary European high culture. Unluckily for some, these tastes would remain the same long after the money ran out.

Governing the Gold Trail

In August 1607, just two months after Cristóbal Martín's arrest (he was soon freed), the Audiencia of Quito received a disturbing report from the mining camp of Almaguer, south of Popayán. Mayor Francisco Caicedo claimed that over the previous few years counterfeit gold had been turning up in a growing number of transactions, large and small. He was not referring to coins, but rather gold dust, the district's only form of common currency. Apparently about 1595, if not before, indigenous traders had begun mixing genuine gold with a mineral substance Caicedo called "Juan Blanco," passing it off to unsuspecting customers. This problem substance, also called "marcasite" (*margajita,* i.e., pyrite), was said to come from the Marmato mines of the Central Cordillera, taken from veins there by native traders who profited from the debasement.

"The Indians are so full of malice," Caicedo claimed, "that they themselves intermix the said golds [*sic*] . . . thereby causing the ruin of good trade in this city and in all the governorship."[32] Alonso Martín Paladinés (literally "of the Palatinate"), a foreign-born Almaguer mine operator, testified that in past times washed and milled Marmato gold "used to clean up with a discount *(refacción)* of one-half peso to yield twenty karats." "But today," Martín continued, "very bad gold circulates in this city and environs and it is because the Indians bring it with *juan blanco* mixed and dirty *(sucio).*"[33] Another witness claimed only Spaniards directly overseeing indigenous panners could now be trusted to trade "clean" gold *(oro limpio),* and merchant Martín Lozano reiterated that indigenous itinerant traders were responsible for the spurious metal. "It is the indios *mindaláes,*" he claimed, "who know where the veins of *juan blanco* are located."

The audiencia was not alone in its concern. Writing from the royal smeltery at Cali in April 1610, Popayán governor Francisco Sarmiento de Sotomayor (1607–14) informed the Indies Council of two things. First, gold dust still circulated as common currency, both within and beyond the province, and second, "John White" was still afoot in the land. In Sarmiento's own words:

> Among the things in this governorship in need of remedy of which I give notice to Your Mercy . . . was the stopping of gold dust from circulating as common money, a thing extremely damaging to Your Majesty's Royal Treasury, because in exchanging it and making payments large and small no one ever smelted it or paid the *quinto* and when a person had need of leaving for other provinces he would take it there for smelting, where he would pay only the fifteenth *(quinzavo)* or twentieth *(veinteno),* whereas they pay in this *caja* [i.e., the Cali treasury] the tenth part, and this they do against Your Mercy's edicts, which mandate that miners smelt [their gold] before it leaves their hands and also that it not leave this province for smelting under penalty of forfeiture.

And beyond the damage to your Royal Treasury resulting from this practice there was a huge fraud and deception in this gold dust which was done by mixing it with a pyrite *(margajita)* they call *juan blanco,* of which there are many mines in this province, so similar to gold dust that one could not tell them apart nor detect the fraud except by way of smelting, which I did in this [smeltery] of Cali to gain experience, and out of one hundred pesos [c. 420 g] of that gold [*sic*] came only thirty [of genuine gold] and the said *juan blanco* was converted to charcoal, such that no one could really know what they were giving or receiving. Many became rich by this evil trade, putting together a hundred or a thousand pesos of gold and mixing in two parts *juan blanco.* And often it was mixed by so many hands that it came to contain no gold at all, and this could not be easily punished since anyone could commit the crime in private without need of a middleman; *thus there came to be more potentates striking their own coins in this governorship than in all of Germany* . . .[34]

Accompanying the report was a brief missive from Quito oidor and recent investigative judge Dr. Diego de Armenteros confirming the continued problems with loose gold and counterfeiting in Popayán, and approving of Sarmiento's proposed remedies. The governor had mandated all gold dust circulating in his district be brought to the royal smeltery and made into quasi-coins, "little pieces" *(pedazos menudos)* of ten-karat gold bearing the royal seal. As was mandated of genuine coins in most of Europe, these low-grade lumps were not to be "quitted of their intrinsic value" (i.e., refined for sale as bullion), an act "reserved for the prince."[35] These measures, said Armenteros, would help restore "good government" in Popayán and would "serve the king."

"John White" was probably iron sulphide, or fool's gold, a common mineral in most mountainous districts worldwide. That "he" began to pass for true gold in Popayán and Quito in the years following 1599 signaled at least two things: 1) declining production of the real thing, and 2) survival of indigenous wile (and possibly underground mindalá trade networks, a subject requiring further investigation). Most salient here, however, is the other problem cited by Governor Sarmiento: the export of gold dust to other districts.

It was not by accident that "John White" came to Quito, and what follows is a brief exploration of how Popayán's goldfields had been transformed into Quito's lifeline by 1599, its major source of bullion and a principal market for both exotic imports and local products. Notary and other records reveal that contemporary Popayán mine owners depended on Bogotá for cotton mantles, a form of court-mandated payment for encomienda laborers, but virtually everything else they bought linked them to Quito.[36] In part because of modern national boundaries separating Ecuador from Colombia, this important link has never been explored in depth by historians.

Gold specifically said to originate in Popayán first appears in Quito's smeltery ledgers in 1549, taxed at a discount rate of 10 percent (gold from Quito districts like Santa Bárbara was charged the full *quinto,* or 20 percent, at the time).[37] In 1569 this concession was extended and improved to the twelfth *(dozavo),* or just over 8 percent, evidence that Quito treasury officials were competing early and openly with northern smelteries for Popayán gold.

As demonstrated in Table 5.1, Popayán gold by the 1570s constituted over 70 percent of all gold taxed in Quito's royal smeltery. Mining production in the southern highlands was also peaking about this time, but "southern" gold that did not escape as contraband was mostly taxed in the smelteries of Zamora, Loja, and Cuenca. The resulting taxes were (usually) remitted to the Quito treasury, as mandated, but the remaining 80 to 90 percent of southern gold production remains difficult to trace. Notarial and other records suggest much of this gold made its way to Quito merchants, but other outlets included Guayaquil (the normal destination for Quito's remittances) and, more significantly for the extreme southern districts, Paita, and from there Lima or Panama.[38]

Table 5.1. *Popayán Gold Registered in Quito's Libros de Fundición, 1569–1576*

YEAR	GOLD PESOS REG. QUITO	GOLD PESOS ORIG. POP.	% OF QUITO FUNDICIÓN
1569	67,505	44,198	65.47
1570	56,660	33,363	58.88
1571	71,923	53,896	74.93
1572	80,610	59,887	74.29
1573	65,505	48,528	74.08
1574	91,618	67,232	73.38
1575	87,595	61,098	69.75
1576	69,416	56,803	81.83

TOTAL (8 years): 590,832   425,005   avg. 71.93% of total

*source ANHQ Real Hacienda, caja 35, vol. 2

Records for the 1580s give fewer details of provenance, but by the mid-1590s nearly 90 percent of the gold smelted in Quito was said to come from Popayán, a dependence made all the more notable since the southern treasuries of Loja and Cuenca were then being remitted directly to Panama and Spain via Paita.[39] Lacking Quito's administrative authority, royal treasury officials in Cali and Cartago meanwhile remained saddled with higher tax rates, precisely the problem cited a decade later by Governor Sarmiento. Thus gold originating as far north as the Quiebralomo mines of Anserma was brought "raw" to Quito in 1599.[40] Other Popayán sources named during these years were Jelima, Chisquío, Almaguer, Pasto, and Mocoa.

Table 5.2. Popayán Gold Registered in Quito's Libros de Fundición, 1595–1600

YEAR	GOLD PESOS REG. QUITO	GOLD PESOS ORIG. POP.	% OF QUITO FUNDICIÓN
1595	52,435	47,299	90.21
1596	67,442	62,410	92.54
1597	57,273	51,965	90.73
1598	58,594	46,129	78.73
1599	56,804	48,088	84.66
1600	51,985	45,884	88.26
TOTAL (6 years)	344,533	301,775	Avg. 87.59% of total

*source ANHQ Real Hacienda, caja 37

Thus Quito defined one aspect of its generally nebulous political authority over the huge governorship of Popayán. By decree the audiencia had helped draw a high percentage of its subordinate neighbor's brute gold production southward, not once, but with increasing efficiency across five decades. Still, renewed tax incentives alone could not have sufficed, no matter what Popayán's governors claimed. To make this much gold move, Quito needed powerful merchants like Cristóbal Martín, and moreover dozens of roving factors like the ill-fated Pedro de Harrona. It had both.

In June 1599 Domingo Sánchez signed for over five thousand pesos' worth of merchandise from a Quito wholesaler. Over the next four years his name appears in Quito smeltery ledgers next to quantities of high-karat Popayán gold dust.[41] Predictably, he carried goods to the gold camps and brought profits home. Northbound commodities included hundreds of yards of luxury textiles from Italy, France, and the Netherlands, trade beads, "Indian feathers" (possibly from Mesoamerica), eyeglasses, and spices, such as saffron and cloves. As this and many other lists of north- and southbound merchandise indicate, even in the backcountry, hundreds of leagues removed from neo-European cities like Quito or Bogotá, one could still find discriminating consumers of various ethnicities. Like the silver of Potosí or New Spain, it was these miners' gold, after all, that fueled Europe's early modern proto-industries, among them the famous linen manufactories of northern France (primarily Rouen) and several Low Country suburbs.[42]

Sánchez also carried over two tons of raw iron, along with some worked bars, all headed for Popayán mining camps.[43] Iron and steel tools were of course critical in developing goldfields, particularly when operations went underground. Blacksmiths naturally followed close on the heels of miners.[44] A 1581 contract, for example, lists twenty-four outbound "mining kits" (*ternos de minas,* a set of three handtools, including the *barra* and almocafre) along with three hundred pounds of raw iron, four jugs of Spanish wine, twenty jugs of olive oil, five hundred pounds of soap, two hundred pounds of wax, fourteen yards of local (Quito) cloth, and nine reams of paper, all to be traded for twenty-karat gold in Pasto and Almaguer.[45]

Iron nails and caldrons may have come from China via Acapulco, but most iron and steel products listed in the Quito Protocols probably originated in the Basque country of Spain, not far from Pedro de Harrona's birthplace. The provinces of Bizkaya and Gipuzkoa were famously rich in concentrated deposits and had numerous hydraulic foundries operating at full capacity in towns like Zerain and Legazpi in precisely these years. Responding to soaring American demand, Basque artisans produced great quantities of high-quality ingots, bars, horseshoes, nails, and fixtures along the many rivers of the Euskal Herria, future crucible of Iberian industrialization. Indeed, although only a 1581 obligation notes specifically, among scores of hatchets, machetes, and horseshoes, six thousand "Biscayan" planking nails, the frequency of Basque names among Quito merchants and miners implies a more than casual connection between the iron mines and foundries of the Old Country and the gold mines and smelteries of Quito and Popayán.[46]

Just such a Basque merchant with numerous ties to Popayán gold camps was Juan de Artiaga. Artiaga was a native of the Gipuzkoan town of Segura, and debts from a 1588 will, all in gold pesos, reveal connections to merchants (some with Basque surnames) and artisans in the city of Popayán, and also to miners working in the gold camps of Pasto, Almaguer, and Jelima. Artiaga earned his living by transporting a variety of

Basque iron workers discover Miracle Cross (Legazpi, Gipuzkoa, c. 1580, anonymous)

luxury dry goods, tools, and bulk commodities like salt and wine on the backs of his twenty-eight mules. In a land too rugged for oxcarts, these hybrid animals were highly prized; minus tack and accessories Artiaga's train was worth over twelve hundred pesos, roughly the value of a large landed estate near Quito or a very fine house in the city. Predictably, Juan de Artiaga appears in a fragment of Quito's smeltery books paying royalties on Popayán gold dust in 1584. He appears to have lived well beyond 1588 (the year of his will) since he shows up again in 1595 and 1596.[47] Apparently the gold kept coming, since by early 1601 Artiaga was able to borrow against a newly purchased country estate, a house on Quito's main plaza, and two slaves.[48]

Not all itinerant traders linking Popayán and Quito were Basques, of course, and not all were as successful as Juan de Artiaga. But whatever their nationality or fortunes, their tracks fill Quito's turn-of-the-century

Façade of La Compañía, or main Jesuit Church, Quito

smeltery ledgers and Protocols. Their suppliers were large wholesalers and audiencia officials, and much to the chagrin of Popayán's governors these men continued to push for and gain discounts on Popayán gold smelted in Quito. The wise, however, regarded the appearance of "Juan Blanco" sometime around 1599 as a portent, a sign that many Popayán gold camps had peaked and were now facing an uncertain future.

Given the indigenous demographic crisis, more mines were closing than opening all across the equatorial Andes. Yet still Quito's audiencia judges and other officials received handsome salaries in gold bullion, paid directly from Royal Treasury receipts into the 1630s. Some of this money was derived from head-taxes on "foreigners" like Cristóbal Martín and Almaguer's Alonso Martín Paladinés; other sums were collected in a similarly parasitic way via sales of offices, criminal fines, and confiscated estates like Pedro de Harrona's.[49] Mule trains continued to ply the Camino Real to Popayán long after 1599, but the writing was on the wall: Quito could no longer trust solely in gold.

Reorientations

The Sweatshop Revolution

The changing economy of Quito circa 1599 is made evident in the life of Rodrigo de Ribadeneira, an encomendero, merchant, and failed governor of Esmeraldas whose wealth and influence rivaled that of the banker Cristóbal Martín. Ribadeneira would die just before bad news arrived from Spain in 1600: the Indies Council had denied him the title "Captain of Infantry" despite an outstanding military career. As has been noted, it is quite possible the 1580s Esmeraldas debacle was to blame.[50]

Ribadeneira's widow, doña Ana de Zúñiga, would now struggle to keep her husband's legacy alive for the benefit of her children. At stake was much more than a posthumous military promotion. In short, Rodrigo de Ribadeneira had enjoyed the "second life," or final generation of the huge encomienda of Chambo, just south of Riobamba, inherited from his wife's prominent and well-connected father. The time had come for the encomienda to revert to the crown, but Doña Ana fought for an extension.[51]

Though no less clever than Cristóbal Martín, Rodrigo de Ribadeneira had followed a more traditional path to colonial wealth and prominence. He soldiered hard, married well, and by his death had successfully fused encomienda tribute and mita labor subsidies and mercantilist credit instruments to forge a thriving textile export business.

Ribadeneira was one of several elite Quiteños who realized that Potosí in the wake of Viceroy Francisco de Toledo's 1570s restructuring would quickly become a merchandise sink of previously unimaginable proportions. Local experience had shown that isolated mining towns, though sometimes deadly for roving factors, were a wholesale merchant's dream. What made Potosí different from Quito's many scattered gold camps was its potential for longevity and its forced concentration of indigenous peoples. Thousands of consumers, thanks to crown-mandated rations, were conveniently removed from subsistence production and textile manufacture. Here was a market both captive and rotating. Furthermore—almost too good to be true for a producer of woolens— Potosí (unlike Popayán) was bitterly cold all year.

Two other contemporary trends aided men like Ribadeneira: 1) the concentration of indigenous populations in Quito's central highlands discussed in previous chapters, and 2), a simultaneous explosion of sheep populations in the countryside. Amazingly, though by no means without negative consequences, Quito's rain-soaked, subalpine equatorial ecology supported both expanding subsistence and even export agriculture as well as a massive ungulate irruption, primarily of sheep and goats.

The possibilities were evident, but time was of the essence if the encomienda subsidy was to be successfully converted into some other form of profit—or at least rent-generating business. Rodrigo de Ribadeneira happened to command both a large encomienda and operational textile mills at this critical juncture. More entrepreneur than aristocrat, he focused on rushing valuable local manufactures to market in Potosí.[52]

In July 1594 Rodrigo de Ribadeneira sent nearly twelve thousand pesos' worth of Chambo woolen and cotton textiles to Upper Peru with the factor Andrés Sánchez de Felgar.[53] Sánchez was expected to complete the Quito-Potosí-Quito circuit within three years, but given the combination of distance and daunting terrain, shipping costs were

A plague of sheep?

troublingly high. Another shipment in December 1595 reveals
Ribadeneira's clumsy attempt to dampen freight charges, which were
figured by the load (carga). Now hired muleteers complained as their
beasts staggered beneath bundles weighing over two hundred pounds.[54]
Profits must have allayed the encomendero's fears, however, as he kept
shipping substantial quantities of Chambo cloth southward in spite of
rising freightage. A July 1597 company with a fellow military man, Captain
Gerónimo Coronel, included some twelve thousand pesos' worth of
textiles and two thousand pesos in carrying fees, the latter a near fourfold
increase over 1594.[55]

    As the pioneering research of John Super demonstrated more than
twenty years ago, neat profits are all but impossible to calculate from the
contracts recorded in Quito's notary Protocols, particularly in these heady
years, but they were undoubtedly high for exporters of scale like Rodrigo

de Ribadeneira.[56] This cunning soldier-turned-merchant seems in any case to have invested a large measure of his gains in new Quito cloth, mostly produced by other indigenous community obrajes in the southern highlands. One was in neighboring Achambo. In January 1598 that mill's administrator promised Ribadeneira fifteen hundred yards of *paños* of various colors and thirty-four rolls of plain white blanket material by June of the same year. As was more or less standard, half the assessed value of the textiles was to be paid up front, within a month of the contract's signing, the other half upon completion and inspection of the goods.[57]

Another similar purchase of Achambo textiles was agreed upon in October 1598, this time 11,500 pesos' worth, strong indication that the pressure to meet export demand was on. And yet local paños in this critical, formative stage were not restricted to monotonous natural or indigo shades, as is often assumed; instead they included such fanciful colors as "holm-oak," "king's cape," "olive-drab," "fly's wing," "argentine" (i.e., silver-gray), and "raisin."[58] Textiles produced in the Sigchos mill in the same year featured approximately the same range of colors, adding "forest green" and blankets dyed a deep "Brazil" (i.e., brazilwood) red.[59] All such fabrics were to be carefully fulled, finished, and squared, all flaws noted and discounted. Presumably Ribadeneira's factors had discovered that mita workers (and perhaps even slaves) in Potosí were as discriminating in their tastes as Quito's multiethnic urbanites. Such consumer discrimination inevitably resulted in either improved quality control or disastrous loss of market share. It is important to remember these were not open markets, but something of vastly greater lucrative potential: momentary apertures in a theoretically closed, monopoly system.[60]

Rodrigo de Ribadeneira was only one of a dozen or so producers and merchants to make a sizable fortune in the Peruvian cloth trade in the years around 1599. Otavalo also had substantial obrajes, and though no longer controlled by encomenderos (they were leased by the crown), they produced a similar range of fabric styles and colors at the turn of the seventeenth century. Merchants might purchase a varied lot of Otavalo bolts at auction, as Hernando de Ceballos did in late February 1599. Here great lengths of coarse frieze *(jerga),* serge *(sayal),* and baize *(bayeta)* were bundled right alongside finer paños dyed "florentine," "indigo," and "stone."[61]

Treadle loom, Peguche, Ecuador

Quito corregidor Diego de Portugal toured Latacunga's community obraje in December 1599, and while there facilitated a two-year contract between its administrator and master weaver. The negotiations regarded the latter's salary, but they reveal other key details of the growing textile business. The new *maestro,* Francisco de la Vega, had learned his trade somewhere in Spain, and was described by witnesses as "able and sufficient" in overseeing the factory. Vega demanded annual compensation of twelve hundred pesos. Witnesses claimed master weavers at the obrajes of Chambo, Chimbo, and Sigchos were similarly paid despite the smaller size of those operations.

The Chimbo and Sigchos masters, for example, each received twelve hundred pesos annually for overseeing some 200 indigenous laborers and eight or nine looms. Meanwhile, Latacunga's obraje employed 324 mita workers on seventeen looms and turned out better products. General Portugal approved Vega's request and a two-year deal was struck.[62] Thus, as indigenous sweatshop laborers' wages were measured in fractions of pesos (which might be immediately commuted to tribute accounts), their overseers could bargain for annual salaries amounting to almost half that of an audiencia judge. Unnamed indigenous women in Quito suffered also, coerced by Spanish householders to perform the arduous task of spinning raw fiber into thread by hand (as many still do today). Such women shared the lot of rural female proto-industrial workers in contemporary central China and the Low Countries.[63]

Although it seems obvious from notary records that the volume of the southern cloth trade increased dramatically in the late 1590s, it remains difficult to pinpoint beginnings. Contracts like Ribadeneira's date to the early 1580s, when several orders were put in for varicolored paños.[64] A 1583 order called for fifteen hundred pesos' worth of paños, *frezadas,* and coarse frieze within ten months. The Protocols for these years are far from complete, but evidence that business was just beginning to pick up comes from a related obligation for the purchase of "forty-six pairs of Mexican cards for priming and recarding and twenty-six pairs of cards from Lima," plus a sizable copper vat. Meanwhile the merchant Alvaro Ceballos supplied this same expanding operation with 504 arrobas of wool, likely collected in an encomienda-commodity-for-luxury-imports exchange.[65]

Although it appears not to have matured until about the second

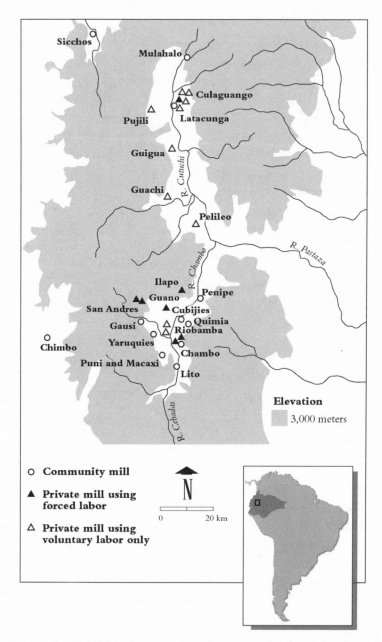

Distribution of central highland textile mills, early seventeenth century. Map drawn from
Carol Cooperrider, from Linda Newson, *Life and Death in Early Colonial Ecuador* (Norman:
University of Oklahoma Press, 1995), courtesy of Linda Newson and the University of
Oklahoma Press.

decade of the seventeenth century, when ordinances like those for the mines were instituted, Quito's cloth industry was already consuming considerable quantities of wool by 1599. Sales of raw fiber and sheep flocks abound in the notary record. A 1597 sale, for example, noted transfer of ten thousand head of presumably Merino sheep near Cayambe, along with three hundred swine.[66] Sales of one thousand to five thousand head of sheep at a time are far more common. In fact, sheep fared so well in Quito's high country that one animal cost less than half a peso at the turn of the seventeenth century.[67]

In part because they were mobile chattels, sheep could occasionally make up a large portion of a woman's dowry. María de San Martín Padilla, for example, brought one thousand head to her marriage in early 1600.[68] Contracts between obraje administrators and sheepowners for wool fiber also abound. Cotton, a key pre-Columbian crop in Quito's deep intermontane valleys and coastal plains, was also in demand; by weight it was almost three times as expensive as wool in the late 1590s.[69]

With the old gold economy visibly sputtering, word of the profitable Peruvian cloth trade spread quickly. New investors crowded in. One was the widow Ynés de Alarcón, who in November 1595 signed an agreement to produce coarse blankets and serge on her estancia at Pelileo, near Ambato. Alarcón's estate was said to already include eight hundred head of sheep, six yoke of oxen, an orchard, and three fields planted with indigo *(yerba de tinta)*. All this was watched over by three resident workers, and an administrator was charged with building looms and petitioning for mita laborers to get things going.[70]

For some unstated reason the Quito widow soon changed her mind and sold the estancia and nascent textile business to a cleric for 1,050 pesos "current silver." As with sales of slaves and other transactions noted above, a closer reading reveals that payment was in fact made in the form of two gold disks and one small bar, plus 300 pesos in silver reales.[71] Similar exchanges must have been carried out elsewhere toward the end of the sixteenth century, but this is rare testimony of locally mined gold being directly invested in textile plant. More frequently, gold collected by merchants from debtors was spent purchasing export goods from established producers.

Along with textiles, hats, footwear, and hides were notable among

Quito's export products. In particular, ballooning demand for both crude
and finished leather goods in Lima and Potosí stimulated both rural stock-
raisers and urban artisans—among them many mestizos and mulattos—to
expand operations. As with cloth, phenomenal growth appears to have
occurred in the late 1590s.

As an example, in February 1599 merchant Alvaro García and an
associate ordered 500 pairs of leather shoes from Miguel Ruíz de la
Yguera. The Quito shoemaker would receive 4 reales for each pair if the
order was filled by the feast of San Juan (late June, also the dry, i.e.,
traveling, season) that year, for a total of 250 silver pesos *(patacones)*.[72]
Similarly, in December 1598 shoemaker Alonso Benítez sold 1,000 pairs of
leather shoes to an export trader (December marked a mini-dry season
also allowing for travel to the coast).[73] Days later the same exporter
purchased 100 tanned hides and 1,000 half-cut rawhides. Within six
months of the 1598 contract Alonso Benítez and another shoemaker had a
new order; they promised merchant Manuel Pinto another 1,010 pairs of
shoes at 3 reales each.[74] The shoe business was so vibrant some artisans
bought slaves in order to keep up. Also, by late 1599—and probably
earlier—Quito tanners were selling locally prepared Cordovans and
goatskins to exporters.[75] As with the burgeoning textile trade, everyone
with cash to invest seems to have wanted a piece of the shoe and leather-
goods business at this moment.[76]

Wool into Wine

Silver would seem to be the natural, desired return product for this flood
of new exports, but in fact itinerant merchants reinvested Peruvian cash in
fresh imports. It so happened that wine, the product that had made
Cristóbal Martín rich, was chief among them. Spanish vineyards, mostly in
southwest Andalusia, had met Quiteño demand for some time, but as early
as November 1581 Peru wine, or "vino de la tierra," appears in the Quito
Protocols, still rather expensive but vastly cheaper than European
imports.[77] "Castilian" wine sold for sixteen to twenty pesos a jug (the *botija
perulera* of c. 8 *l*) in Quito in the last two decades of the sixteenth century.
It remained popular for some years—perhaps for qualitative reasons like
flavor or snob appeal—but with time this Old World product would be

largely displaced by the vintages (or plonk) of Arequipa, Pisco, Ica, and other Peruvian oases. Indeed, what must have been passable jugs of *vino de la tierra* could soon be had for ten to twelve pesos, a savings of one-third or more, but still roughly equivalent to the cost of an average horse.[78]

This new "dependency" on Peruvian wine had not come about as a result of Quiteño sloth or ineptitude, but was rather the result of uncontrollable ecological factors. Numerous attempts had in fact been made to establish vineyards in the several mid-altitude valleys of the equatorial Andes since conquest. Various letters and crown-ordered reports note vines in the Chota-Mira Valley by the 1570s, for example, and there is mention of plantings near Pasto in 1583.[79] Likewise, in early 1587 two Quiteños attempted to establish vineyards at a site called Alchipiche, apparently without success, and later the same year another attempt was made in the nearby Guayllabamba Valley.[80] A 1588 will notes yet more attempts at both grapevine and olive plantings in the hot Catamayo Valley west of Loja by Jérez de la Frontera native Alonso de Carvajal.[81] But wine, olives, and other Mediterranean products, such as raisins and some desired varieties of figs (both of which routinely show up in the Protocols as accompanying wine from Peru) could never be produced locally.

These general economic reorientations—gold for luxuries to wool for wine—should not obscure local complexities and instances of interpenetration. Despite the faltering gold economy, Quito's northern and southern trade circuits were not independent of one another. Silver profits from the cloth-and-leather trade to Potosí, for example, were routinely reinvested in wine destined for the gold camps of Popayán. In a late–1599 contract a resident of the mining camp of Almaguer signed for thirty-eight jugs of Peru wine in a Quito store.[82] The factor Juan de Artiaga, mentioned above, frequently carried wine to Popayán as early as the 1580s. In Quito Peruvian wine, at twelve pesos a jug, was even making inroads among artisans.[83] By 1595 one finds vintners selling full botijas peruleras for ten and a half pesos each to a range of private citizens on credit, suggesting a drop in prices and wider social acceptance.[84]

As with most dealings in mood-altering products, profits seem to have been remarkably high in the wine trade. A general figure would be difficult to calculate, but not unusual was a mid-1600 settling of accounts on a nearly four-thousand-peso contract from 1598 that yielded two

satisfied merchants a 50 percent return.[85] Still, despite the relative
proximity of Peruvian vineyards, spoilage seems to have been
disconcertingly common. In 1595, for example, a shipment of 150 jugs
included thirty-two (c. 21 percent) "touched with vinegar." Here two
merchants, one based in Potosí, had aimed to profit from a low-cost
product from the Chancay Valley north of Lima. Unfortunately for them,
its ten-peso-per-jug retail value was deeply eroded by the mistakes of the
winemaker.[86] Like gold mining or textile marketing, the wine business
clearly had its own share of risks and uncertainties. Quiteños of means
appear to have taken such risks in stride, at least in the promising years
around 1599.

Had he lived so long Pedro de Harrona would have been amazed by the
changes under way in Quito's commercial and productive sectors by the
turn of the seventeenth century. Though still somewhat isolated by south
Peruvian or central Mexican standards, Quito was a vibrant
city and colony, dynamic, rich, and driven to consume at
all social levels. It was also a macro-region caught
shifting from a marginal gold economy wracked by
rebellion, fraud, and other uncertainties, to a more
centralized one based largely on textile manufacture for
export. Always indigenous tribute—in both goods and
labor—underwrote the Quiteño experiment in high living,
but adventurous overland traders were also responsible for the
region's economic dynamism. First to tap truly global market
opportunities, they rode an extraordinary wave of gold- then
silver-fueled prosperity. For a time they realized profits rarely
seen in the monopoly-encumbered markets of the Old
World.

AN ANONYMOUS DESCRIPTION
OF GUAYAQUIL

The whole city has sixty-one houses, four of them inns . . . Creole and Spanish [male] householders living in the city number 152; seventy-three of them are married, mostly to creoles, that is, most of the women are natives of the land. Beyond these there are thirteen widows and twelve married men whose wives are in Spain. Most of the married men are non-creole merchants who long to return to Spain. These householders have 112 male children and seventy-seven female, [and also] 216 male slaves, most of them black, but some mulatto; and 117 black and *mulata* slave women. Of free black and mulatto men there are seven, three of them married; free black and *mulata* women, thirteen. . . . In the ten Indian pueblos [in the surrounding countryside] there are 657 [male] tributaries; caciques, the wounded, and elders above fifty years of age exempt from tribute number 116. Married women number 647 and widows 150; boys under eighteen number 572 and girls 434. . . . In this province [of Guayaquil] there are no warlike Indians, nor maroons, nor other known enemies; if a few slaves escape, it is easy to catch them. Currently the city has nine principal men, captains and old soldiers who know war, and also many valorous citizens who can serve Your Majesty when the need arises. In general the householders and all those who reside in Guayaquil have harquebuses, blunderbusses, swords, daggers, and halberds, and some even have breastplates, morions, and other steel and iron body armor, and steel-plated wooden bucklers. The encomenderos also have horses, lances, and leather shields. In Guayaquil's ports Your Majesty keeps no [permanent] galleons nor other warships; they come up from Callao only when corsairs threaten, or to carry soldiers to Chile from time to time; they also come to victual and supply the armadas. The port of La Puná could be protected by two forts, one near each of its two piers, and a terreplein up to the edge of the estuaries and mangroves, for the rest is naturally fortified by the mangroves and their roots. There remains only the river entrance, and this could be defended by the

artillery of the forts. In times of fear of pirates they have made
bulwarks and trenches in the said places with ease, since wood is
plentiful.

—Anonymous report to the king, 1604

Translated extracts from Pilar Ponce Leiva, ed., *Relaciones Histórico-geográficos de la Audiencia de Quito* (Madrid: CSIC, 1991–93), 2:10–48.

SIX: Pirates, Soldiers, Cannibals

Oh, beastly cruelty, insane furor
Infamous crime, infernal motive!
As I write, my pen falls from my hand
With an ice cold tremor.

(Juan de Castellanos, "Discourse on Captain Francis Drake," 1589)[1]

In early 1598, as Dutch corsairs threatened to raid the Spanish Pacific for the first time, a wounded Quito veteran wrote the Council of the Indies requesting a pension. Alonso Carillo Espínola had valiantly battled English pirates near Guayaquil on the island of Puná in 1587, but he had yet to be compensated. Lame since this forgotten engagement with what Quito clerics and officials liked to call "Lutheran heretics," Carillo was a twenty-year Indies hand, a kind of soldier of fortune—or rather, misfortune—who had participated in numerous north Andean campaigns. The piles of similar requests now housed in Spanish archives suggest that many hard-luck soldiers shared this man's fate in Quito, city and colony, circa 1599.

Carillo's semiautobiographical "proof of merit" account was typically diverse. He had served in New Granada in the insanely resilient search for

El Dorado and had distinguished himself against Pijao and Páez rebels in the mountains north and east of Popayán. Still, Carillo considered his 1587 stand against the English corsair Thomas Cavendish and his followers on Puná Island his greatest achievement, even if all he had managed to do was catch a bullet in the leg. By his own account he had proudly and defiantly "left the said skirmish badly wounded with a musketball they gave me in the right thigh."[2]

In the decade since this glorious sacrifice in defense of Quito's principal port, Carillo had only barely managed to get around the highland capital on horseback. It was not getting any easier with age. But this was not his first wound, nor indeed his first pirate battle. According to other witnesses and his own testimony, not only had Carillo taken a poisoned dart in a New Granadan campaign (in the same right thigh, meriting an alert scribe's "ojo," or "look here"), but he had also been shot—in the other thigh—in a skirmish with French corsairs some ten or fifteen years earlier near Coro, Venezuela.

The Council of the Indies, for reasons all its own but perhaps spurred to generosity in Philip II's final hour, chose to reward the old soldier and his unlucky legs with an annual pension of four hundred pesos. It was a fortunate break given Carillo's second, suspiciously Italian-sounding—but also potentially illustrious—surname ("Spínola"). The crown could perhaps afford to indulge him now that he was not likely to survive another decade.

Memories of the conquest era had largely faded to history and even legend in Quito by 1599, yet experiences like Carillo's served to remind sheltered highlanders of all ethnicities that war still beckoned beyond literally every horizon. While such soldiers tended to exaggerate, particularly when asking for a *merced,* or favor from the crown, marauding pirates, native rebels, and African maroons were hardly imaginary enemies. These days mysterious ships were sighted near Punta Santa Elena or Paita with increasing frequency; unarmed cargo vessels were suddenly disappearing, presumably captured by new and mysterious foes. Then, as happened in 1587, an escaped slave might swim ashore to tell a tale of pirate captivity and evil designs, throwing the kingdom into a panic. And just as that was sinking in, news of a bloody Jívaro raid arrived, followed by word of yet another failure in Esmeraldas.

Unsettling also was the sight of scarred and angry soldiers like Alonso Carillo, and perhaps no less so the arrival in Quito after 1599 of their branded Pijao and Páez captives. The Inkas had been routed some two or more generations past, yet still it seemed the borders of the Kingdom of Quito could not be fixed. Again, the audiencia's experience was in effect the whole Spanish empire's in miniature. Perhaps this embattled affinity was in part what held them together.

Others clamored to be compensated for services against the pirate enemy of 1587, among them several indigenous *costeños*. One was don Baltázar Zaman, cacique of San Estéban de Charapotó, a village near Quito's secondary port of Manta. (Zaman may have been the brother of Pedro Zama, mentioned in chapter 1.) He petitioned the Indies Council like Carillo, but earlier, in 1594. Apparently Zaman, having received word that "Tomás Candi" and his thieving heretics were heading north, had mustered one hundred armed men and rushed to Manta's defense.[3] Earlier requests for compensation in the form of a larger jurisdiction and tribute relief had been ignored, but this only convinced the cacique of the necessity of his physical presence in Madrid. Somehow Zaman managed to gather the funds needed for this great journey, but before reaching Cádiz or Sanlúcar he had the bad luck of being aboard a Spanish vessel caught and robbed by English corsairs off Cape St. Vincent. (What a revelation it must have been to find Iberian waters just as vulnerable to foreign attack as Quito's.)

Despite his troubles don Baltázar Zaman of Charapotó at last reached King Philip's court. There, one witness proved most helpful. He was fifty-year-old Andrés Díaz de Ribadeneira, brother of Rodrigo de Ribadeneira, Quito's prominent encomendero-entrepreneur and failed governor of Esmeraldas. While reconnoitering the Esmeraldas coast in search of his brother back in 1587, Díaz de Ribadeneira had happened to put in at Manta with several dozen soldiers just as Thomas Cavendish was heading off to New Spain. Díaz claimed that when he and his men made port they were astonished to find Zaman loyally standing guard with his hundred native warriors, all "well-armed with bows and arrows" in anticipation of a pirate landing.

Although Cavendish failed to stop at Manta, the cacique's men had camped out for forty days at the edge of town, aiding Díaz's soldiers in

various tasks and awaiting marching orders from the local corregidor.
Other written testimonies added that Zaman and his subjects had always
and unhesitatingly supplied friendly South Sea vessels with water, hens,
swine, fruits, and other refreshments when they put in at Manta, and that
he was in general a much-respected and loved native lord. Díaz, backed by
an accompanying squadron commander, Juan Fernández, added that
Zaman had in fact gone above and beyond the call by supplying his
starving men with a morale-lifting cargo of bacon, a salty godsend for his
mostly Spanish-born and not tropically seasoned troops. In short, if anyone
deserved a merced, it was don Baltázar Zaman. And he had survived the
pilgrimage to Madrid to argue his case! Although it is unclear if anything
came of it, the Council of the Indies recommended that Quito officials do
something to reward the faithful cacique.

In the years around 1599 several ranking officers were also petitioning
the crown for mercedes to compensate service against assorted South Sea
corsairs. Such a man was Captain Pedro Reynalta Coello, a Lima-based
naval commander. He claimed in a 1601 letter to king and council not
only to have helped defend Potosí's port of Arica against Cavendish in
1587, but also to have served more recently with General Beltrán de
Castro in the celebrated 1594 capture of Englishman "Richarte Aquines"
(also known as Richard Hawkins). The key engagement had taken place
near the great beach of Atacames, Esmeraldas, the spot where Sebastián de
Yllescas later entertained the Sánchez de Cuellar castaways. In fact, the
Elizabethan corsair had just made contact with Yllescas and the maroons
of Esmeraldas, and his landing there had in part goaded otherwise
belligerent crown officials to support the novel methods of Quito's Dr.
Barrio.

Seeking more than a promotion, Captain Reynalta hoped his anti-
pirate service would buttress his petition for the job of corregidor of
Chimbo, a plum post in these years of growing textile production in
Quito's central highlands.[4] His commander, General Castro, had already
received one of the district's most lucrative textile-producing encomiendas
for his troubles. Perhaps something similar would befall the first mate.

Promising not to settle too quickly into the role of colonial seigneur,
however, Reynalta ended his letter to the Indies Council by offering to go
south to Chile to fight the newest foreign menace on the Pacific coast,

what he called "Irish or Hollander corsairs." These would turn out to be of the latter sort, the first of them captured near Valparaíso in November 1599. Thanks to the growing threat of foreign sea raiders and cyclical rebellions of indigenous and maroon communities, Quito's neofeudal economy lived on. Three revealing episodes may serve to illustrate the resilience of the martial urge and some of its consequences for Quito, city and colony.

Pirates

Foreign poachers of Quito gold and Potosí silver had appeared in the Spanish Pacific as early as 1577. In March of that year, aided by African maroons entrenched in eastern Panama, English corsair John Oxenham had trekked across the isthmus and taken a bullion-laden vessel from Manta near the Pearl Islands. Quito merchants, needless to say, were concerned; some lost significant sums of money.[5] Disorganized and unlucky, Oxenham was quickly captured and ultimately executed at the Inquisition's behest, but soon his countryman Francis Drake arrived in the South Sea. Drake came the long way, via the Strait of Magellan, and he made maximum use of his swift little English-built galleon, later immortalized as the *Golden Hind*. This well-armed vessel, along with the not inconsiderable element of surprise, enabled him to pillage vulnerable ships and terrify coastal residents all along this vast, unguarded flank of the Spanish empire.

Aside from laying dubious claim to California, Drake is best remembered on this, his so-called famous voyage of global circumnavigation, for capturing the Panama-bound *Nuestra Señora de la Concepción* (also known as *Cacaplata*) off the Quito coast in March of 1579. The feat was enough to make Drake a rich and notorious man, but it is also worth remembering that just days earlier his men had seized eighteen thousand pesos' worth of Quito gold and New Granada emeralds from an unarmed Guayaquil bark.[6] As Oxenham had also discovered, there was Quito gold to be had in the age of Potosí silver.

Drake's legacy was to sow lasting fear in Spanish America, reflected in the contemporary epic poetry of Juan de Castellanos and in shrill

Manuscript record of Quito gold recovered from John Oxenham's 1577 pirate raid near Panama (courtesy of the National History Archive, Quito)

dispatches between the Peruvian viceroy and Quito's *audiencia* throughout the 1580s and 1590s. Still, there is no evidence of the giddy paralysis often claimed by Anglophone historians of piracy. Unblinking merchants, accustomed to losing the occasional cargo to shipwreck, fire, and assorted other "acts of God" simply added the word "corsair" *(corsario)* to the list of South Sea shipping hazards and moved metals and merchandise apace. That they did so without formalized marine insurance policies is all the more striking.

After Drake came Thomas Cavendish, another Elizabethan corsair who, along the way toward repeating Drake's circumnavigation, would unwittingly leave a more lasting imprint on Quito's fringe in the summer of 1587. As with the Drake scare about a decade earlier, merchants mostly took this unwanted visit in stride; according to notary records, at least, trade seems hardly to have been affected. Meanwhile, in other quarters—as among professional soldiers like Alonso Carillo—the effects of the Cavendish raid would reverberate for decades.

Perhaps guided by a wily or terrified prisoner, Cavendish's pirates had landed on the large but sparsely populated island of Puná, in the Gulf of Guayaquil, in early June. The foreigners were looking to refit their vessels, first of all, but they also intended to search out booty or ransomable captives in the near hinterland. Since Drake's depredations war had been declared between England and Spain, making Cavendish and his fellow raiders privateers rather than pirates in the technical sense. Nevertheless, it is quite clear that pecuniary rather than nationalistic motives were foremost on their minds.

Whatever we might call them, Cavendish and his followers would unwittingly provide battle-starved locals with merit claims that, if heard, could be worth their weight in gold. For others, the pirate raid would serve as a costly lesson in unrequited love of king and country.

Young Thomas Cavendish had barely cut his teeth in an early voyage to Virginia when he decided to circle the globe in 1586. This audacious expedition, carried out in three relatively small vessels, would touch on Sierra Leone in West Africa, then Brazil, then a doomed Spanish colony meant to guard the Strait of Magellan, and finally several lesser settlements in Chile and Peru before landing at Puná Island. Here, beginning around the first of June 1587, the exhausted corsairs spent a week careening, or

Thomas Cavendish, Elizabethan corsair, from Philip Nichols, *Franciscus Dracus redivivus*, Amsterdam: 1596.

repairing the hulls of their vessels, and reconnoitering the nearby Quito coast. Gathering food was a priority, but Cavendish's first act was to take over port facilities and houses belonging to a very wealthy coastal cacique named Francisco Tomalá. It is not known for certain what role he played in this affair, but he was not captured.[7]

Before dawn, June twelfth, Cavendish and his companions were surprised to find themselves attacked furiously by two companies of Spanish militiamen, one from Quito, the other from Guayaquil, and perhaps a hundred indigenous and African-slave auxiliaries. According to Cavendish's chronicler, Francis Pretty, this engagement with Spanish forces was but one of several unpleasant asides in a largely successful enterprise, crowned, as it were, by the capture five months later of the silk-laden Manila galleon *Santa Ana,* off Baja California.

Cavendish's ship *Desire* would alone reach Plymouth in September 1588. There would be joyous celebrations, though not for him. As it happened, with the help of Drake and inclement weather, Spain's Invincible Armada had just been vanquished in the English Channel. On the Spanish side, however, and particularly for residents of Quito and Guayaquil, the 1587 Cavendish encounter was noteworthy. In particular, the corsair's cruise served as a rare opportunity to prove valor or cowardice (or at least to claim such), and to conjure up again the spirit of Santiago in a largely conquered land.

As with the many failed Esmeraldas campaigns, service of any kind, including the victualing of soldiers and sailors, could be loudly proclaimed in letters to the king across succeeding decades, with presumably genuine hopes of remuneration. At most the mercedes received for such spontaneous acts of fealty consisted of an encomienda or lifetime annuity. At very least—short of no aid at all—one got a general recommendation, the sort of boon that might help secure a bid for a potentially lucrative government post.

One result of this continued, provincial neofeudalism was that Guayaquil's defenses went unimproved in the wake of Cavendish's stop. This was to prove a disastrous oversight in the years following 1599, but at the time such a prospect was hardly debated. It seems that in the late sixteenth century a quick run for war prizes was welcomed by costeños and *serranos* alike, but even after repeated badgering from Peru's viceroy, the elite of Quito refused to make any sustained effort to defend their number-one port. Perhaps in relating the details of the 1587 encounter one may gather why.

An anonymous manuscript now housed in Spain's National Library, almost certainly written by Guayaquil corregidor Gerónimo de Reynoso, provides a concise summary:

Relation to be sent to the Royal Audiencia of Quito of what occurred in the victory of the Island of Puná against the English:

- First, left this city of Guayaquil for the Island of Puná Wednesday, 10 June, vespers of San Bernabé.

- Arrived at the pier *(embarcadero)* secretly the same day at midnight and arrived at the estancia called Los Guayabales half a league from the enemy, where we halted that night and dispatched two sentinels to the enemy's camp.

- The following day, Friday, twelfth of same [June], left said port at two in the morning with said field in order and arrived in view of the enemy an hour before dawn and [set the] ambush with order, the hour having arrived; the camp picked up and marched with all necessary silence toward the wharf, which is next to the house of Don Francisco [Tomalá, wealthy cacique and lord of the island] and at the entrance to the said landing pier the 'Santiago' was given by a sentinel there, who later died, and charging forward, all going out together into the plaza, and there giving battle to all the enemies occupying the church and said house and a foundry which the enemies had constructed, all which was in the 'plaza,' as the sailors say, where the ships were beached, with all the artillery trained on the said plaza, house, and church; the battle *(refriega)* lasted two hours, during which we skirmished with the enemy on land and sea and the enemy left, retiring with great haste to the sea and to embark in the ship's boat *(chalupa)*, [but] the skirmish continuing in the church and houses there died more than thirty English, and from appearances even more; four were taken alive, two of whom are in the power of Captain Juan de Galarza, the other two in my [custody]; yet they continued to fire from the sea, remaining in the engagement [with] many shots from artillery and muskets [raining] on the plaza where the said skirmish took place [but] God was served that no harm was done to ours more than in one soldier named Betanzos of the company that came from the city who died of a gunshot wound, less five or six other soldiers who escaped wounded.

• The damage done to the enemy is as follows:

> First their launch, which was hauled ashore and hit by two artillery shots, was burned.

> Their sails, which they had brought ashore for mending, were burned.

> Their pipes [casks], which they had on land to take water, were burned, being some thirty, with another 600 jugs of water, [which we] broke.

> All the tools of the forge were destroyed.

> Some twenty muskets, among halberds *(partesanas)*, blunderbusses, and other arms, were taken.

• A black man whom they had taken captive on the Lima coast escaped unto us on this island, knowing us to be Spaniards, and advised us that the enemy had in their fleet some two hundred men of war, less sea folk, [and also that they had] three vessels, the *capitana* very good and large, the *almiranta* somewhat smaller, and a bark and small *fragata* which they bring for patax [light shuttling vessel] and the launch we burned.

• We left this city [Guayaquil] for Puná Island some eighty men with those of this city and those of the company of Juan de Galarza; we left afterwards for this city [i.e., returned to Guayaquil] since the black man gave us notice that this following Sunday they thought to come to this city and assault it, so we have come with haste to guard it . . .[8]

A valuable counterpoint to Reynoso is Francis Pretty, whose account was published in Richard Hakluyt's 1600 compilation, *Principal Navigations:*

> The second day of June in the morning [old style date], by and by after breake of day, every one of the watch being gone abroad to seeke to fetch in victuals, some one way, some another, some for hennes, some for sheepe, some for goats, upon the sudden there came down upon us an hundred Spanish souldiers with muskets and an ensigne, which were landed on the other side of the Iland that night, and all the Indians of the Iland with them, every one with their weapons and their baggage after them: which was by meanes of a Negro, whose name was Emmanuel, which fled from us at our first landing there. Thus being taken advantage we had the worst: for our companie was not past sixteene or twentie; whereof they had slaine one or two before they were come to the houses: yet we skirmished with them an houre and an halfe: at the last being sore overcharged with multitudes, we were driven down from the hill to the waters side, and there kept them play for a while, until in the end Zacharie Saxie, who with his halberd had kept the way of the hill, and slaine a couple of them, as hee breathed himselfe being somewhat tired, had an honourable death and a short: for a shot strooke him to the heart: who feeling himselfe mortally wounded cryed to God for mercie, and fell downe presently dead. But soone after the enemie was driven somewhat to retire from the bankes side to the greene: and in the ende our boate came and carried as many of our men away as could goe in her, which was in hazard of sinking while they hastened to it: And one of our men whose name was Robert Maddocke was shot through the head with his owne peece, being a snap-hance, as hee was hasting into the boate. But foure of us were left behinde which the boate could not carrie: to wit, my selfe Francis Prettie, Thomas Andrewes, Steven Gunner, and Richard Rose: which had our shot readie and retired our selves unto a cliffe, untill the boate came againe, which was presently after they had carried the rest abourd. There were sixe and fortie of the enemies slaine by us, whereof they had dragged some into the bushes, and some into olde houses, which wee found afterward. Wee lost twelve men in maner following:

Slain by the enemie:
  1 Zacharie Saxie
  2 Neales Johnson
  3 William Geirgefield
  4 Nicholas Hendie
  5 Henry Cooper
killed with his peece: Robert Maddocke
burnt: Henry Mawdly
drowned:
  1 Edward the gunners man
  2 Ambrose the musitian
taken prisoners:
  1 Walter Tilliard
  2 Edward Smith
  3 Henry Aselye

The selfe same day being the second of June, we went on shoare again with seventie men, and had a fresh skirmish with the enemies, and drave them to retire, being an hundred Spaniards serving with muskets, and two hundred Indians with bowes, arrowes and darts. This done wee set fire on the towne and burnt it to the ground, having in it a number of three hundred houses: and shortly after made havocke of their fieldes, orchards and gardens, and burnt four great ships more which were in building on the stockes.[9]

Although the first part of Pretty's summary—up to the listing of casualties—rings true when compared with Spanish accounts, the last paragraph is pure fabrication, revenge taken on the page rather than the battlefield. But clearly both sides took liberties in remembering these events: local defenders reckoned they killed thirty men instead of five, the pirates forty-six instead of one. Perhaps a more critical detail bears clarification. The key to the Spanish "victory," although both sides were ashamed to admit it, was the African slave "Emmanuel," or Manuel; he had been captured in a timber-carrier heading south from Guayaquil, and apparently knew the Guayas Estuary and Puná Island intimately. In other words, he was the wrong person to lose track of and his untimely escape was most responsible for Cavendish's defeat and Quito's gain. Although he appears to have been most deserving of all participants, there is no record of Manuel being rewarded by Spanish authorities for this singular act of heroism.

What about the others? Cavendish would get his revenge off Cabo San Lucas in a few months, but local residents of the Audiencia of Quito chose Pretty's path by taking the battle to the page. Given the great distances separating them from their sovereign, such people knew the pen to be sharper than the sword. Indeed, the gold standard for reward was set by the man who filed the concise, if exaggerated, report above, Guayaquil corregidor Gerónimo de Reynoso. This is how the Peruvian viceroy responded to his very professional, "bullet format" letter:

> The good luck you had with the English corsairs on Puná Island
> and the reports you have given me surrounding this matter have
> greatly contented me and I value it all, and with good reason since
> with zeal to serve our Lord and His Majesty you ventured with such
> determination and will to give these enemies the punishment
> *(castigo)* they deserved, from which resulted the deaths you noted
> and the imprisonment of four, which has been of great importance
> in finding out their designs, [and] there will be a general procession
> to give thanks to the Divine Majesty, whom I also trust will
> compensate you in some way for such good success, and in order to
> thank you [myself] for this service, seeing what could be done, I
> have found nothing more apropos than the freeing up of the
> *repartimiento* [encomienda] which pertained to Francisco de Fuentes,
> citizen of the city of Trujillo, which was vacated by his death, [and] I
> have entrusted it to you for two generations, wishing that the rents
> would be greater, [but] be certain that I will always keep in mind
> what you have done and will always view it with much pleasure.
> May Our Lord guard you,
> *Los Reyes [Lima], August 28, 1587*
> *The Count of Villar*[10]

The leader of Quito Company, Juan de Galarza, also sought rewards, though apparently Viceroy Villar was not to be his benefactor. Galarza's petition to the Indies Council, written six years after the Cavendish raid, is preserved in Seville.[11] Forgetting the actions of Manuel the slave and inactions of Pretty and his compatriots, Galarza reveled in his memory of the now-distant engagement. Judging from his letter one would think he had almost single-handedly vanquished the corsairs, juggling harquebus, rapier, and royal standard as he fearlessly cut through enemy lines, forced retreat, burnt sails within view of humiliated foes, smashed earthenware water jugs, and even scuttled a frigate. All told, Galarza claimed he (and a few good sidemen, of course) had killed twenty or twenty-five of the English heretics and captured "the four." Like the corregidor, he claimed only one Spanish death on that glorious day.

In the meantime Galarza had had another chance to distinguish himself, or so he claimed, in helping suppress the 1592–93 "rebelión de las alcabalas," Quito's brief and abortive challenge to crown authority (discussed below). In compensation for all this, but mostly for keeping Cavendish and his followers from achieving "the evil end they sought," Galarza begged another "life," or generation, on his encomienda. He got it. Thus the indigenous inhabitants of Guano, a village near Riobamba, would continue to render tributes to the pirate fighter's heirs well into the seventeenth century.[12]

Lesser lights were not so lucky. An example was Captain Pedro de Castro, who was still pleading with Madrid for a merced in 1592, and getting no response.[13] Like Galarza, he had tried to pad his appeal with evidence of distinguished service in other campaigns, in his case a turn against "Turks" and Moriscos in the 1568–70 Alpujarras Revolt, at the great canyon fortress of Lanjarón. As with fellow Alpujarras veteran Martín Alonso Merlo, who had stumbled in Esmeraldas, apparently past service against "the infidel" was not enough. Silence was the Indies Council's usual method of avoiding responsibility for overseas veterans, but the worst one could hope for was this simple, Kafkaesque reply: "No ha lugar." In essence? "Your claim does not exist." As late as 1599 a Pasto widow pleaded for an extension of her husband's encomienda rights to their minor son on grounds that his father was a veteran of the Puná raid; the Indies Council said nothing.[14]

Others got some credit, though hardly as much as they thought they deserved. Such a man was Gonzalo Gutiérrez de Figueroa, who in 1590 wrote the Indies Council from Quito seeking compensation for his service against the corsair.[15] In begging, as was customary, for means "to eat,"

Gutiérrez de Figueroa added mention of two years battling the maroons of Esmeraldas, but avoided detail since those campaigns had all ended in humiliation and failure. Much more glorious was his participation in the Spanish victory at Puná. The same Juan de Galarza, heroic captain of Quito Company, testified that Gutiérrez had not only displayed personal valor in engaging the pirates, but had successfully goaded several reluctant Guayaquil volunteers into action, promising they would "win honor" in serving God and king.

In the predawn attack, Gutiérrez de Figueroa had led an assault on Cacique Tomalá's now fortified house, hoping to flush out the countless enemies holed up inside. After setting fire to the structure in a hail of harquebus fire, two or three foreigners emerged disoriented from the smoke and quickly fell into his clutches. Apparently it did not bother Galarza that Gutiérrez claimed partial credit for the killing of thirty Englishmen and for helping to sink one of their vessels. (In fact the English had intentionally scuttled the *Hugh Gallant,* discussed by Pretty but here related to Gutiérrez by an African man and three native captives dropped off by the pirates at Machala.) In sum, Gutiérrez de Figueroa appears to have sincerely believed his participation had been critical in helping spare Guayaquil from looting and certain destruction. For his troubles (and connections to prominent figures) the Indies Council granted a "favorable recommendation."

Shortly after the Puná raid the extent of Quito's devotion to coastal defense was tried again, and the resulting decisions would come back to haunt the audiencia in the decades immediately following 1599. Apparently the viceroy, the same count of Villar who had so generously rewarded Guayaquil's corregidor, had just got word of another pending invasion. News had it that upon arriving in the Plate Estuary the newly appointed bishop of Tucumán (in Upper Peru) had been abducted by English corsairs under a certain "Captain Roberto." Carried overland with great haste to Lima, the bishop's report claimed the rogues, whose clutches he had boldly escaped some way down the Argentine coast, were acting on behalf of a certain "conde que llaman Comerlan" (also known as the earl of Cumberland). In any case, the pirates were last seen in February 1587 at 42 degrees south latitude, headed for the Strait. It was now late July and the enemy was due to pop up in Peruvian waters at any moment.

In truth the corsairs, headed by Captains "Roberto" Withrington and Christopher Lister, had managed only to reach 44 degrees south before storms and short provisions forced a slow and ugly retreat to England.[16]

Ignorant of this, however, on 22 September 1587 the viceroy's call to arms was read aloud in Quito. All "householders and feudataries" were to march without delay to the coast where they would defend Guayaquil against this next wave of English corsairs. A kind of pledge of allegiance was quickly signed by all such individuals, including Puná veteran Juan de Galarza, and many prominent women of the town.[17] Yet a number of service-eligible signers, many of them merchants and bureaucrats, hastened to add conditions and complaints to their statements of fealty. First, the winter flood season was beginning, and these folk, "accustomed to the lifestyle and climate of the sierra," claimed they simply could not withstand the rigorous temperatures and humidity of a Guayaquil "winter"; the trip itself, they argued, would kill most of the capital's principal citizens, quite a waste if no pirates showed up. Furthermore, if such an attack were to occur, all the weapons of Quito and Guayaquil combined were insufficient to beat off an enemy as well armed and brazen as a Cavendish or a Drake (*"Oh, beastly cruelty, insane furor, etc."*).

These excuses were not wholly convincing, but Quito's audiencia nevertheless agreed. Its judges recommended instead total evacuation of Guayaquil in case of pirate emergency, adding that the viceroy's plan presented hidden dangers: aside from climate issues, draining Quito of its notable residents could bring forth disaster in the highlands in the form of a massive indigenous rebellion. Given that the prolonged authority void of the Alcabala Revolt a few years later produced no such uprising (see below), this was probably less than likely. Yet the viceroy ultimately backed down. In the course of his agonizingly slow and unsatisfying correspondence with Quito (and many other Peruvian cities with coastal interests but tight purses) the count had apparently received no further news of corsairs. Now, in early 1588, he simply demanded that loyal Quiteños find means of supporting fifty harquebusiers for four months; they should be ready at any moment to defend Guayaquil.

Citing "the great importance of this business," Viceroy Villar's tone in his last response suggests deep disappointment. He had hoped Quito would opt to protect its port with more than the ad hoc forces mustered with luck and "God's grace" at Puná. Still, the locals were probably right. Pirates were a relatively rare menace in the South Sea, the humid coast was indeed a deathtrap for many highlanders, and rat-infested pile-and-thatch "cities" like Guayaquil could stand being sacrificed to flames from time to time. Certainly this passive approach to defense would have its cost, driven home in 1624 when Guayaquil was razed by Dutch corsairs.[18] But what was this against the year-to-year burden on the flow of commerce and indigenous tribute of supporting a garrison and building a stone fortress, Cartagena-style? By the mid-seventeenth century Quiteños would be forced to subsidize such Caribbean expenditures, a late but bitter taste of the cost of crown defense projects against a growing maritime menace. Meanwhile, sporadic pirate attacks on the Quito coast would serve, like raids on backcountry maroons and indigenous rebels, as rare opportunities for male subjects to distinguish themselves and beg recognition.

Soldiers

Occasionally there were urban opportunities for Quito's self-styled hard men to prove their mettle in the years around 1599. Sometimes they saw action serving warring elite factions. Indeed, with both crown and local citizens unwilling to support formal garrisons or standing troops of any kind, soldiers like Alonso Carillo were—in the absence of an emergency muster to fight pirates, maroons, or indigenous rebels—entirely dependent on elite sponsorship.[19] Between skirmishes they were squires and bodyguards, but on the streets of Quito (and also Bogotá, Lima, and Potosí) they frequently got into trouble gambling, drinking, brawling, and abusing vulnerable women. Sometimes they played the role of hired assassin. As noted above, several pirate- and maroon-fighters claimed service in helping to quash Quito's 1592–93 tax revolt in their letters to the king. What had happened in this episode? And what role did Quito's beleaguered soldiers play?

French historian Bernard Lavallé has examined the so-called Alcabala Revolt in greatest detail, and his conclusions do little to improve the image of Quito's itinerant armed men. In fact, these idle soldiers, many of them described by contemporary authorities as "luckless mestizos," had become

something of a social powder keg by 1592. Conquistador "wanna-bes,"
Lavallé calls them the colony's losers, low-born men who had somehow
"missed out on the American dream."[20] Be this as it may, the implementation of the royal sales tax, accomplished in New Spain with little fuss by
1574, had been resisted in Peru at the highest levels. The rate had been sub-
stantially reduced (from 10 to 2 percent) to dampen the effect, yet crown
officials feared uprisings in the still politically unstable Andes. They were
right to be concerned, of course, since it was here in places like Quito and
Cuzco that implementation of the encomienda-strangling New Laws had
touched off civil war less than two generations earlier.

Still, by the 1590s Quito was not known for shirking royal directives,
at least not without going through the usual motions and claims of
obedience. It just so happened that at the moment of forced
implementation the self-described "very noble and loyal" city of Quito
happened to be wracked by unusually bitter elite divisions. These had
formed mostly between the creole-dominated town council and the
Spanish-dominated high court during the ham-handed administration of
interim audiencia president Manuel Barros de San Millán (1587–92—not
to be confused with Dr. Barrio of Esmeraldas fame).

Barros had upset the applecart, as it were, by digging mercilessly into
the pockets and private lives of Quito's ruling class. Fancying himself the
king's enforcer, he went about calling in long-forgotten gold taxes, fining
and even exiling encomenderos for mistreatment of indigenous tributaries,
and picking on and prosecuting beloved members of the clergy for
supposedly egregious behavior. In turn, they accused him of being, among
other things, a homosexual. Since at the time homosexuality was
considered a crime punishable by the Inquisition, the charge was not a
light one. But mutual name-calling, however serious the potential
consequences, was just the start of it.

Though relatively prosperous thanks to gold and long-distance trade,
Quito had nevertheless fallen to a state of political decadence by the late
1580s. Cognizant of the colonies' unhealthy combination of mineral wealth
and physical separation from Europe, Philip II and his ministers sought to
curb corruption and hence disloyalty by appointing outsiders, usually
peninsular Spaniards, to many judicial and ecclesiastical posts. In Quito, in
part because it was a second-tier colonial capital (its audiencia ranked

CHAPTER 6

210

below that of Lima, for example), these attempts had not had the desired
effect. In a nutshell, by the time Judge Barros arrived powerful creole elites
and crown appointees had gotten used to being in bed together, sometimes
literally. Ignoring a sheaf of royal directives, several Quito audiencia judges
had married daughters of merchants and encomenderos and most, if not all,
openly engaged in contraband commerce.

Factions developed quickly in response to Barros's reforming zeal and
Quito's soldiers, hoping as always to improve their fortunes, stood armed
and ready on both sides. When the formal alcabala decree arrived from
Lima in July of 1592 the powder keg blew. At first there was only petty
vandalism and saber rattling. Then, in September, President Barros ordered
an outspoken and popular Quito treasury official jailed. Soon after several
soldiers broke him out amidst cheers. Meanwhile, word of the "mutiny"
had reached Lima. Anxious to enforce the crown's will, Viceroy Hurtado de
Mendoza responded by dispatching several hundred troops under command
of a trusted pirate-fighter, General Pedro de Arana. Arana arrived in the
southern highlands in December 1592, where he set up a temporary base.
Here, from the strategic but relatively distant town of Riobamba (then on
the standard Quito-Guayaquil road), he negotiated with the rebels and the
audiencia until early April 1593.

Arana's decision to hang back rather than march into the city with an
iron fist proved wise. At his arrival in Riobamba, Quito was in the midst of
an uproar following the assassination of the treasury official who had just
been freed. The royal offices of the audiencia had been besieged in turn
and the interim president was temporarily held captive. It was only the
now very real threat of crown retaliation that spared Barros and his most
ardent supporters from a violent end. Another form of retaliation would
come eventually.

In January 1593 Quito's archdeacon tried to calm the situation with a
public procession, hoping to remind the disputants of their shared faith. It
was to no avail; skirmishes involving gangs of soldiers continued to keep
the city on edge. Finally, in March the embattled Barros was unseated by
the new, incoming audiencia president, Esteban Marañón, who was also
armed with the formidable title of Royal Inspector, or *visitador general*. As
Barros was marched off to Lima under guard to face a humiliating sodomy
investigation, Marañón invited General Arana to Quito to establish martial

law. Finding the city unexpectedly calm and quite weary of the conflict, Arana sent most of his three hundred troops back to Lima. To head off new violence and firmly reestablish crown authority, several dozen suspected rebels were prosecuted straightaway. As expected, the elite members among them, including several ranking encomenderos and aldermen, received sentences of exile and fines. Seventeen others, almost all of them "luckless" soldiers of the kind described above, were hanged.

A general pardon and pledge of allegiance was signed in Quito in July of 1593, almost a year to the day after the arrival of the crown's tax decree. As these and other documents plainly reveal, elite and plebeian Quiteños were contrite, embarrassed, and divided; the city's reputation throughout the Viceroyalty of Peru was also deeply tarnished.[21] A rigorous tax-collection system was instituted immediately, but there would be another, greater punishment for this collective act of insolence: the city of Quito would not be allowed to choose its own aldermen for *one hundred years*. That sentence, handed down by the Council of the Indies after a long and tortuous investigation, was executed in 1599.

Quito's Alcabala Rebellion was certainly less violent and destructive than one might expect from an urban tax revolt, but this was the sixteenth and not the eighteenth century (and this was Spanish America, not the Netherlands). More specifically, populations were smaller and less racially mixed (although some Quiteños singled out mestizo men as culprits), and the crown much less inflexible. Also, as Lavallé has shown, the new sales tax was not the principal issue being decided here. Consequently, with the exception of the soldiers, what might be called plebeian participation was minimal throughout. Mostly there was tension, and among elites nagging fear of a generalized indigenous uprising.

In the final analysis the tax rebellion, now memorialized in both Quito's and Ecuador's histories as an early cry for independence, appears—in the context of its own times—to have been little more than an untimely and embarrassing standoff between intransigent local elites and crown officials. In short, cool heads did not prevail, and petty retaliatory violence spiraled out of control. On the other hand, the uprising served as pretext for several dissatisfied individuals, most of them unemployed soldiers of one sort or another, to express anger at the crown for forgetting them. Some of these complaints were silenced at the gallows. Yet even those soldiers who had chosen the "right" side in 1592–93 would find themselves remembered by both crown and countrymen in a way that was not to their liking.

In mid-November 1599 Quito's corregidor, General Diego de Portugal, wrote Spain's new king to inform him of two things. First, local observation of his father's funeral had been properly "ostentatious," and second, 285 men had been mustered for service in "the pacification and rescue of the Kingdom of Chile, in danger as it is of being lost following the death of Governor Martín García de Loyola."[22] The first project had come off without difficulty, and without great cost to the treasury (Quito merchants and encomenderos were of course under intense pressure to express their fealty). The second endeavor, however, had found fewer loyal champions. At first, Quito's remaining men-at-arms would not budge. As the corregidor himself put it, the soldiers' enthusiasm had been sorely undermined by "the vice and easy life *(regalo)* of this land," and also "the ill fame of the Chile campaign."

It was true that even vagabonds did not go hungry in bounteous Quito, city of eternal spring. It was also a commonplace that one did not come back from the windswept and bleak Chilean Front; even its formidable stone *presidios* had to be staffed with criminals. Ultimately, General Portugal decided to threaten all able hands with imprisonment if they did not "volunteer" within thirty days. Dodgers would be formally exiled and declared "infamous." Despite the seriousness of these threats, the general was forced to offer supplies and other incentives, and he felt compelled to personally accompany his 285 harquebusiers, all "very skilled" in the use of these weapons, to Guayaquil. There he would wait nervously until their transports' sails disappeared beyond the horizon. This ritual of exiling misfits to Chile would be repeated several times in the course of the seventeenth century.

Before the 1599 departure a few of these men, Quito's suddenly reluctant soldiers, had wills, donations, and other documents notarized on Puná Island. Among other things, the documents contain faint echoes of fatalism. Young Hernando Yáñez could think of no one else to donate his meager belongings to but a niece. Meanwhile, Diego Hernández de la Reyna gave power of attorney to his wife, declaring rather melodramatically: "I go as a soldier to the rescue of the Kingdom of Chile in the company of Garcí-Díez de Ortega."[23]

A late sixteenth-century soldier's motto: "With sword and compass, more and more and more and more" (Bernardo de Vargas Machuca, *Milicia Indiana,* [Madrid: 1599]).

The will and inventory of Seville-born Diego Quixada offers a bit more to contemplate, including some sense of the material side of a late sixteenth-century soldier's life. Among his belongings Quixada claimed a harquebus "six palms long" and a large *pistolete,* accessories for both weapons including a silver-trimmed glass powder flask. A jug held three or four pounds of extra powder, and should his firearms fail Quixada also carried a steel sword, a buckler, and a helmet. Unlike many of his companions, the skilled harquebusier would ride a silver-gray horse (assuming the animal survived the several-month voyage to Chile). Quixada's marriage had proved sterile, but he had produced an illegitimate daughter by an indigenous servant girl working in the household of a prominent Quito lady. Quixada's wife would receive "a certain quantity of gold dust, some silver in reales, and a pair of gold earrings"; the daughter would get two hundred silver pesos and a small amount of gold.[24]

Whatever their battlefield experience in the Americas thus far, the Quito volunteers of 1599 would face an enemy in Chile unlike any they had encountered before. The foe was not to be Dutch pirates, but rather indigenous rebels. As in Jívaro country and Esmeraldas, persistent Spanish military initiatives and gold-lust in the Southern Cone had been contested and rejected since about 1550. Yet the Mapuche and neighboring groups were not like their "Amazonian anarchist" and coastal maroon brethren-in-arms.

By the 1590s various Chilean bands had coalesced to form a vast confederacy south of the Bío-Bío River. This unified resistance, with the Mapuche at the core, was dubbed "the Indomitable State" *(el estado indómito)* by contemporary warrior-poet Alonso de Ercilla. According to historian R. C. Padden, much of the *estado's* power derived from the growing force of mounted native defenders, said to number in the hundreds by 1594.[25] As in the Great Plains of North America, the so-called Columbian exchange had greatly increased the mobility of some local peoples.

Despite theft and adoption of Spanish horses, however, Mapuche military strategy remained largely unchanged. Rather than face the enemy on the open field, as preferred by European-trained opponents, mounted and otherwise, native cavalrymen continued to attack by stealth, sapping bedraggled colonists' and soldiers' strength and resolve through repeated ambushes in remote canyons. They also made excellent use of terror via long-distance night raids. To rub in the humiliation of defeat, the Mapuche sometimes ate their captives and placed their bones and skulls on display. In short, harquebusiers like Diego Quixada would have their work cut out for them. No doubt as General Portugal and his elite supporters hoped, few such men would return to the "easy life" of Quito.

As this and preceding episodes suggest, by 1599 the military entrada or "punishment" (castigo) had become a critical rite of passage for the young and sometimes old men of the colonies, a necessary probe of masculinity enacted—and indeed replicated for generations—across the seemingly endless fringes of empire. Here at the margins of Quito, in encounters with pirates and rebels of many nations and ethnicities, loyal Spanish subjects of all classes and hues found means to re-create (mostly against the crown's wishes) the conquistador economy. Most did so also to give meaning to their lives as men. At times these would-be heroes and lunatics (recall Landa and Barreto's ill-fated 1572 mutiny in Jívaro country) had to be forcibly pushed to the frontlines. More often, however, they went of their own accord.

It would not be much of an exaggeration to call men like Quito's hobbled pirate- and Indian-fighters Spanish America's knights-errant. There were thousands of Alonso Carillos in Greater Peru and Mexico at the turn of the seventeenth century. Yet like the equally transient and unstable conquistadors before them, the consequences of these second- and third-generation soldiers' actions were no joke. In their often misguided and frequently unsuccessful marauding they killed and displaced many thousands of native Americans. The extent of their role as disease vectors remains unclear. Seen from the other side of any given "wild frontier," however, a side the documents rarely permit us to envision, all this must have looked very different. Out here, as in the backlands of Chile, the hunter could easily become the hunted.

Cannibals

On Thursday, 13 July 1600, in the midst of the confirmation feasts of the Yllescas brothers of Esmeraldas, three indigenous headmen stood before the Audiencia of Quito to present a petition. They humbly requested compensation for the rescue of one Spanish and four African captives from the "infidel Indians" of Barbacoas, the lowland Pacific province northwest of their home. These men were native lords of the highland town of Tulcan, just south of Pasto. Having heard of the new and unusually friendly policies of Quito's Dr. Barrio, don García, don Mateo, and don Miguel Tulcanaza decided to try their luck at court. They hoped to gain some concessions with this independent show of fealty.

In their own words:

> We had news that on the sea coast pertaining to the Indians of that
> land [Barbacoas] there were many Spaniards and blacks who escaped
> from a large ship loaded with merchandise lost on that coast and in
> order to comply with our obligations in the service of God and
> your [highness] we sent runners to search that land for the lost
> Spaniards and blacks and having news that they were in the province
> called Alpan, the cacique of which is named Alpan; in his power
> were a Spaniard, a black man, and a black woman, and with all
> diligence we sent for them by two routes, one from the new town
> of Quinchol to don Rafael, Indian chieftain, your constable in the
> said province, who, having arrived at the province of Alpan with
> blankets, shirts, hats, salt, and the other things we had given him to
> carry to the said provinces and to the said cacique to humor him,
> and by way of ransom *(rescate),* being as he is an Indian of the
> backcountry, an infidel and great butcher of human flesh, God was
> served that he had not eaten them yet, and happy with that which
> we had sent him, he handed over the said Spaniard and the two
> slaves to don Rafael, so that he could bring them before us . . .[26]

As it happened, there had been other survivors of the wreck of the *San Felipe and Santiago* off Mangrove Point on the night of 6 January 1600. Whereas shipmaster Alonso Sánchez de Cuellar and his party of nineteen had been feasted and embraced by the Esmeraldas maroons, these other castaways had found themselves in the clutches of those "wild Indians" described by the inept pilot.

In the quote above the caciques mention only three individuals, but they had in fact also managed to ransom two other African women from a chieftain other than Alpan. These last two ransomed captives had been baptized Ana and Juliana, both native to some part of the vast West Central African region slavers called Angola. The other Africans were Antón, of the Biafada district (the Geba Estuary in Upper Guinea), and María, a Congolese who had learned to speak some Spanish in the course of her forced peregrinations. The lone Spaniard was named Juan Ortega de la Torre, native of Burgos.

The four Africans were presumably on their way to the Callao slave market when the great merchant ship ran aground. Juan Ortega was to take up the office of Accountant of the Edicts of the Holy Crusade in Lima. This official of the only state institution directly linked to the Old World "reconquest" would be the only one of his captive cohort freed in the New. Despite having survived such incredible tribulations— tribulations that killed, apparently, almost everyone else but the Sánchez de Cuellar band and these five—Ana, Juliana, Antón, and María would all be sold back into captivity in Quito at public auction. In the words of Judge Barrio de Sepúlveda, proceeds from the sale of the "rescued" slaves would go "to ransom the souls of [the Barbacoas] infidels, prisoners and captives of the Devil." As if to add further insult, the audiencia, with Dr. Barrio out front, rewarded the Tulcan caciques with a paltry one hundred silver pesos and a terse dismissal.[27]

We can only imagine the tales these African-born survivors of shipwreck and captivity among reputed cannibals must have told their countryfolk in the houses and fields and mines of Quito. Instead we have only the Spaniard Juan Ortega's account of the Barbacoas episode. Ortega recalled how, a little after two weeks sailing, the ship had struck ground and sank; how he and all the passengers had so fortunately been evacuated to shore. He then recalled the eight days' march south, halted by the rivers and the many sick women, children, and slaves (he makes no mention of the burned ship's boat), and the sending ahead of the Sánchez de Cuellar scouting party. Ortega remained with the larger group for three months, he said, struggling to lay hands on sufficient food and water without falling into the clutches of the much-feared "cannibal Indians."

After some seventy days of this the pilot, accompanied by his wife, mother, and seventeen others, took off toward Portoviejo, possibly on a raft (some members of this group may have also survived). Another two weeks passed, every day marked by the unconfessed deaths of castaways black and white, children, women, and men. Ortega lamented the absence of priests among them, adding that the suffering was such that "a father could not save his child, nor a husband his wife, nor a wife her husband."[28]

Recognizing the hopelessness of their situation, reduced now to only twenty-eight survivors, sixteen Africans of both sexes, two Spanish women, and ten Spanish men, Ortega and a few others decided to act. He chose to cast his lot with María and Antón and after saying a prayer they headed north on foot along the coast. Emaciated and probably on the verge of hallucinating, they reached the mouth of a large river after fifteen days spent wandering through tidal flats and mangroves. There they were captured by thirty-two indigenous men in six canoes, "stripped of what little clothing [they] had," and ferried naked up a great river (apparently the Patía, since Ortega says it was nearly a quarter-league wide in spots). Their captors paddled through the night, and early the next morning they arrived in the village of the cacique Alpan, lord of a province he called Posbí (perhaps just north of modern Barbacoas, Colombia).[29]

María and Antón were given to lesser lords, while Ortega was kept for some reason (probably his ransom potential) in the household of Alpan. The captives remained here in the Barbacoas jungle interior forty-seven days, "serving them with great fear for our lives, they being bellicose infidels who eat human flesh." In the course of the next several weeks Ortega got a taste of the enslavement that must have been all too familiar to María and Antón. The indignant Spaniard claimed he was kept naked and "made to work, bringing them maize and wood from the forest, [they] beating me with sticks and throwing canes at me, saying 'this one's for the Christian,' and [giving me] many other tasks and frights."[30] Eight days after being seized the captives' spirits were further dashed when they were informed that a war party had gone to assassinate the remaining survivors languishing on the beach below. Not only was all hope of redemption lost, but now Ortega understood that a feast would eventually be prepared, and he was to be served as the main course (he says nothing of the fate, real or imagined, of María and Antón).

For this purpose Ortega was taken some weeks later to the house of an indigenous widow in the neighboring province of Pogotaiú. Here he waited anxiously for four days as vats of manioc beer fermented and pots were readied; on the fifth day he was to be dispatched and butchered. But "God was served" that a friendly Amerindian named don Rafael Guasip and a helper arrived from the recently "Christianized" indigenous town of The Nativity of Our Lady of Cunchul (the Tulcanazas' "Quinchol"); they carried enough of the right sort of dry goods to ransom the incredulous Spaniard and his African companions. (The cannibal feast was halted, the scribe taking Ortega's testimony suggests, thanks to Dr. Barrio's wise decision to establish ties with don Rafael's subjects at Barbacoas's edge less than two years earlier.)

Whether Alpan's supposed cannibalism was an established (or revived, or new) cultural practice or a simple, visceral threat intended to terrify outsiders, particularly Christians, we will probably never know. Whatever ultimate destiny they had been saved from, the redeemed captives— including the other two African women mentioned above—were given clothing and shelter and guided up steep and narrow foot-trails to the frosty realm of the Tulcanazas, a cluster of villages nestled in moorlands over three thousand meters above the sea. After some weeks of recovery and acclimatization the caciques accompanied the Barbacoas castaways along the Royal Road to Quito, several days' hard journey to the south.

In concluding his testimony the ex-captive Ortega railed against "the evils and offenses the barbarians of that land commit against the Divine Majesty and against Your Highness." But, he added, "having begun to undertake such a holy work [of conversion and 'reduction'] it should be concluded and finished such that those souls be converted and not condemned." How reminiscent of the Mercedarian missionary Cabello Balboa's rhetorical inversion of "freedom" and "captivity" in the context of 1570s Esmeraldas. Or of Licenciado Auncibay's similarly contradictory depiction of an enslaved black utopia in Popayán. Who were the true captives here, and who their redeemers? For the historian it is difficult to distinguish between words actually uttered by Ortega and ones that might have been suggested to the scribe by the propagandist Dr. Barrio: "What is more, with great ease they [the Barbacoans] could be reduced and attracted to the Holy Catholic Faith, and besides, the land is plentiful with food and very rich in gold . . ."[31]

This last bit of inside information was critical; the survivor of cannibal captivity now played mercantilist spy, hinting at the promise of Barbacoas as a new mining frontier for the Audiencia of Quito. He had called it "a land very rich in gold and people," people who could have saved the castaways had they been loyal Spanish subjects. (Alpan's people had informed Ortega that the castaways' situation was known to them soon after the wreck. They had simply avoided contact until the foreigners' numbers were sufficiently reduced by famine and disease.)

Based on information apparently gathered from his rescuers, Ortega estimated the Barbacoas region's indigenous population at some five thousand. "The land is good," he claimed, "purely mountainous jungle (montaña) but not impassable, with many ravines through which flow many rivers, and all with much gold." "The Indians themselves," he continued, "fill bird quills daily with more than a peso's worth of gold, without even knowing how to work it." It is highly unlikely that the Barbacoans were as ignorant of metallurgy as Ortega claimed, but whether they worked gold or not, like the Jivaroan peoples of Amazonia it seems they hardly needed it. The land was said to be rich with foodstuffs, as well: maize, plantains, pineapples, manioc, sugarcane, papayas, guavas. Beyond these cultigens (many of them presumably borrowed from European plantings) fish, fowl, and wild game abounded. Suddenly, against the horrors of cannibalism shone the fantasy of bonanza; the contradiction was almost imponderable.

In early September 1600 the Audiencia of Quito sponsored a reconnaissance mission into the area around the mouth of the Mira River, approximate site of the wreck of the *San Felipe and Santiago*. It was headed by a resident of the Otavalo-area village of Carangue named Hernán González de Saa. He was to accompany caciques of the highland village of Tulcan and the lowland villages of Mallama and Lita into the promising but still dangerous land of Barbacoas. The only other Spaniard to accompany the mission was Juan Gómez of Pimampiro, a native of the Extremaduran town of Bobonal, near Badajoz.

It was doubtful that any shipwreck survivors remained among the bellicose "Malabas" of the lower Mira region, but rumors of live captives again began to circulate after the rescue of Ortega and the others. By now officials were as much concerned with preventing Africans from mixing with indigenous peoples as with rescue per se; the judges cited "the great damages and inconveniences that might result from leaving blacks there."[32] No doubt they had Esmeraldas in mind. Hoping for information, if nothing else, the royal exchequer sent the rescuer/slave-catchers off from Quito with a new sort of "gift" for their lowland interlocutors: fifteen pounds of gunpowder and twenty pounds of lead.

The going was slow. González de Saa and his followers only reached Tulcan by 20 November (the document says December, but this is apparently a mistake, as subsequent events clearly take place in early December). After demonstrating the various written mandates to the caciques and their assigned Spanish priest, or *doctrinero,* the group set off with more than thirty highland Andeans as auxiliaries for a sub-province of Barbacoas called Camonbí. After about a week's march the expedition reached the town of Quinchol, home of the men who had bartered for Juan Ortega and the four African slaves. Awaiting them there were two caciques from the interior, don Hernando Nasdip of the Nurpe, or "Nulpe" band, and don García Guapilde of the province of Camonbí. Nasdip and Guapilde informed González de Saa and his followers that a neighboring group, the Guasmingas, had annihilated the remaining castaways some two months earlier. Nevertheless, they had also heard that five African captives, a woman and four men, were still alive and in the power of the cacique Alpan. The earlier ransom mission had been incomplete.

González de Saa agreed to meet the caciques and their people some days later at a site called Yamban, in the territory of Camonbí, some fifteen leagues from Quinchol. This place, said to buttress "the great pile-dwellings *(barbacoas)* that gave the district its Caribbean-derived Spanish name, was deep in the backcountry, and apparently some of the auxiliaries from Tulcan and Lita began to feel uneasy. The next day caciques don García Tulcanaza and don Hernando Taquez chose to return to their highland home with a number of their retinue.

González de Saa set out with his reduced expedition, still including some thirty-five highlanders under don Miguel Tulcanaza and don Juan Taquez, and another thirty "recently reduced" native men from the "Vicious Valley" (also known as the lower Mira River basin, near Lita). They marched five leagues before making camp in an uninhabited area, then did the same the next day after a six-league push. Finally, on the third day, after two more leagues' hacking and trudging, the expedition reached "a populated stilt-house," whose inhabitants "received us with great love, and gave us what they had." This glorious reception was followed by another day's march, another five leagues, and another encampment in wilderness.

After yet another six leagues on foot over punishing terrain, González de Saa and his group reached "a great stilt-house where there must have been more than forty souls, and they received us with much love and gifts of that land." Next day, after two leagues more, they arrived in the province of Camonbí and the house of a "principal," or lesser lord subject to don García Guapilde. This individual, according to González, "received us and gave us lodging with much love and goodwill, making us many gifts, and ordering all his people to come see us."

On the following day another forty indigenous persons arrived at the house, bringing a variety of presents. A special council was called. González de Saa asked how he and his party might find and "remove" the African (or possibly Spanish) captives mentioned by the elder cacique, Guapilde. In response, the inhabitants of Camonbí repeated that they had heard of the Guasmingas' annihilation of the shipwreck survivors some two months back, but believed they had also taken four African men alive. The African woman, they said, was in the hands of the cacique Alpan, Ortega's former captor. His settlement lay two days' journey farther in.

The natives of Camonbí offered to accompany González de Saa's expedition to the beach near the shipwreck site to confirm these stories— as had been ordered by the audiencia. Unfortunately for González, don Miguel Tulcanaza, the highland cacique, balked at the suggestion of a canoe journey into Guasminga territory. The expedition now reached an impasse stickier than the worst Barbacoas swamp. Frustrated, González de Saa tried to reason with don Miguel, reminding him how close they were to completing their mission. The cacique would not budge, claiming that he was following a secret order given by his overlord delivered before his return to the highlands. He even produced a letter signed by don Hernando Tulcanaza stating that "by no means" was don Miguel to take his people beyond Camonbí. Judging his remaining auxiliaries insufficient for the task at hand, González de Saa was forced to plot his party's return to the sierra.

In the meantime, the cacique Alpan, apparently without any

encouragement, sent the African woman mentioned above to González de Saa's company with an indigenous escort/messenger. The message was an invitation to visit him in his own household. The terrified captive, whom González de Saa does not bother to name, but was clearly African-born ("bozal"), must have been positively stunned by this turn of events. Having barely set foot in the Americas, she was already a bargaining chip in a strange game of frontier politics. Using the few Spanish words she knew, she told the less-than-compassionate González de Saa that her captors had killed two other African women (the testimony does not say why, but cannibalism is not mentioned). Most importantly for the expedition leader was the captive's claim that somewhere in the jungle four African men remained alive. González de Saa renewed his plea to don Miguel Tulcanaza not to abandon the enterprise, but the cacique, following his own orders, would not change his mind. The auxiliaries from Lita were sent home, but González played one last card: he sent don Rafael, cacique of Quinchol, and two of his followers to meet with Alpan and seek information regarding the lost men.

When the Quinchol troop returned with nothing but the same story of the Guasminga massacre and the four living captives González de Saa despaired. Worse still, the go-betweens carried angry words from Cacique Alpan of Posbí. As had been requested of him in the earlier communication, he had mustered many canoes and rafts, not to mention eighty warriors, to accompany the highlanders' expedition to the coast. When no one came, he felt snubbed. González de Saa and his followers had not only broken their word, they had taken advantage of Alpan's generosity with the free handover of the captive African woman. The Quinchol ambassadors claimed that "filled with regret he returned to his land, very angry and ashamed."[33] Having made no friends and only "freeing" one of the five known captives, an equally angry and ashamed González de Saa returned to Quito to report on his activities in Barbacoas.

Predictably, he blamed the Tulcanazas for the mission's failure. Then again, they may well have saved his life. It had been the same Alpan, after all, whom they claimed to have stopped short of making a meal of the Spaniard Juan Ortega de la Torre. In any case, González de Saa offset the bad news with geographical notes, some promising, some menacing:

The people of this province are of great stature and some go
clothed, and they are feminine and well-featured, and they wear a
cloth *(manta)* from the waist to the knees made of tree bark, and the
rest of their body is nude, and the said province is very rich in gold,
very fine, and the natives trade it in dust-grains and nuggets and
they carry it on their persons as jewelry, all signs that there are
mines of the said gold in this province, and there are many areas of
red earth where it [i.e., gold] grows *(donde se cria),* and it is a land of
genuine jungle, of hot but moderate climate, and with very swift
rivers and rivulets large and small, and it is very abundant in
foodstuffs: maize, plantains, *chonta*-palms, pineapples, fish, wild boar,
turkey, and guan *(paujil);* and these natives eat three varieties of
vipers, the first large and black, more than a fathom in length, and
others very painted with diverse colors, thin and only a half-fathom
in length, and still others smaller, between green and brown, with
wide heads like toads, and these are the most venomous, such that
being bitten one escapes only by miracle; and this land is not too
mountainous, especially near the coast, and the province of Alpan is
bordered by the province of Aspipuis . . .[34]

The year 1599 had marked the beginning of a most ambivalent conquest
of this refractory strip of lowland South America claimed by Quito. The
1600 wreck of the *San Felipe and Santiago* and aftermath simply thrust the
region under a magnifying glass during a key moment of transition. As
echoed by the captives' testimonies, both hope and despair abounded.
Many baptisms had taken place, to be sure, but promised roads and
towns—and most importantly, mines—were slow in coming. Dr. Barrio
had pushed hard for conversion and diplomacy after so many failed
entradas, but his methods, though clever, never quite got the job of
conquest done to the satisfaction of Quito's old soldiers, nor ultimately
the crown.

The Province of Barbacoas, said to be subject to Quito but
technically within the semi-independent governorship of Popayán, had
been among Dr. Barrio's several fronts in the "bloodless" Pacific lowlands
campaign, but its future would diverge radically from that of neighboring
Esmeraldas. Supported by hawkish governors and less soul-searching (or

even interested) monarchs, a new generation of largely creole neo-conquistadors would make war on caciques like Alpan, annihilating them by the dozens to force open a new gold-mining frontier.[35] Luckier, perhaps, Esmeraldas would fade to its old state of quasi-anarchy, largely untouched by prospectors and settlers until the late eighteenth century.

Black and white and on both sides of this at once imaginary and strangely resilient backcountry border, the hapless castaways of the *San Felipe and Santiago* had witnessed and unwittingly participated in a watershed moment in the history of the Audiencia of Quito. In the course of their trials many frontiers—those separating north from south, highlands from lowlands, white from black, Christian from pagan, and most of all captive from redeemed—had been tested, penetrated, broken, and redrawn.

EPILOGUE

Quito was many things in 1599. It was a city recognized as the unequivocal beacon of regional political, religious, and commercial authority. It was also a haven of sorts for thousands of indigenous peasants and more than a few European outcasts, a parade ground for conspicuous consumer-philanthropists, a woman-centered popular marketplace, a mustering-ground for restless soldiers. It was also a highland hinterland, stretching north beyond Cali and south beyond Loja, now town, now village, now countryside, then mountain wilderness, every corner transformed by waves of plague, dislocation, deforestation, and explosive European livestock and cultigen reproduction. Here and there the highlands were already scoured of mineral wealth. In the north, where the search continued despite sharp decline in native populations, colonists were becoming more African each day. Finally Quito was a vast unknown, an untamed or unpopulated fringe of snowcaps, desert coast, and jungle. In a few places, such as the vast Jivaroan heartland of Upper Amazonia, Quito's arrogance had been successively defied, attacked, and ultimately nullified. Cartographic claims aside, this place, like the "cannibal coast" of Barbacoas, was not Quito at all.

Borders, like identities, only concretize when challenged, and Quito's fringe challenges at the turn of the seventeenth century were many. They were mounted by pirates, rebels, maroons, and even the stubbornly independent governors of Popayán. Taken together these conflicts reflect deeper transformations under way in Quito circa 1599. Among the most salient were the shifts from the gold to textile economy in the highland core and the equally profound (yet likewise incomplete) shift from martial to mercantile means of gaining wealth and status throughout the audiencia. More than ever Quiteños turned from the dangerous search for gold and sinecures to new and risky but less often life-threatening market opportunities of the immediate sort. Some, like Rodrigo de Ribadeneira, bridged the two, using encomienda subsidies to produce textiles for export. Others, less fortunate, soldiered on to Chile, an extraterritorial destination synonymous with death.

Changes not fully explored in this book but evidently under way in Quito circa 1599 occurred in interior realms as well, in spaces less accessible to modern historians. In the hearts and minds of many residents, rich, poor, and of various colors and both sexes, a new religion was taking root. An admittedly impressionistic reading of wills and related evidence suggests the edicts of Trent, reiterated in Quito's 1594 synods, had begun to sink in. The new rules would of course be interpreted in myriad ways, not all of them in line with European theologians' intentions, but their effect was real. Pietism, memorialized in Quito's stunningly diverse Baroque architectural and artistic corpus, was viewed as the most likely path to Christian redemption. Souls were depicted on canvas as chained babes in the Devil's thrall, pleading with Christ's Virgin Mother to intercede.

The seemingly paradoxical intertwining of spiritual freedom and bodily captivity, a kind of Baroque Catholic trope discussed here in the context of African slavery, would manifest itself in other ways. Nunneries, once poor and perfunctory copies of peninsular compounds, suddenly proliferated and their ranks swelled. In the seventeenth century they would be among Quito's most powerful economic players. As women in Quito, Popayán, and other cities grew wealthy, some as widows, some as chaste matriarchs, they could afford for the first time to embrace new ideas and forms of female devotion emanating from Madrid and Rome. To judge from the few documents I have examined, Quito's nuns and *beatas* took their female slaves and indigenous servants with them, presumably transforming their experience of Baroque Christianity as well.

Strictly male orders like the Society of Jesus also expanded

dramatically in Quito after 1599, establishing a huge presence in city, countryside, and at what might be called the "tribal" margins of Amazonia.
Low-interest loans to the cash-starved laity, supplemented by pious donations of land and other real property, would subsidize the Jesuit program to
develop urban schools, rural haciendas, textile mills, and a vast missionary
complex downriver from Jívaro country in the Province of Mainas. The
older, more established orders did not sit idly by. Quito's Franciscans,
Dominicans, Mercedarians, Augustinians, and other regulars wrangled with
the Jesuits and with each other for souls, both urban and "barbaric."

Alongside the regulars, the secular clergy and popular sodalities also
flourished, fueled by a similarly renewed sense of urgency and what might
have been seen as a more clearly marked path of devotion. The record suggests this post-Tridentine fervor crossed ethnic, class, and gender boundaries, and together most Quiteños (however hypocritically in particular
cases) set about building their version of the city of God on the flanks of
Pichincha Volcano. Their example was in part followed by the similarly
pious citizens of Cuenca, Loja, Pasto, Popayán, Ibarra, and other highland
towns. On the other hand, some rural doctrineros simply wanted—and
gained—sinecures. By the late seventeenth century the creole Jesuit historian Pedro de Mercado would serve in a sense as greater Quito's Jonathan
Edwards, chastising sinners and memorializing saints in his copious annals.
Guayaquil remained, meanwhile, a ramshackle coastal entrepôt periodically
sacrificed to pirates. Like most port cities and mining towns in Spanish
America, Guayaquil came to be associated—in the highland imagination,
at least—with moral degeneracy. The image has persisted.

Many other themes deserve closer examination: the growth of Quito's
mixed heritage population, changes (and continuities) in indigenous
religious beliefs and language, formation of enslaved and free African and
African-American communities in city and countryside, convent life,
heterodox sexuality, marriage strategies among women of elite versus
popular status, childhood, the heterogeneity and mobility of the clergy, the
articulation of estates, ranches, and urban markets, environmental
consequences of sheep and cattle ranching, the particulars of the textile
economy, and so on. Certainly these and other issues will be addressed in
due course, but what does *Quito 1599* add to current understandings of
colonial Latin America, at least for the early period?

First, like any given city and administrative district within the larger Spanish empire, Quito's early trajectory was both singular and representative. Many of its "weird" particulars, like the 1592–93 Alcabala Revolt, have been highlighted to emphasize the former. Comparatively, though, the shifting economy of Quito circa 1599 should serve as a reminder of the potential for dynamic adaptation far from the great centers of administrative and economic power (not only the regional hubs of Lima and Potosí—and in another sphere, Mexico City—but also Seville and Madrid). Clearly Quiteños—mostly merchants, but also encomenderos, high officials, and a variety of others—were constantly jockeying for position in a wide range of commercial and productive enterprises. At least one hard-headed banker emerged, and virtually all "investors," broadly speaking, seem to have brushed off crown directives— like the ban on silk imports via Mexico—that interfered with the pursuit of profits. Similar commercial dynamism and flexibility, sharp reorientations toward more lucrative colonial markets, and periodic challenges to crown and merchant-monopoly authority characterized the River Plate district, Venezuela, and other parts of Spanish America in the seventeenth century. Quito may have been unusual only in its earliness and extremes. If notary records are any guide, Quito's economy circa 1599 was certainly dynamic and diversified; its special motor, at least up to this point, had been the gold of Popayán.

Furthermore, the same notary records suggest early development of a sophisticated consumer culture that, like Baroque Catholicism, spanned the social hierarchy and more or less blanketed the colonized region. My sense is that although a previously unrecognized gold boom and consequent development of far-flung merchant networks provided the initial spark, by 1599 credit-based consumption was as critical to the continued expansion of the regional economy as production for export. To some extent each probably drove the other. In the city, indigenous market women were as quick to profit from the prevailing shopping-spree mentality as major wholesalers. Similar patterns of cross-class consumer capitalism must have arisen elsewhere, particularly in the gold- and silver-rich Andes of this period. (An often overlooked feature of all colonies believed to contain mineral wealth has been their capacity to generate hope and, for the merchant, hype.)

Also critical in the comparative context was Quito's constantly changing relationship with its own periphery, or rather, peripheries. At the geographical fringes—in this case usually densely forested lowland regions rumored to contain gold—crown, church, and would-be settler authority was hotly contested. Sometimes maroons won out, as in Esmeraldas, sometimes native groups, as in Jívaro country or Barbacoas. There was also room for mestizo-led rebellions from time to time, although as in backcountry Peru and New Granada none succeeded. The pirate menace was of even lower frequency, or periodicity, yet the very foreignness of the attackers served to provide a rare patriotic rallying point. Rather than being settled and developed as a result of these challenges, Quito's vast, unprotected coast became just another proving ground for honor-starved men of all colors and classes. This was more or less akin to the experience of contemporary western New Spain, but quite unlike that of the pirate-infested and hence heavily fortified Spanish Caribbean. Also, as proved true throughout Iberoamerica, frontier chaos and urban cohesion were at best imperfectly linked; that is, the latter did not result from the former. Tensions at the core were revealed in part by Quito's love-hate relationship with its lower-class mercenary-frontiersmen, ultimately shipped off to Chile in 1599, and bitter elite divisions were as evident here as in contemporary Potosí.

In general outline at least, these types of localized core-periphery relationships were hardly unique to Quito, or even to secondary colonial districts more broadly. Similar stories of valor, shattered femurs, accidental martyrdom, and razor-thin escapes from certain death could be heard in Guadalajara, Charcas, Manila, or Guatemala, but also in the viceregal capitals of Lima and Mexico City. Throughout contemporary Brazil, and certainly in the capital of Salvador, they were the stuff of everyday life.

In the Spanish case, the quick toppling of indigenous inland empires and subsequent implementation of more or less peaceful regimes has led many historians to neglect ongoing or cyclical fringe conflicts. However justified this approach may seem in terms of "neo-core" patterns of demography, economy, and so forth, contemporary writings reveal that it was the violence and uncertainty lingering beyond every horizon that most preoccupied residents of *every part* of Spanish America in this period.

In trying to make sense of colonial affairs, including, for example, the constant jockeying between second-tier audiencias and viceroys—and likewise audiencias and subject governors—it would perhaps be advisable to keep in mind the power of this besieged, "frontier" mentality at the Spanish American core. Frontiers, imagined and real, were always a gold mine for astute politicians. Their defense, subjugation (including conversion), and exploitation were the very stuff of colonial government. There is another side to this story, of course. That the maroons of Esmeraldas and the Jivaroans of Amazonia—like their many counterparts all over the Americas—remained autonomous and in fact defined Quito's limits despite the known presence of gold in their territories should also serve as a reminder that despite significant European advantages (in technology, biological immunity, access to information, and so forth) conquest was not inevitable. Certainly Quito's Dr. Barrio, who benefited personally from frontier policymaking, would have been first to admit this.

In the highland core, meanwhile, conquest and the limits of crown, church, and settler authority were contested in other ways. African slaves and their descendants were cruelly exploited, verbally denigrated, physically mutilated, and even murdered, yet through it all they cut various new and unexpected paths to freedom and self-respect. The spectrum of resistance (an admittedly embattled concept, but applicable in this case) ranged from grand marronage to the purchase of relatives with personal savings.

Individual slaves' experiences varied tremendously within Quito's broad boundaries, but in general the scale of slavery was small. This was true of most of contemporary Iberoamerica, and it may be that a similar range of actions, reactions, and adaptations to the early slave experience could be found in the ports, mines, fields, and cities of New Spain, New Granada, central Peru, and Brazil. More careful study of slavery "at the fringe" in this early period would certainly be welcome. That African and African-American physical captivity was linked to elite spiritual redemption in early Quito only highlights, I think, the strangely intimate nature of the institution of slavery in the Baroque period.

Quito's hundreds of thousands of native peoples faced similar hardships in the early colony, and as one ought to expect, they proved equally resilient. One of the ironies of historical documentation, however, is that the majority of indigenous Quiteños are less accessible to us as individuals than slaves. Clearly like certain slaves the most resourceful among them managed to turn the tables on would-be exploiters, spiritual guides, and "protectors." Into the Inka-noble void stepped native lords, intermediaries of dubious lineage but apparently prodigious political and economic talent. Indigenous women were no less active than men in this and other colonial pursuits and enterprises.

For the mass of indigenous men subject to encomienda and mita abuses, on the other hand, mobility was key. Families often followed. As in many other parts of the Andes, the resulting shell game played by migrants and native lords would continue to frustrate Spanish authorities throughout the colonial period. Yet as demonstrated by the ongoing Pijao and Páez wars of the north, indigenous resistance of the violent sort was not limited to the initial period or jungle fringe. Subtracting the ravages of epidemic disease, one could easily imagine a massive native uprising and successful expulsion of the Spanish in the Quito district as late as the 1620s, a prospect far less likely (though not unthinkable) in contemporary Lima or Mexico City. In short, elite fears expressed during the Alcabala Revolt of 1592–93 were not spurious.

This book contributes to these and other themes of comparison and also adds something new to the edifice of document-derived knowledge of early colonial Latin America. But I would like to return to a more general and ambiguous issue raised in the preface: what might be called the fluidity of history and the contingent experience of the individual. It is not out of simple love of anecdotes (although I admit a fondness) that I have attempted to highlight individual lived experiences: the strange careers of the "Belgian millionaire" Cristóbal Martín, for example; or the branded Pijao youth Xi, sold to a Quito hatmaker at the turn of the seventeenth century; or the young Congolese woman baptized María who survived enslavement, the middle passage, and shipwreck in the Pacific, only to be captured by cannibals. Rather, I continue to be deeply bothered by an enduring conundrum. In short, how is it that human lives, or at least their texts, never match the structured contexts we receive or (as historians) build for them?

Establishing context, that is, taking into account contemporary patterns of war, disease, marriage, economy, nutrition, technology, religion, and so on, is obviously critical to any attempt at understanding individual trajectories. On the other hand, context, because its aim is averages, can never really explain a life; we get only ranges of possibility, at best. (One need only look at one's own life and imagine the facile judgments of future historians to see this.) Certainly this problem of reconciling seemingly aberrant individual lives with perceptible currents of history is a very old one, and I do not pretend to have solved it. I doubt in fact there is a solution, and instead my hope is that by having mixed in bits of lived experience that seem to match or at least reflect broader findings and expectations with several that clearly do not, readers of this book will have been compelled to avoid easy conclusions (hence this "inconclusive" epilogue). Based on my experience—both in and out of the archives—the past can be counted on as much as the present to surprise and trip us up. In the case of Quito in and around the year 1599, why should we expect the various bundles of diverse, overlapping, and intersecting lives, laws, beliefs, and activities that we call collectively "colonial society" to constitute anything but a squirming, evolving enigma, an organic cryptogram? Perhaps the beguiling portrait of the Esmeraldas ambassadors says it all.

NOTES

PREFACE

1. The painting has graced the covers of several books over the years, but the only authors to offer much of an explanation are Thomas B. F. Cummins and William B. Taylor, "The Mulatto Gentlemen of Esmeraldas, Ecuador," in *Colonial Spanish America: A Documentary History,* ed. Kenneth Mills and William B. Taylor (Wilmington, Del.: Scholarly Resources, 1998), 147–49.

2. The pioneering work in this genre, at least in English, is Ray Huang's *1587: A Year of No Significance* (New Haven, Conn.: Yale University Press, 1987).

3. The first term is borrowed from Jeremy Adelman, ed., *Colonial Legacies: The Problem of Persistence in Latin American History* (New York: Routledge, 1999); the second from Inga Clendinnen, *Ambivalent Conquests: Maya and Spaniard in Yucatan, 1517–1570* (Cambridge: Cambridge University Press, 1987). An example of the contact-era focus in Andean historiography is Kenneth Andrien and Rolena Adorno, eds., *Transatlantic Encounters: Europeans and Andeans in the Sixteenth Century* (Berkeley: University of California Press, 1991).

4. The phrase is taken from R. Brian Ferguson and Neil L. Whitehead's introduction to *War in the Tribal Zone: Expanding States and Indigenous Warfare* (Santa Fe, N.Mex.: School of American Research, 1992).

INTRODUCTION

1. See Esteban de Marañón's 1598 "Relación de la renta que hay en la catedral de Quito, etc." in *Relaciones Histórico-Geográficas de la Audiencia de Quito* (hereafter *RHGQ*), ed. Pilar Ponce Leiva, 2 vols. (Madrid: CSIC, 1991–92), 1:575–88.

2. For a cogent discussion of these and related issues, see Stuart B. Schwartz and Frank Salomon, "New Peoples and New Kinds of People: Adaptation, Readjustment, and Ethnogenesis in South American Indigenous Societies (Colonial Era)," in *South America*, vol. 3, pt. 2, *The Cambridge History of the Native Peoples of the Americas*, ed. Salomon and Schwartz (Cambridge: Cambridge University Press, 1999), 443–501.

3. Frank Salomon, *Native Lords of Quito in the Age of the Incas* (Cambridge: Cambridge University Press, 1986), 75. See also David G. Basile, *Tillers of the Andes: Farmers and Farming in the Quito Basin* (Chapel Hill: University of North Carolina Press, 1974), 109–15.

4. Gregory Knapp, *Andean Ecology: Adaptive Dynamics in Ecuador* (Boulder, Colo.: Westview Press, 1991).

5. Fast-disappearing swatches of "old growth" Ecuadorian páramo have been analyzed by Philip L. Keating in, for example, "Effects of anthropogenic disturbances on páramo vegetation in Podocarpus National Park, Ecuador," *Physical Geography* 19 (1998): 221–38; and "Changes in páramo vegetation along an elevation gradient in southern Ecuador," *Journal of the Torrey Botanical Society* 126:2 (1999): 159–75.

6. See Thomas F. Lynch, "Earliest South American Lifeways," in *South America*, vol. 3, pt. 2, *The Cambridge History of Native Peoples of the Americas*, ed. Salomon and Schwartz, 197.

7. A classic general study is Betty J. Meggers, *Ecuador* (London: Thames and Hudson, 1966). See also the more recent summaries of Segundo Moreno Yánez and others in vol. 1 of Enrique Ayala Mora, ed., *Nueva Historia del Ecuador*, multiple vols. (Quito: Corporación Editora Nacional, 1983–2002); and those in *Pacific Latin America in Prehistory: The Evolution of Archaic and Formative Cultures*, ed. Michael Blake (Pullman: Washington State University Press, 1999).

8. Izumi Shimada, "Evolution of Andean Diversity (500 BCE–CE 600)," in *South America*, vol. 3, pt. 1, *The Cambridge History of the Native Peoples of the Americas*, ed. Salomon and Schwartz, 369–71, 416–19, 430–36.

9. See, for example, Anne Christine Taylor, "The Western Margins of Amazonia from the Early Sixteenth to the Early Nineteenth Century," in *South America*, vol. 3, pt. 2, *The Cambridge History of the Native Peoples of the Americas*, ed. Salomon and Schwartz, 188–256; and P. Pedro Porras, *Investigaciones arqueológicas a las faldas de Sangay* (Quito: Tradición Upano, 1987). See also the revised edition of Betty J. Meggers's classic *Amazonia: Man and Culture in a Counterfeit Paradise* (1971; Washington, D.C.: Smithsonian Institution Press, 1996), and the many writings of Donald Lathrap.

10. For recent ethnohistory of Popayán-area groups just before and after conquest, see Ximena Pachón, "Los Guambianos y la ampliación de la frontera indígena," in *Frontera y poblamiento: estudios de historia y antropología de Colombia y Ecuador*, ed. Chantal Caillavet and Ximena Pachón (Santafé de Bogotá: IFEA/Sinchi/U.de los Andes, 1996), 283–314.

11. See, for example, Juan and Judith Villamarín, "Chiefdoms: The Prevalence and Persistence of 'Señoríos Naturales' 1400 to European Conquest," in *South America,* vol. 3, pt. 1, *The Cambridge History of Native Peoples of the Americas,* ed. Salomon and Schwartz, 577–667. See also the marvelously illustrated essay by Warwick Bray, Leonor Herrera, and Marianne Cardale Schrimpff, "The Malagana Chiefdom, A New Discovery in the Cauca Valley of Southwestern Colombia," in *Shamans, Gods, and Mythic Beasts: Colombian Gold and Ceramics in Antiquity,* ed. Armand Labbé (Seattle: American Federation of Arts/University of Washington Press, 1998): 121–61.

12. Alfred Métraux, *The History of the Incas* (1961; New York: Schocken, 1970), 161–64; Carolyn Dean, *Inka Bodies and the Body of Christ: Corpus Christi in Colonial Cuzco, Peru* (Durham, N.C.: Duke University Press, 1999), 185–99.

13. A breathtaking photo-essay is Keith Muscutt's *Warriors of the Clouds: A Lost Civilization of the Upper Amazon of Peru* (Albuquerque: University of New Mexico Press, 1998).

14. In an account of the Imbabura town of Pimampiro a priest mentions ongoing mountain-top "witchcraft" c. 1591; Ponce Leiva, *RHGQ* 1:483.

15. A curious variation on this story is found in Juan de Betanzos, *Narrative of the Incas,* trans. Roland Hamilton and Dana Buchanan (1557; Austin: University of Texas Press, 1996), 182–83.

16. On *mitmajkuna,* see Salomon, *Native Lords of Quito,* 158–67.

17. For a brief synopsis, see "The Quitan Campaign" in John Hemming, *The Conquest of the Incas* (New York: HBJ/Harvest, 1970), 151–68. An eyewitness account of subsequent battles between Spanish factions in the 1540s is Pedro Cieza de León, *The War of Quito,* trans. C. Markham (London: Hakluyt Society, 1913).

CHAPTER I

1. Survivor testimonies are in Archivo General de Indias (hereafter cited as AGI) Quito 25:45. Royal proclamations from 1593 and 1604 prohibiting trade in East Asian goods between Mexico and Peru (with specific mention of Quito) are reprinted in *Colección de cédulas reales dirigidas a la Audiencia de Quito, 1601–1660,* ed. Jorge Garcés (Quito: Archivo Municipal, 1946), 56–59.

2. Little is known of the artist, but he was apparently in demand and well paid, as suggested by a 1592 commission to construct and adorn a c. 3.6-m-high-by-3-m-wide tabernacle for Chimbo cacique Diego Pilamunga for twelve hundred pesos (Archivo Nacional de la Historia, Quito [hereafter cited as ANHQ], PN 1:3 DLM, ff. 317v–18v).

3. Adam Szászdi, "El Trasfondo de un cuadro: 'Los Mulatos de Esmeraldas' de Andrés Sánchez Galque," *Cuadernos Prehispánicos* (Valladolid, Spain) 12 (1986–87): 93–142. See also Rocío Rueda Novoa's excellent unpublished thesis, "Sociedad negra y

autonomía: La historia de Esmeraldas, Siglos XVI–XVIII," Tesis de Maestría, Universidad del Valle (Cali, Colombia), 1990; Rafael Savoia, "El negro Alonso de Illescas y sus descendientes (1553–1867)," *Actas del primer congreso de historia del negro en el Ecuador y sur de Colombia* (Quito: Centro Cultural Afro-Ecuatoriano, 1988): 29–80; José Alcina Franch, "El problema de las poblaciones negroïdes de Esmeraldas, Ecuador," *Anuario de Estudios Americanos* 31 (1974): 33–46; J. L. Phelan, *The Kingdom of Quito in the Seventeenth Century* (Madison: University of Wisconsin Press, 1967), 3–22; Linda A. Newson, *Life and Death in Early Colonial Ecuador* (Norman: University of Oklahoma Press, 1995), 262–67; Luis Andrade Reimers, *Las esmeraldas de Esmeraldas durante el Siglo XVI* (Quito: Casa de la Cultura Ecuatoriana, 1978); and Jacinto Jijón y Caamaño, *El Ecuador interandino y occidental antes de la conquista castellana,* 2 vols. (Quito: Editorial Ecuatoriana, 1941), 2:415–547. For printed primary documents, see José Rumazo González, ed., *Colección de documentos para la historia de la audiencia de Quito,* 8 vols. (Madrid: Afrodisio Aguado, 1948–50), vol. 4. (1949); José Alcina Franch y Remedios de la Peña, ed., *Textos para la etnohistoria de Esmeraldas: trabajos preparativos, v. 4* (Madrid: Universidad Complutense, 1976); and Miguel Cabello Balboa, "Verdadera descripción y relación de la provincia y tierra de las Esmeraldas," *Obras* (1583; Quito: Editorial Ecuatoriana, 1945).

4. The Yllescases appear throughout Seville's sixteenth-century notary Protocols in connection with the Indies trade, particularly in tax farming; but see also the merchant Alonso de Yllescas's 1538 contract with Fernando Colón, the admiral's son, and a 1551 contract to recover gold from a factor in Lima, in *Documentos Americanos del Archivo de Protocolos de Sevilla, Siglo XVI,* multiple vols. (Madrid: Tipografía de Archivos I. Olózaga, 1935), 4:202, 357.

5. A later witness would refer to Alonso de Yllescas as the most "astute, valiant, and bellicose" of the maroon leaders of Esmeraldas (AGI Quito 25:45, 4:6, testimony of Pedro de Arévalo). Arévalo also claimed the African castaways took up native "rites, ceremonies, and dress."

6. Cabello Balboa, "Verdadera descripción," 25.

7. AGI Quito 20b, 2:18, 17-xii-1550. Following a refrain heard throughout Peru, Hernández claimed that local indigenes had closed up mines to spite Spaniards. Similar is AGI Quito 20b: 51, 24-i-1566, where the Guayaquileño Alvaro de Figueroa promised to conquer Esmeraldas in exchange for concessions.

8. See Ponce Leiva, *RHGQ* 1: 66–71, 312–13.

9. AGI Quito 22:1, 1-ii-1578.

10. In his "Verdadera descripción," Cabello Balboa makes repeated reference to the incredible tracking abilities (and ability to cover tracks) of the maroons and their indigenous neighbors; see, for example, 14–17.

11. Ibid., 75.

12. Szászdi, "El Trasfondo de un cuadro," 107.

13. Both Urquizo's and López de Zúñiga's versions of these events are in AGI Quito 23:26, 18-ii-1589.

14. AGI Quito 22:56, 22-v-1585. Espinosa calls Gonzalo de Ávila "español."

15. AGI Quito 23:26, 18-ii-1589.

16. Alonso de Espinosa to the Audiencia of Quito, 22 May 1585, in Rumazo González, *Colección de documentos para la historia de la audiencia de Quito,* 4:11–12.

17. For a sense of the disorder that characterized Quito's audiencia in these years, see chapter 6, below, and Bernard Lavallé, *Quito y la crisis de la alcabala, 1580–1600* (Quito: Corporación Editora Nacional, 1997), 66–75. López de Zúñiga would be named corregidor of Quito, only to be caught up in the 1592–93 tax revolt.

18. AGI Quito 23:11, 17-xi-1587. Merlo counted himself among the vanguard in this brutal 1570 siege, turning point of the eastern campaign, and he had wounds to prove it. Perhaps crossing the threshold between bravery and rashness, he had entered the Morisco fortress with a few other men by way of an underground passage he had discovered, the "mine" *(mina)* through which the rebels supplied themselves with water. In the resulting scuffle he had managed to capture five "Turks" found among the rebellious false converts, and these he had ceremoniously handed over to don John of Austria, Philip II's half-brother and overall leader of the Alpujarras "punishment." Pleased with these efforts, don John had the foreign prisoners executed, as per royal edict, and promised rewards to compensate the bloodied ensign. But whereas the king's half-brother would go on to greater things, taking scores of genuine Turkish galleys at Lepanto in 1571, the deeply scarred Alonso Merlo would fade to obscurity and poverty. As Captain Suazo later testified in Antequera, Merlo was so badly wounded in one arm and one leg he had to be evacuated to the nearby town of Baza prior to formal recognition. Merlo was not listed among the many heroes and casualties of La Galera in former Barbary captive Luis del Marmol Carvajal's riveting eyewitness account, *Rebelión y castigo de los moriscos del Reino de Granada* (1600; Malaga: Editorial Arguval, 1991), 215–20. The "mine" he entered is described on p. 216.

19. AGI Quito 23:22, 23-vii-1588.

20. The prominence of metal items in these gift lists should not be read as a sign of absolute dependency; Cabello Balboa claimed that Alonso de Yllescas had introduced the forge to the indigenes of Esmeraldas (c. 1550s), and he noted the use of bellows made from the "tanned hides of wild pigs" ("Verdadera descripción," 15). Given the frequency of shipwrecks in the region, salvageable iron for points and other items must have been at least occasionally available.

21. Szászdi, "El Trasfondo de un cuadro," 126.

22. AGI Quito 25:36, 25-v-1600. His petition for the title "Captain of Infantry," though supported by the Peruvian viceroy, was turned down by the Council of the Indies.

23. Their petitions for compensation are in AGI Quito 25:38, 10-vii-1600, and 25:39, 2-ix-1600, respectively.

24. AGI Quito 25:39, 2-ix-1600, f.3v. Evidence of Espinosa's return to Esmeraldas comes from a 24 February 1590 letter from Quito Mercedarian Juan de Salas (AGI Quito 77), repr. in Joel L. Monroy, *El convento de la Merced en Quito, 1534–1617* (Quito: Escuela Tipográfica Salesiana, 1931), 47.

25. Richard Hawkins, *Observations of Sir Richard Hawkins, Knight, or Voyage into the South Sea* (1622; New York: Da Capo Press, 1968), 124. Four years before Hawkins's visit, Juan de Salas (see n. 24) claimed that "if the English should come this way and commandeer this port [San Mateo Bay], it would do great harm to all this land." The friar went on to note that the Afro-Esmeraldeños had inquired about these English, giving rise to a suspicion that the foreigners had already made contact, perhaps with the "lost" Trinitarian, Alonso de Espinosa.

26. AGI Quito 25:4, 3-iii-1598. Dr. Barrio revealed a kind of "domino-theory" strategy, encouraging conversion of indigenous groups abutting the highlands first, then moving downstream. He hoped, for example, to use the converted cacique of Lita, on the upper Mira River, as an entrée into the Cayapas heartland. On the difficulties of locating these maroon neighbors with precision, see Warren R. DeBoer, "Returning to Pueblo Viejo: History and Archaeology of the Chachi (Ecuador)," in *Archaeology in the Lowland American Tropics: Current Analytical Methods and Recent Applications,* ed. Peter W. Stahl (Cambridge: Cambridge University Press, 1995), 243–62.

27. ANHQ Real Hacienda, caja 36, bound libramientos, f.21.

28. Ibid., f.21v.

29. Ibid., f.28v.

30. AGI Quito 25:45, 4:10–11.

31. AGI Quito 25:45, 5:3.

32. AGI Quito 25:45, 4:5.

33. AGI Quito 25:45, 4:16, 2-xii-1600.

34. New evidence regarding this enigmatic culture is emerging; see, e.g., Warren R. DeBoer, *Traces Behind the Esmeraldas Shore: Prehistory of the Santiago-Cayapas Region, Ecuador* (Tuscaloosa: University of Alabama Press, 1996).

35. Szászdi, "El Trasfondo de un cuadro," 142.

36. ANHQ Fondo Especial, caja 1, vol. 1, no. 15. Hincapié claimed that Yllescas had been very ill.

CHAPTER 2

An earlier version of this chapter appeared as "Captivity and Redemption: Aspects of Slave Life in Early Colonial Quito and Popayán," *The Americas* 57:2 (October 2000): 225–46.

1. ANHQ PN 1:6 DLM, 19-vii-1594, ff.24–28v. See also ANHQ PN 6:9 RDO pt.2, c.30-x-1598, f.812–15, will of Ysabel de Hermosilla, widow of Martín de Pino de Oro. Hermosilla left wealth to various church organizations and some items to indigenous and apparently mixed-heritage servants, including meal grinding stones and empty wine and olive jugs, but her slave María Bran, whom she had purchased for five hundred pesos "current silver" (see n. 40), was to be sold to fund a chaplaincy for the master's benefit. A codicil for Ynés de Alarcón (ANHQ PN 1:6 DLM, 19-iv-1596, f.397) asked that her two slaves, twenty-two-year-old Ysabel Biafara and twenty-year-old Antonio Bañol, be sold to fund a *capellanía*. Similar is the June 1600 bequest of Ysabel de la Torre, whose husband had been missing for some time; she summed up her situation as follows: "at this conjuncture I find myself with [nothing but] 650 pesos current silver or a bit less, proceeds of the black Juliana [Angola] and her children [five-year-old Nicolás and one-year-old Francisca], whom I sold . . . because I had nothing else to hand to remedy my want." Upon her death de la Torre charged a Dominican prelate "to say, as soon as possible, as many masses for my soul as the remaining silver pesos allow" *(tantas misas, quantos pesos)* (ANHQ PN 1:12 ADV, ff.689, 708). In 1601 Lucía Pimentel, wife of an Italian painter living in Quito, pledged proceeds from a slave sale for masses (ANHQ PN 1:18 FGD, f.521). On the mechanics of chaplaincies in contemporary Spain, see William A. Christian, *Local Religion in Sixteenth-century Spain* (Princeton, N.J.: Princeton University Press, 1981), 107; and Carlos Eire, *From Madrid to Purgatory: The Art and Craft of Dying in Sixteenth-Century Spain* (Cambridge: Cambridge University Press, 1995), 200–209. On the formation of early modern conceptions of Purgatory and economy generally, I have consulted Jacques Le Goff, *The Birth of Purgatory* (Chicago: University of Chicago Press, 1984), and *Your Money or Your Life: Economy and Religion in the Middle Ages* (New York: Zone/MIT, 1988). For very recent work in a similar vein for colonial Latin America, see Nancy E. van Deusen, "The 'Alienated' Body: Slaves and *Castas* in the Hospital de San Bartolomé in Lima, 1680–1700," *The Americas* 56:1 (July 1999): 1–30.

2. A Mercedarian friar in Quito in early 1601 hoped to trade his recalcitrant Angolan slave for another, "for his service, given that he is an elderly and ill clergyman in need of someone to serve and accompany *(acompañar)* him" (ANHQ PN 1:17 ALM, 28-v-1601, f.301v).

3. See, for example, AGI Quito 20b, 3:25, 1557 letter from Puná Island cacique "don Diego [Tomalá]" to Indies Council, and 22:16, 14-xii-1568 letter from Latacunga cacique don Sancho de Velasco to Council requesting rents, a coat-of-arms, and "dos negros con espadas andando con su persona."

4. Fragmentary Protocols in the Archivo Central del Cauca (hereafter cited as ACC) for the years 1583–1605 record sale of ten slaves in Almaguer and forty-five in Popayán. The Almaguer sales included two couples with children and two single men. In Popayán sixteen women and twenty-two men changed hands, along with six girls and four boys. Only one enslaved African couple is mentioned, but a bill of sale for "black slave" Martín de Trejo notes he was "married to an Indian named Lucía"; he was said to have "gone maroon for a time." ACC Notarías 1:1 23-x-1590, f.3 (immediately following bound Almaguer record).

5. In 1592 Popayán's Dominican brothers sought to trade Juan Criollo for "a black woman" *(una negra)*, saying they preferred a female touch in "washing the clothes and preparing the food" of the monastery. ACC Notarías 1:1 14-x-1592, ff.319v, 321. Frederick Bowser, in *The African Slave in Colonial Peru, 1524–1650* (Stanford, Calif.: Stanford University Press, 1974), Appendix B, records sale of c. 1,300 slaves in Lima, 1580–1600, with the percentage of women sold over the longer term (1560–1650, total 6,890 individuals) approaching 40 percent. It should be noted that the city of Quito was not a port of entry like Lima/Callao, but rather a final, interior destination; slaves entered the kingdom via Guayaquil and the northern and southern highlands, and many never reached the administrative capital. Some 300 "blacks" were said to be working in Popayán gold mines by c. 1560, and 1573 and 1576 *relaciónes* of Quito suggest a population of only c. 100 slaves in the city (of c. 300 householders), along with several hundred free mulattos and "zambaigos." Quito's slave population c. 1600 was probably more than twice this number, especially considering the fact that by 1604 a Guayaquil census recorded, in a city of only 152 householders, an enslaved population of 333 (sex ratio c. 1.85:1 [216 men to 117 women]), and only 20 free people of color (7 men, 13 women; see interlude 6). Here the high number of men reflected the thriving port city's demand for stevedores, lumberjacks, shipbuilders, sailors, polemen, and so forth. See Ponce Leiva, *RHGQ,* 1: 56, 221, 262, 264; 2: 16.

6. There are occasional hints of more specific origins: one "Congo" slave was called Francisco Catacamango (ACC PN 1:2 10-xii-1603, f.867), and three "Angolas" were listed as Pedro Maquango and Pedro and Antón Malembo (ANHQ PN 1:16 ALM, 19-v-1600, ff.55v–58). I have generally followed John Thornton's list of ethnic categories, in *Africa and Africans in the Making of the Atlantic World, 1400–1680* (Cambridge: Cambridge University Press, 1992), xvi, 184–92.

7. A few 1603 Popayán sales substitute "chontal" for *bozal,* an apparent reference to the supposedly uncouth habits of the Chontal Maya of isthmian Mexico; see, for example, "vendo por negros chontales sacados de Guinea" (ACC Notarías 1:2, ff.790v, 792, 793v).

8. ANHQ PN 6:10 DRD, 10-ii-1601, f.108v ("tiene una señal que es una 'A' en el brazo derecho").

9. ANHQ PN 1:1 DLM, ff.5, 386, 426, 433; 1:3 DLM, ff.56v, 101v, 158v; 1:9 GA, ff.109v, 87v, 230v, 540v; 5:1 JBM, ff.1124v, 1300; 6:5 DRO, f.603; 6:6 DRO, f.85v. By the early eighteenth century one even finds descriptions like "black, the color of a slave" *(negro color esclavo)* (ANHQ Fondo Especial, doc. 1226, f.170 [Guayaquil, 1740]).

10. ANHQ PN 1:5, DBL, 20-vii-1593, f.4.

11. ANHQ PN 1:4, DBL, 14-ix-1596, f.571v.

12. ACC Notarías 1:2 25-x-1605, f.339 (the only real difference is the widow's renunciation of her heirs' rights to "the captivity of the said Diego"); ANHQ PN 1:18 FGD 8-ii-1601, f.79. A Quito man freed Lima-born Catalina in 1601 citing "good and loyal services"; her age is not given, but she had spent most of her life raising the man and serving his recently deceased mother. As per the mother's wish, Catalina was freed upon her death (ANHQ PN 1:18 FGD, 1-iii-1601, f.111).

13. ANHQ PN 1:1, DLM, 3-xii-1585, f.316; 1:13 ADV 15-viii-1600, ff.446, 468, 933.

14. ANHQ PN 1:5, DBL, 29-iii-1596, f.380. Closer examination suggests a less optimistic appraisal, as the Dominicans disputed ownership of the properties and furnishings were minimal (a bed, two chairs, and a couple of empty chests). La Paz seems to have spent most of her income freeing her daughters, Juliana and Agustina.

15. ANHQ PN 1:13 ADV 24-x-1600, f.1082.

16. ANHQ PN 1:5, DBL, 20-v-1595, f.124v. Another free mule skinner, Francisco de Palacios, borrowed over three hundred pesos in cash from a merchant to pay off other debts and maintain his mule train (ANHQ PN 1:5, DBL, 23-xi-1595, f.230, and f.331, 20-ii-1596). Juan Çagas worked the Popayán road, charging ten pesos per mule load of "Chinese cloth" (ANHQ PN 1:18 FGD, 22-iii-1601, f.196v). Slaves worked these routes as well (see, for example, ANHQ PN 1:15 DLM, 24-ix-1602, f.499), and some were purchased along with mules and merchandise for the long journey to Potosí, where they were sold (see, for example, ANHQ PN 1:13 ADV, 10-x-1600, f.1018; 1:19 FGD, 1-ix-1601, f.666v.).

17. ANHQ PN 1:16 ALM 8-xi-1600, f.308 (said the merchant-lender: "to redeem himself of the vexation and annoyance of prison he wishes to repay me"); ANHQ PN 1:2 DLM, 16-ix-1586, f.1435v. I suggest Larrea's wife was indigenous since the skirt *(anaco)* was an indigenous-style garment from Quijós Province, in the Oriente, but women of African descent also wore such garments. Esteban Rodríguez, "moreno libre" of Popayán, signed for forty gold pesos' worth of textiles and knick-knacks in 1592 (ACC Notarías 1:1 27-xi-1592, f.368). Likewise "moreno horro" Sebastián García, who signed for fifty-eight pesos' worth of fine accouterments, including lengths of brown broadcloth, velvet, taffeta, and silk, along with a hat and a bit of musk (ACC Notarías 1:1, 4-i-1593, f.388).

18. Jorge Garcés G., *Libros de Cabildo de Quito,* 9 vols. 1573–1574. (Quito: Archivo Municipal, 1934), (3-vi-1573), 4:42. Ruth Pike, in "Sevillian Society in the Sixteenth

Century: Slaves and Freedmen," *Hispanic American Historical Review* 47:3 (August 1967): 344–59, noted the case of a mulatto slave making the rounds in Seville in 1598 with his master, the *almotacén* of the meat market (349).

19. ANHQ PN 1:4 DBL 16-xi-1596, f.614, and Archivo Municipal de Quito, Miscelánea #93, "tierras de Carangue," f.13. Hernández also testified on behalf of a rent-seeking Cayambe cacique, don Gerónimo de Puento; see AGI Quito 23:5, 26-iv-1586, f.24v. Another propertied "brown" Quiteño was Pedro Ramón, called a "householder and resident" *(vecino y morador)* in his will (ANHQ PN 6:6 DRD, 27-i-1597, ff.65–66v). Ramón was dying of wounds apparently suffered in the course of a dispute, but he appears to have been as strong-willed a character as Hernández. Pedro Ramón was a parishioner of the Santa Bárbara barrio, but asked to be buried in the Chapel of the Kings, "in the Great Church, where I am a brother." He owned a house and estancia near the village of Quinche, northeast of Quito, along with seven mares, two studs, and a saddle with full tack; he left these things, along with two iron bars and a sword he was still paying for, to his wife and four children. Ramón was married to an indigenous woman named Francisca Començaña, and he himself may have been Afro-Amerindian, son of "brown Juan," farrier, and "Ysabel." Like other propertied Quiteños, he claimed to have enjoyed the services of indigenous mita workers on his farm—and he owed them back pay on the eve of his death.

20. ANHQ Real Hacienda, caja 37, vol. 2 (1593 alcabalas), f.102v. Villorin apparently had to pay these taxes, since "indios" were exempted by law. Another person of color, Julian Larrea, "color moreno," was said to owe alcabalas for selling a solar in the Barrio San Blas (135v). Bowser, in *African Slave in Colonial Peru,* notes numerous cases of free women of color operating retail stalls and inns in early Lima and Cuzco (106–9). As in Quito, vendors of African descent, despite their obvious enterprising spirit, were frequently penalized by discriminatory legislation.

21. ANHQ PN 1:6 DLM & MA, 8-i-1596, f.329. See also the *concierto* between Quito householder Melchor Villegas and Miguel Sánchez, "moreno horro," involving oversight of mita farm laborers and care of four hundred swine; payment would consist of one-fifth of annual herd growth (PN 6:5 DRD, 12-xii-1596, f.623). A more vague service agreement appears in the case of a twenty-year-old mulatto named Francisco, who signed on with Joaquín de San Román (as squire?) for one year at twenty pesos current silver (ANHQ PN 6:4 DRD, 2-iv-1596, f.133v.).

22. I follow Bowser's interpretation of this bizarre phrase (*African Slave in Colonial Peru,* 84). Bowser credits Fernando Ortiz with deciphering it in Spanish. ANHQ PN 1:3 DLM, ff. 807, 852; 1:5 DBL, f.53; 1:6 DLM, f.146v; 1:9 GA, f.361v; 5:1 JBM, f.1285v; 6:6 DRD, f.221v; 6:9 RDO, f.529. When Francisco Cobó of Buga sold "Pablo Criollo, native of Cape Verde" in 1601, a Quito scribe revealed his discomfort with the lie, or at least confusion, writing: "abido en buena guerra," crossing it out and replacing it with "buena paz" (i.e., "just peace"), then crossing that out to write again "buena guerra" (ANHQ PN 6:10 DRD, f.604).

23. ANHQ PN 1:1 DLM, ff.56, 410; 1:3 DLM, f.169v; 1:6 DLM, ff. 146v, 191; 5:1 JBM, f.1112; 6:5 DRO, f.494; 6:6 DRD, ff.359v, 392; 6:7 DRD, f.931; 6:8 DRD, ff.171, 376; 6:9 RDO, f.921; 6:10 DRD, f.151. By way of contrast, mules, the most valuable livestock traded in contemporary Quito, tended to be described lovingly in bills of sale; for example, as "a mule, bay in color, aged four years more or less, healthy and without defect or illness" (ANHQ PN 1:17 24-x-1601, f.659v.); "a fat, black riding mule, with bridle, feet healthy *(sana de pies y manos)*, and without a single vicious habit *(resabio)*" (ANHQ PN 1:16 ALM 27-ix-1600, f.280v.); or, of thirty-two carrying mules sold in Popayán: "tame and healthy, with no sicknesses or wounds" (ACC Notarías 1:2 9-ix-1605, f.291).

24. ANHQ PN 1:16 ALM 3-vi-1600, f.99v.

25. ANHQ PN 1:9 GA, ff.361, 817v, 6:6 DRD, f.173v; 6:7 DRD, f.612. In 1605 the nuns of Popayán's Encarnación convent were forced to refund the buyer of the slave "don Diego" when it was discovered that he had "been ill for more than a year with an obstruction and tumor in the stomach" (ACC Notarías 1:2 9-v-1605, f.142v). Cuenca-born Andrés, twenty-two, was said to suffer from "epilepsy and a bad heart" (ANHQ PN 1:16 ALM 13-v-1600, f.90v); María Angola, twenty, was said to have fully recovered from "an ulcer in her mouth" (ANHQ PN 6:10 DRD 9-v-1601, f.392v).

26. ANHQ PN 1:3 DLM, f.257; 1:6 DLM, ff.434, 582; 1:9 GA, f.448v; 5:1 JBM, f.154; 6:5 DRO, f.603; 6:6 DRD, f.221. The term *cimarrón* was applied to cattle, for example, ACC Notarías 1:2, f.829 (24-x-1603).

27. ANHQ PN 1:14 DBL 14-i-1600, f.71v.

28. ANHQ PN 1:15 DLM 29-x-1600, f.280. In this case the couple forced sale to live united, but others were not so lucky (see, for example, ibid., f.394).

29. ANHQ PN 1:13 ADV, ff.851v, 866v, 1121v. Twenty-year-old Francisco Angola was sold in leg irons in early 1600 for similar reasons; he was traded for four hundred pesos and a book (ANHQ PN 1:14 DBL, f.51v). On cicatrisation in later New Granada, see James F. King, "Descriptive Data on Negro Slaves in Spanish Importation Records and Bills of Sale," *Journal of Negro History* 28 (1943): 204–30.

30. ANHQ PN 1:13 ADV 14-ix-1600, f.960v. Like many chronic runaways, Hernando's person was described in detail in this power of attorney authorizing his capture: "he has a lame finger on one hand and is missing several upper and lower teeth in the front; he is very tall and has a thick beard."

31. ANHQ PN 1:10 FGD & DBL, 16-iii-1598, f.254.

32. AGI Quito 76, no. 31 (24-i-1580), f.5, mentioned in letter of Bishop Peña to Council.

33. ACC Notarías 1:1 23-x-1592, ff.326v, 378v; ANHQ PN 1:13 25-x-1600, f.1084. Ynés had been given two hundred lashes and faced four years in exile.

34. Maroons had holed up in a site called Matarredonda, on the upper Patía, north of Pasto by 1590, however. See AGI Quito 24:36 (8-iv-1596), Captain Juan de Mideros of Almaguer to Indies Council.

35. For contemporary price trends on the Gulf Coast of New Spain, see Patrick J. Carroll, *Blacks in Colonial Veracruz: Race, Ethnicity, and Regional Development* (Austin: University of Texas Press, 1991), 34–36. For highland New Spain, see Colin A. Palmer, *Slaves of the White God: Blacks in Mexico, 1570–1650* (Cambridge, Mass.: Harvard University Press, 1976), 34–35.

36. ANHQ PN 1:5 DBL, 3-x-1594, f.40v, *carta de libertad* for "negra" Victoria Andrada, apparent self-purchase for 650 pesos current silver. Slaves used by a husband to replace his wife's (spent) dowry in 1604 Popayán were similarly overvalued, prices in 20-k gold pesos (for example, Juana Bran, appraised at 400 gold pesos, would probably have sold for c. 300 pesos if offered on the open market); ACC Notarías 1:3, 11-ix-1604, f.990.

37. ANHQ PN 6:3 SH, 7-xii-1587, f.172. In early 1596 a wheat estancia near Alangasí, including tools, oxen, and threshing horses, sold for 300 pesos current silver, about the price of an adolescent slave (ANHQ PN 1:6 DLM, f.335). By way of contrast, a placer gold claim traded for only 150 pesos low-karat gold dust in 1603 Popayán, a reminder that labor was everything in this industry; ACC Notarías 1:2, 29-x-1603, f.840v (the "mine" was a patch of ground 30-x-60 *varas* at the base of the "cerro de minas de Chisquío").

38. ANHQ PN 1:6 DLM, 20-viii-1597, f.536; and 1:16 ALM, 5-v-1600, f.41.

39. ANHQ PN 1:4 DBL, 17-viii-1596, ff.523–23v. Pedro de Atienza for Gil de Billarubia, cancelled 5-vii-1597.

40. ANHQ PN 5:1 JBM, 7-ii-1600, f.52v. The *peso de plata corriente* was worth 340 *maravedis,* or 10 *reales;* the "piece of eight," or *tostón,* was worth 272 maravedis.

41. ANHQ PN 1:11, 9-i-1600, ff.9v–11v.

42. ANHQ PN 1:17 ALM, 16-ii-1601, f.91v.

43. For example, ANHQ PN 1:1 DLM, 31-xii-1582, f.5. Here Juan Caro *(presbítero)* sent two gold disks worth 111 pesos fine gold with Quito merchant Juan Núñez to purchase a "negro o negra" aged five to twelve in Tierra Firme (i.e., Panama City or Nombre de Diós).

44. ANHQ PN 6:2 SH, 23-vii-1583, ff.991–91v. In reverse cases, slaves became currency, as in the 1583 swap of "nine bars assayed silver and a black" for a half-share in "a vessel named the San Juan," carrying merchandise between Panama and Lima (ANHQ PN 6:2 SH, 27-vii-1583, ff.994v–95).

45. ANHQ PN 1:17 ALM, 8-vi-1601, f.310v.

46. ANHQ PN 6:2 SH, 19-viii-1583, f.1130v; 1:12 ADV, ff.435, 656; ACC Notarías 1:1,

16-xii-1592, f.373. Francisco Adán was being traded for merchandise by Popayán Corregidor de Naturales Miguel Fonte, who had just purchased him (f.337) for 170 pesos from Juan Albarrán of Buga; the wide price disparity suggests an attempt to influence this important political figure. See also ANHQ PN 1:11 ADV, 19-ii-1600, f.221v, where Juan Criollo (35) was traded for 506 pesos' worth of cloth from a local textile mill. On another occasion an entire slave family was traded for sugar in Popayán; ACC Notarías 1:2, 10-x-1603, f.812.

47. ANHQ PN 1:20 FLM, f.37, and see, for example, a Popayán "escritura de empeño" in which two slaves were pledged to secure 579 gold pesos; ACC Notarías 1:1, 14-vii-1592 (see also ACC Notarías 1:2, 19-vi-1603, f.736v.); ANHQ PN 1:15 DLM, 6-ii-1602, f.449. Note also a repossession/auction in ANHQ PN 6:10 DRD, 15-v-1601, f.420v.

48. *Libros de Cabildos Quito II* (10-vi-1551), 2: 412.

49. ANHQ PN 1:6 DLM & MA, 10-vi-1596, f.428v, and 28-iii-1596, f.354v.

50. ANHQ PN 1:13 ADV, 17-x-1600, ff.1058v-62v; 1:14 DBL, 24-x-1600, ff.260v, 263, 264v.

51. ANHQ PN 1:12 ADV, 16-vi-1600, f.665; 1:17 ALM, 12-ix-1601, f.509v., 1:18 FGD, 9-vi-1601, f.411v. (by contrast, a forty-year-old ethnic Wolof named Lorenzo sold for only two hundred pesos, a reflection of both age and fighting spirit—he was not only a chronic fugitive, but had also gotten himself four years exile for beating an indigenous fellow; (ANHQ PN 1:20, 22-iii-1601, ff.74-77v.). See also the sale of a skilled slave by farrier Sebastián Carrasco, ANHQ PN 1:16 ALM, 7-xi-1600, f.336.

52. ANHQ PN 1:13 ADV, 3-1-1601, f.1374. Audiencia attorney Dr. Pineda de Zurita had perhaps similar hopes of skill-enhancement when he placed two enslaved men and one woman in his newly opened frieze factory in December 1600; similar were the area's several enslaved sugar makers. ANHQ PN 1:16 ALM, 9-12-1600, f.344. See also mention of the slave-staffed obraje of Hernando Cevallos c. 1608 (Fernando Jurado N., "Algunas reflexiones sobre la tenencia de los esclavos en la colonia: 1536–1826," *Boletín del Archivo Nacional*, no. 22 [Quito: Sistema Nacional de Archivos, 1992], 96). These cases contradict J. L. Phelan's bold but groundless claim that: "Neither Negroes nor mestizos worked in the obrajes of Quito" (*Kingdom of Quito in the Seventeenth Century*, 72.) Slave labor was common in the obrajes of contemporary Mexico; see Palmer, *Slaves of the White God*, 73–74.

53. ANHQ PN 6:10 DRD, 2-viii-1601, f.615v. As a reminder that such contracts still resembled captivity, Soto would receive the first salary installment only after six months' work (the clothes came up front). He also had to promise to "serve [the master] and do all that he mandates and orders"; backing out at any time would be punished with a one-hundred-peso fine.

54. ANHQ PN 1:14 DBL, 9-ix-1600, f.233v.

55. ANHQ PN 1:5 DBL 3-x-1595, f.192.

56. ANHQ PN 1:9 GA 23-iii-1599, f.645. Another such agreement is found in ANHQ PN 6:7, vol. II, DRD, 10-vii-1597, f.486, where two native Angolan slaves, Juan and Manuel, were to learn shoemaking in two years from Sebastián Suárez. Their master, Diego de Molina Sotomayor, would pay for food and clothing, but the slaves would lodge with the shoemaker and carry out unspecified tasks *(tareas)*.

57. ACC Notarías 1:1, 4-v-1592, f.117v.

58. ANHQ PN 6:1 AN, 11-iv-1581, f.34v. Other apprenticeship agreements in these years involved adolescent native Andeans and mestizos, often charged with vagabondage and petty theft, ordered by the city council to learn a trade as part of a criminal sentence.

59. Evidence of similar penetration of the contemporary New Spain market is in Carroll, *Blacks in Colonial Veracruz,* 30–31.

60. For example, ANHQ PN 6:2 SH, 6-ix-1583, f.1016; here Martín Hederr of the southern gold camp of Zaruma disputed the loss of seventeen slaves to an unscrupulous factor, Tomás de Vergara. Vergara was said to have traded some of the slaves for a sailing vessel, which he then took to New Spain. Hederr (a German?) purchased other slaves in Quito with gold ingots about the same time (PN 6:2 SH, 13-ix-1583, f.264v [marked '267']). ANHQ PN 1:1 DLM, 27-vi-1585, f.311v, notes the sale in Quito of fourteen-year-old Cristóbal Criollo, formerly of the gold mining cuadrilla of Captain Díaz Sánchez de Narváez in the Patía River Valley (between Pasto and Popayán), for 410 pesos current silver (other slaves had apparently been traded for gold dust in Pasto).

61. Ponce Leiva, *RHGQ* 1: 530. Arias Pacheco claimed that this type of payment in installments had not proved feasible in placer districts, which yielded less gold ("minas de oro corrido que se lava con las bateas y no son de tanto aumento").

62. Peter Bakewell, *Miners of the Red Mountain: Indian Labor in Potosí, 1545–1650* (Albuquerque: University of New Mexico Press, 1984), 191–93. Bakewell describes Spanish attitudes toward Africans in the south-central Andean context, but does little to question these prejudiced views about race and supposed climate suitability. The same sort of solutions to indigenous labor problems proposed in Quito and Popayán were considered in the late sixteenth century, but as in the cases of Zaruma and Zamora, Africans never came to constitute more than a supplementary workforce. Most slaves were engaged in refining and, in the case of Potosí, minting tasks. On sixteenth-century conceptions of high-altitude physiology in Peru, see Thayne Ford, "Stranger in a Strange Land: José de Acosta's Scientific Realizations in Sixteenth-century Peru," *Sixteenth-Century Journal* 29:1 (spring 1998): 19–33. A widely distributed Spanish treatise on innate human characteristics and the effects of climate more generally was the physician Juan Huarte's 1575 *Examen de ingenios para las ciencias* (altered after Inquisition censure in 1584).

63. Ponce Leiva, *RHGQ* 1: 550 (relación of Pedro González de Mendoza). Despite legal restraints, African men did marry native women in gold-mining zones in these years, for example, "a black slave named Juan married to an Indian woman," mentioned in a dowry inventory from the far southern gold camp of Santa María de Nieva in 1584 (ANHQ PN 1:1 DLM, 18-xii-1584, f.296). A single female slave named María served the same household.

64. Ponce Leiva, *RHGQ* 1: 567–68.

65. Numerous such petitions flowed from the pens of Popayán governors and elite citizens; see, for example, AGI Quito 16. A fragment of Almaguer's notary Protocols notes mixed native/African work gangs circa 1583; ACC Notarías 1:1, 8-ix-1583, f.22v ("mi quadrilla de yndios y esclavos").

66. Ponce Leiva, *RHGQ* 1: 518–26. "Tomás Moro" is cited on p. 524. More's idea of utopia was rather authoritarian for modern tastes, and slavery was a prominent institution in his imagined community. Unlike European slavery in More's time, however, utopian slavery was not an inherited condition and did not involve massive importation from other lands, but rather relied on war captives and criminals, such as adulterers. See Thomas More, *Utopia* (1516; Cambridge: Cambridge University Press, 1980), 80–83. Even more curious is that unlike Auncibay's Popayán, gold was scorned in Utopia and reduced to common uses, like the manufacture of chamber pots and, incredibly, the fetters and chains of slaves (62–63). Bowser, in *African Slave in Colonial Peru*, 13–25, describes a number of similar proposals put forth by Peru's viceroys before Toledo's implementation of the mita system in the mid-1570s. As in Quito, none of these grand plans came to fruition due to the crown's unwillingness to directly subsidize the slave trade.

67. Auncibay's own ideas of what constituted "civilization" are not fully articulated, but Ortiz de la Tabla notes that he was known for his frequent denunciations of Quito's encomenderos as "more merchants than gentlemen." He himself was denounced by others as a philanderer and father of illegitimate children by both indigenous and slave mistresses. See Javier Ortiz de la Tabla Ducasse, *Los Encomenderos de Quito, 1534–1660: orígen y evolución de una élite colonial* (Sevilla: EEHA, 1993), 135, 165.

68. Ponce Leiva, *RHGQ* 1: 521.

69. Ibid., 523–24.

70. Ibid., 526. The Quito Cabildo established punishment codes for African slaves as early as the 1540s: Spanish masters were fined if their slaves were discovered living in indigenous villages, caciques were fined and then jailed for retaining runaways as servants, and the slaves themselves were subject first to one hundred lashes, then to loss of all toes on the right foot, and finally death upon a third offense (in José Rumazo González, ed., *Libro Segundo de Cabildos de Quito*, 2 vols. [Quito: Archivo Municipal, 1934], 2:18). Runaways were a continuing concern, and in January 1551 the cabildo mandated that any runaway slave captured after more than eight days'

absence would be punished corporally. Women would be given one hundred lashes and men would have their "genital members and testicles cut off." For simply being found in the native marketplace *(tianguez)*, black men and women were to be given one hundred lashes at the post. For carrying a sword while not in the company of the master, enslaved men were to be given fifty lashes. Most tellingly, the cabildo banned relationships between African men and indigenous women, saying that "it does great harm to the natives that black men lie with *(se echen con)* Indian women." It was ordered that any indigenous woman known to have had sexual relations with an African slave be tied to the public pillory, given one hundred lashes, and further humiliated by having her head shorn *(la trasquilan);* the man would suffer the loss of his genitals (ibid, 2:387). Evidence that such punishments were in fact carried out comes from the governor of the southernmost gold districts, Juan de Salinas Loyola. In 1572 he claimed that Spanish masters controlled their African slaves with lashes, but also punished marronage and other crimes *(delitos)* with genital mutilation: "The most effective punishment for them, in order to domesticate them, has been to cut off the genital member." Quoted in Alfonso Anda Aguirre, *Indios y negros bajo el dominio español en Loja* (Quito: Abya-Yala, 1993), 259.

71. For context on Sandoval, see A. J. R. Russell-Wood, "Iberian Expansion and the Issue of Black Slavery," *American Historical Review* 83:1 (February 1978): 16–42. For a discussion of early Mexican critics of the slave trade, see Palmer, *Slaves of the White God,* 168–70.

72. See Peter Marzahl, *Town in the Empire: Government, Politics, and Society in Seventeenth Century Popayán* (Austin: University of Texas Press, 1978), 45. Enriqueta Vila Vilar, in "La sublevación de Portugal y la trata de negros," *Ibero-Amerikanische Archiv,* N.F. Jahrgang 2, Heft 3 (1976): 171–92, notes that a mid-seventeenth-century estimate of slave populations in Spanish South America counted only 5,000 slaves in Popayán and some 6,500 in the rest of highland Quito. Slaves were only identified as gold miners in the Popayán case, however, referred to as "negros de batea," or "black panners" (176). More than 21,000 other "negros de batea" were said to be working in other parts of northern New Granada (mostly Antioquia, it seems) at this time. Quito was said to "consume" 250 slaves per year and Popayán 200. The accuracy of these estimates is not well known due to a lack of census data for comparison, but Vila Vilar suggests they offer a good general guide in terms of scale.

73. For a brief description of this scandal see Marzahl, *Town in the Empire,* 143–46.

74. ANHQ Religiosos, caja 1, 16-x-1613, f.5 ("de los quales sirven de sacar oro en las dichas minas treynta y tres bateas"). This phenomenon of referring to workers as tools is also noted in the colonial sugar industry of northeastern Brazil. Stuart B. Schwartz mentions the use of the term *fouce* (scythe) to refer to a male-female cane cutting-and-binding pair; see his "Plantations and Peripheries," in *Colonial Brazil,* ed. Leslie Bethell (Cambridge: Cambridge University Press, 1987), 77.

75. Marzahl, *Town in the Empire,* 24, gives production figures for the crown-administered gold mines of Chisquío, just west of Popayán, between 1618 and 1631. The Chisquío mines, worked by about twenty-one native Americans held in encomienda, reportedly produced about 20 pesos of gold per week, or 1,040 pesos per year, again a relatively small sum. In terms of individual productivity, the 50 or so pesos per year produced by each indigenous miner at Chisquío was roughly comparable to the approximately 40 pesos produced by a slave of the Encarnación cuadrilla. Variations in work schedules, weather, or ore quality (or the honesty of the overseer) could easily account for the difference, but both operations were exceptional in their corporate ownership. The Chisquío mines were owned by the crown and supplied with crown-controlled encomienda labor; the only overhead costs were tools and a food-and-clothing ration for the indigenous workers, and a stipend to the mine administrator.

76. ANHQ Religiosos, caja 1, 16-x-1613, ff.5–6. The censo income was listed as 819 pesos of 20-k gold per year. The market value of the slaves probably exceeded 15,000 20-k gold pesos (estimating 300 pesos per slave).

77. Ibid., f.5.

78. Some of these slaves may in fact have been part of a 1592 grant from Popayán's second Bishop (Marzahl, *Town in the Empire,* 13), but see, for example, ANHQ PN 6:5, 22-viii-1596, f.426v, where Quito apothecary Pero Hernández donated a nine-year-old *mulata* named Magdalena to serve his daughter, Ynés, professing at the city's Conceptionist convent (cf. 1:13 ADV, 22-ix-1600, ff.965, 1266). In 1601 General Francisco de Cevallos donated twenty-five-year-old Catalina Angola and her two children to a young female cousin "as dotal goods, with which she may take estate *(tomar estado)* in matrimony or religion" (ANHQ PN 1:17 ALM, 21-ii-1601, f.94v). Also in 1601 nuns entering Quito's Santa Clara convent brought slaves, which were then sold by the nunnery's administrator to raise cash to lend at interest (ANHQ PN 6:10 DRD, ff.501v, 570). At the wish of nun Juana de Santa Clara (a.k.a. Juana de la Cueva) slave Francisco Nadu (Nalú), sold at discount to Quito's crown accountant, was promised freedom upon her death, whenever it may occur, presumably for the unburdening of her conscience.

CHAPTER 3

1. Immediately prior to his execution Atawallpa was said to have wept for his children in faraway Quito as he struggled to describe them by signs; see Hemming, *Conquest of the Incas,* 78.

2. ANHQ PN 6:10 DRD, ff.85v–99v, and Tamara Estupiñán, "Testamento de don Francisco Atagualpa," *Miscelánea Histórica Ecuatoriana* 1:1 (1988): 9–67 (the key property, called Cumbayá, lay just northeast of Quito). Using a c. 1582 padrón for San Sebastián parish, Salomon, in *Native Lords of Quito,* 168–72, suggests that the prince had until his death maintained something like an imperial court made up of regional lords and numerous wives.

3. ANHQ PN 1:12 ADV, 16-vi-1600, ff.665–76v. Xi had been captured while running along the banks of the Narváez River, but his ten years' enslavement would begin on the date of sale in Quito. He had been trying to aid a nine-year-old boy named Honenio in escaping an attack on a place the Spanish called "Slaughterhouse Hill."

4. Adam Szászdi, *Don Diego Tomalá, Cacique de la Isla de la Puná: Un Caso de Aculturación Socioeconómico* (Guayaquil: Museo del Banco Central, 1988).

5. See, for example, Cristóbal Landázuri, *Los curacazgos prehispánicos: agricultura y comercio, Siglo XVI* (Quito: IOA/Banco Central del Ecuador, 1982); and Udo Oberem, *Don Sancho Hacho: un cacique mayor del Siglo XVI* (Quito: Abya-Yala, 1993).

6. Salomon, *Native Lords of Quito*, 125.

7. Oberem, *Don Sancho Hacho*, and Karen Vieira Powers, *Andean Journeys: Migration, Ethnogenesis, and State in Colonial Quito* (Albuquerque: University of New Mexico Press, 1995); Powers, "A Battle of Wills: Inventing Chiefly Legitimacy in the Colonial North Andes," in *Dead Giveaways: Indigenous Testaments of Colonial Mesoamerica and the Andes*, ed. Susan Kellogg and Matthew Restall (Salt Lake City: University of Utah Press, 1998), 183–213; Powers, "The Battle for Bodies and Souls in the Colonial North Andes: Intraecclesiastical Struggles and the Politics of Migration," *Hispanic American Historical Review* 75:1 (February 1995): 31–56; and Powers, "Resilient Lords and Indian Vagabonds: Wealth, Migration, and Reproductive Transformation of Quito's Chiefdoms," *Ethnohistory* 38 (1991): 225–49. Joanne Rappaport has done similar work in a more ethnographic vein in the case of the Tierradentro Páez and Cumbal Pasto caciques of modern Colombia (though within the sixteenth-century Audiencia of Quito); see *The Politics of Memory: Native Historical Interpretation in the Colombian Andes* (Cambridge: Cambridge University Press, 1990), and *Cumbe Reborn: An Andean Ethnography of History* (Chicago: University of Chicago Press, 1994).

8. The cacique's wishes were dictated in Quechua, but unfortunately for modern philologists verbally translated to Spanish for the benefit of the scribe. Chantal Caillavet, "Ethno-histoire écuatorienne: un testament indien inédit du XVIe siècle," *Caravelle* 41 (1983): 5–23. See also Salomon's commentary, *Native Lords of Quito*, 124–25.

9. The rules were not always consistent in this regard, but generally *hijos naturales* were children born of potentially suitable marriage partners (i.e., women of the lordly class) and *bastardos* of servants or slaves.

10. On llautu in seventeenth-century Cuzco, see Dean, *Inka Bodies and the Body of Christ*, 129–30.

11. The same practice is mentioned in the wills of Quito Spaniards, for example, ANHQ PN 1:17 ALM, 4-xii-1601, f.558 ("ofrendas" for the funeral of Toledo-born Diego Suárez Pacheco, in the San Francisco compound, were to include six "wax hatchets,"

twenty-four candles, six sheep, and two jugs of wine) and a mestiza, Ysabel de Hermosilla, ANHQ PN 1:17 ALM, 30-vii-1601, f.567 (ofrenda of bread, wine, sheep, and maize). For comparable practices in Spain, see Fernando Martínez Gil, *Muerte y sociedad en la España de los Austrias* (Madrid: Siglo XXI, 1993), 429–32.

12. A copy of the will, transcribed from the notary books housed in Ecuador's Central Bank Archive, is reprinted in Landázuri, *Los curacazgos prehispánicos,* 206–15.

13. The many problems of conversion in a similarly multilingual, early colonial context have been explored in depth by Vicente Rafael, *Contracting Colonialism: Translation and Christian Conversion in Tagalog Society under Spanish Rule* (Ithaca, N.Y.: Cornell University Press, 1988).

14. Lockhart, *Of Things of The Indies: Essays Old and New in Early Latin American History* (Stanford, Calif.: Stanford University Press, 1999), 98–119.

15. ANHQ PN 6:9 DRD, ff.750–52. Apparently her husband had accompanied a merchant to Guayaquil with a sack of pesos and was not seen again (Cañar's only named heir was an orphan boy she was raising; she was also a *cofrada* in the Chapel of the Virgin of the Remedies). Many of these wills were examined by Frank Salomon in "Indian Women of Early Colonial Quito as Seen through Their Testaments," *The Americas* 44 (1988): 325–41, but he makes little reference to the trading activity implied by debt inventories. Salomon suggests fabrics said to be from "Huancavelica" were in fact from "Huancavilca," near Guayaquil. Though quite probable, this remains to be proved, since spelling in the Protocols is generally consistent with the former, highland Peruvian site (an exception is mention of "una pieza de ropa de Guangavilca de Guayaquil la liquida labrada con seda" in the will of a Pasto-born indigenous woman [ANHQ PN 6:10 DRD, 10-iii-1601,f.100], and "vestidos de Guayaquil" in ANHQ PN 1:17 ALM, 21-viii-1601). More famous for its mercury, Huancavelica does indeed seem an unlikely regional cloth exporter, but given contemporary imports of Guánuco woolens and Arequipa wines, and the tendency of Spanish merchants to shuffle unsaleable bundles of merchandise over great distances, the possibility cannot be ruled out. Salomon also appears to have been unaware that silks and other items designated "de la china" really were from China. For a more detailed examination of Quito's market women in the seventeenth century, see Kimberly Gauderman, "Women Playing the System: Social, Economic, and Legal Aspects of Women's Lives in Seventeenth-Century Quito" (Ph.D. diss., University of California, Los Angeles, 1998), 173–251. On the value of textiles in Inka times, see John V. Murra, "Cloth and its Function in the Inka State," in *Cloth and the Human Experience,* ed. Annette Weiner and Jane Schneider (Washington, D.C.: Smithsonian Institution Press, 1989), 275–302.

16. ANHQ PN 1:8 FGD, ff.847v–49. The document is unclear as to how these items were to be liquidated upon her death. Perhaps the market for such things is represented by women like Juana de Torres, a mestiza who filed a will in mid-1596;

she would leave behind one new Huancavelica outfit, two more embroidered ones from Quijós, and a silver topo. These were to be sold to fund masses for her soul "whom I name as heiress," but older clothes and blankets were donated to a poor indigenous woman named Luisa, and indigenous-style jewelry to her priest (ANHQ Notaría 6:5 DRD, f.328).

17. ANHQ PN 1:10 DBL, f.724v.

18. AGI Quito 76:50, 8-v-1597. On similar efforts of Andean women to block or avoid the one-two punch of racism/sexism in contemporary urban Peru, see Elinor C. Burkett, "Indian Women and White Society: The Case of Sixteenth-Century Peru," in *Latin American Women: Historical Perspectives,* ed. Asunción Lavrin (Westport, Conn.: Greenwood Press, 1978), 101–28.

19. ANHQ PN 1:3 DLM, ff.126v–29v.

20. She may also have owned an enslaved African woman; see ANHQ PN 1:3 DLM, f.238 (widow named María Rodríguez sells María Criolla, thirty, single, born in Quito, for five hundred pesos *plata corriente* to Juan Méndez, 30-xi-1591).

21. ANHQ PN 1:4 DBL, ff.515v–16. Salomon provides a closer analysis of Amores's legacy; see his "Indian Women," 334–35.

22. ANHQ PN 6:5 DRD, ff.497v–99.

23. ANHQ PN 1:6 DBL, f.588v.

24. ANHQ PN 6:6 DRD, ff.84v–86.

25. Indigenous men also must have engaged in trade in greater Quito, especially the famed *mindaláes* described in various contexts by Frank Salomon, but their tracks are scarce in surviving records. One such indigenous male Quiteño linked to pre-Columbian merchant families seems to have moved into the arts by 1581. Juan Pacima, "silversmith and *mindalá,*" perhaps continued to trade in some way, but the land deal in which his name appears fell through (ANHQ PN 6:1 AN, f.157). Another indigenous silversmith and Quito native, Juan Masaña, sold an urban solar to Elvira Carguaviche for fifty pesos in April 1596, evidence at least of successful male participation in the city's intra-indigenous real estate market (ANHQ PN 6:4 DRD, f.135v). The 1598 will of "Alonso," a native barber-surgeon, revealed, along with a small amount of land, livestock, and clothing—and of course the tools of his trade, lancets and basins—a variety of small debts owed him by various persons. These debts seem to have been for merchandise, but Alonso was also owed seven years' back pay (now over two hundred pesos) for service to the Dominican monastery. He hoped his brother, Juan Agualongo, would see that all these matters were settled for the benefit of his wife, Beatriz Tulisichig, and their four children (ANHQ PN 6:8 DRD, ff.231–32v; cf 1:4 DBL, f.459 [1596 will of indigenous zapatero Pedro Caxas]). In spite of the loans, in this case there is no indication of mindalá heritage or connections.

26. ANHQ Criminales, caja 1 (8-iii-1589) one large folio.

27. Galley service in the Mediterranean was akin to a death sentence, but this was hardly the case in the context of the sixteenth-century Pacific.

28. Newson, *Life and Death in Early Colonial Ecuador,* 293.

29. Encomendero Diego de Alvarado claimed: "I rented the Indians of [my encomienda of] Pizavaro to the said [neighboring encomendero] Martín de Larraínzar to harvest wheat and maize and mine gold from the year 1599 to the last, 1603, for the price of the wheat, maize, and gold [collected]" (ACC Notarías 1:2, 11-iii-1604, f.916).

30. The classic study is Ortiz de la Tabla Ducasse, *Los encomenderos de Quito.*

31. Aquiles R. Pérez T., *Las Mitas en la Real Audiencia de Quito* (1947; Guayaquil: Universidad de Guayaquil, 1987).

32. Newson, *Life and Death in Early Colonial Ecuador,* 191.

33. ANHQ Real Caja 37, v.3, f.311v. Newson, *Life and Death in Early Colonial Ecuador,* 192, notes that mitayo wages were officially raised to about twenty reales, or about two and a half silver pesos per month in 1591.

34. ANHQ PN 1:7 FGD, f.178; company agreement between merchant Diego de León Cieza, on behalf of the San Diego convent, and Antonio de la Mulla, operating the kiln for his mother, Leonor de Mateos. Leonor de Mateos would receive half the lime produced as rightful owner (to be disposed of as she desired), the company the other half as reward for mustering mitayos.

35. See also AGI Quito 22:17 (1-viii-1579), in which the caciques of Tuza, Guaca, and Tulcan petitioned for an end to mita service in Quito. In this case "ordinary" mita service required long-term resettlement and many dangerous river crossings. Officials and encomenderos with agricultural interests in Cuenca and Loja actively shielded their charges from crown mita service in Zaruma as early as the 1580s. See AGI Quito 22: 45 (28-i-1584), f.30v.

36. ANHQ PN 1:18 FGD (1601), ff.407, 441v, 823v (1:19).

37. ACC Notarías 1:1, ff.71v–79v, 115v–127v, 220–222v, 270v, 312–313v, 339v. For similar agreements in Quito, see, for example, ANHQ PN 1:17 ALM (1601), ff.105v, 136v. Compensation for these indigenous men working for Quito tailors and gilders (10 to 12 silver pesos per year) fell well below that promised in Popayán. A Chimbo native renting himself to Quito Vicar General Jorge Ramírez Arellano received only 3 silver pesos and a papal indulgence, but was also promised "good treatment," food, and medicine (ibid., f.150v). Later, an indigenous couple from Cartago joined Ramírez's retinue for 30 pesos per year (ibid., f.621v). By contrast, the same vicar paid a native Spaniard 120 pesos per year to serve as squire (ibid., f.170). Skilled indigenous workers could make much more than the average indenture: in 1600 a Quito

shoemaker hired Juan Destradillo for 50 silver pesos per year plus board (ANHQ PN 1:14 DBL, f.172.) Women also participated, as when an indigenous Pastuza exchanged her labor with Leonor Rodríguez of Quito for two suits of local cloth, a papal indulgence, board, and the promise of medical care (ANHQ PN 1:14 DBL, 24-iv-1600, f.104v). By far the most unusual indenture agreement in Quito around this time was that of Juan Chino, "of the Chinese nation" (de nación chino), who signed for two and a half years service with two Spaniards to clear 104 pesos' worth of debts (ANHQ PN 1:20 FLM, 8-i-1603, f.6). To my knowledge, Juan was the only East Asian living in Quito at this time. Elinor Burkett discusses similar agreements in contemporary Arequipa in "Indian Women," 111.

38. Karen V. Powers, "Land Concentration and Environmental Degradation: Town Council Records on Deforestation in Uyumbicho," in *Colonial Lives: Documents on Colonial Latin American History, 1550–1850,* ed. Richard Boyer and Geoffrey Spurling (New York: Oxford University Press, 2000): 11–17. Salomon, *Native Lords of Quito,* 48–51, discusses pre-Hispanic highland resource management using Uyumbicho as the core example. See also Newson's summary of land-grabbing in the Quito basin to c. 1600 in *Life and Death in Early Colonial Ecuador,* 181–84.

39. Salomon, *Native Lords of Quito,* 54.

40. AGI Quito 25:18 (31-iii-1599).

41. Salomon, *Native Lords of Quito,* 150, 170. I substitute "surplus" for "tribute" following John V. Murra's many and influential studies on the topic, most recently in "Did Tribute and Markets Prevail in the Andes before the European Invasion?" in *Ethnicity, Markets, and Migration: At the Crossroads of History and Anthropology,* ed. Brooke Larson and Olivia Harris (Durham, N.C.: Duke University Press, 1995), 57–72.

42. Salomon, *Native Lords of Quito,* 160–63.

43. Ibid., 181.

44. Newson, *Life and Death in Early Colonial Ecuador,* 4–5.

45. Luis Fernando Calero, *Chiefdoms under Siege: Spain's Rule and Native Adaptation in the Southern Colombian Andes, 1535–1700* (Albuquerque: University of New Mexico Press, 1997), 88–89.

46. AGI Quito 16, no. 8 (3-xi-1564), f.1.

47. AGI Quito 24: 2 (30-iv-1593), f.11v.

48. Copies of cédulas and related documents are in ANHQ PN 1:12 ADV, 16-vi-1600, ff.665–76v.

49. ANHQ PN 1:13 ADV, 17-x-1600, ff.1058v–1062v; 1369v; 16-ii-1601, f.89v.

50. See, for example, the sale in Popayán of "the service of a Pijao Indian slave for a term of ten years" for 60 pesos current gold dust (ACC Notarías 1:2, 24-i-1604, f.892).

This document also provides an unusually detailed physical description of the unbaptized slave, a young man named Diuhu (no age given): "he is of medium build, round-faced, missing one tooth in the lower jaw, with a scar above the right eyebrow and another next to the right ear." In 1601 María Pijagua, an eighteen-year-old Pijao woman, was rented to a Quito leather-worker for thirteen years at a cost of 150 pesos (ANHQ PN 1:12 ADV, f.304v).

51. ANHQ PN 1:13 ADV, f.957v.

52. AGI Quito 26:55 (14-iv-1606).

53. This failed mission is summarized by Hemming, *Conquest of the Incas,* 457–58.

CHAPTER 4

1. Chants, or *anent,* selected from Philippe Descola, *The Spears of Twilight: Life and Death in the Amazon Jungle,* trans. Janet Lloyd (New York: New Press, 1996), 392, 399. "Hollow spears" is a reference to modern firearms, *emesak* the vengeful dead soul of an enemy, and *natem* an hallucinogenic effusion made from the bark of *Banisteriopsis* vines.

2. Michael J. Harner, *The Jívaro: People of the Sacred Waterfalls* (1972; Berkeley: University of California Press, 1984), 1. Harner wrote to correct some of the errors of Rafael Karsten's monumental *Head-Hunters of Western Amazonas: The Life and Culture of the Jíbaro Indians of Eastern Ecuador and Peru* (Helsinki: Societas Scientiarum Fennica, 1935).

3. Juan de Velasco, *Historia Moderna del Reyno de Quito y Crónica de la Provincia de la Compañía de Jesús del mismo Reyno,* tomo I: 1550–1685 (1790; Quito: Reyes y Reyes, 1940).

4. Harner, *Jívaro,* 21. The "gold-down-the-throat" story continues to be repeated unquestioningly by other ethnographers; see, for example, Clayton and Carole Robarchek, *Waorani: The Contexts of Violence and War* (Fort Worth, Tex.: Harcourt Brace, 1998), 85. Mention of this grisly sort of "payback" does, interestingly enough, predate Velasco. See Jorge Juan and Antonio Ulloa, *Discourse and Political Reflections on the Kingdoms of Peru,* ed. John J. Te Paske and trans. with Besse Clement (Norman: University of Oklahoma Press, 1978), 110–11.

5. Harner, *Jívaro,* 26.

6. Salomon, *Native Lords of Quito,* 97–106. The La Tolita smiths made utilitarian fishhooks from gold-copper alloy.

7. Adam Szászdi, "Preliminary Estimate of Gold and Silver Production in America, 1501–1610," in *Precious Metals in the Age of Expansion,* ed. Hermann Kellenbenz, Papers of the Fourteenth International Congress of Historical Sciences, San Francisco, CA (Stuttgart: Klett-Cotta, 1981), 151–223, also summarizes these records. His calculation

of total production for the period (p. 177) is slightly lower, at 105,222 pesos, 6 tomines.

8. See, for example, Marshall Saville, *The Gold Treasure of Sigsig, Ecuador* (New York: Heye Foundation, 1924).

9. José María Vargas, *La economía política del Ecuador durante la Colonia,* 2d ed. (1957; Quito: Banco Central, 1980), 187–94.

10. Georgius Agricola, *De re Metallica,* trans. Herbert Hoover (1556; New York: Dover, 1950), 157.

11. Pedro de Cieza de León, *The Discovery and Conquest of Peru,* ed. and trans. A. P. and N. D. Cook (Durham, N.C.: Duke University Press, 1998), 268–70. Ponce Leiva, *RHGQ* 1:238. Note also that Quito's *libros de fundición* are missing for precisely these years (1542–47), which also coincide with the Peruvian Civil War. The Italian merchant Girolamo Benzoni seems to have visited the mines of Santa Bárbara around 1547–50, but gave no details. See his *La historia del Nuevo Mundo* (c. 1570; Guayaquil: Banco Central, 1985), 123.

12. As late as 1600 gold dust produced by encomienda workers in Santa Bárbara was brought to Quito's royal smeltery (ANHQ Real Hacienda, caja 37). See also geographer Theodor Wolf's reconnaissance of the area in *Viajes Científicos por la Republica del Ecuador,* 3 vols. (Guayaquil: Imprenta del Comercio, 1879), 2:21–26, 51–52.

13. Zaruma was about a week's travel by land and sea from Guayaquil. "Oro de Zaruma" appears in Quito's smeltery records for the first time in 1557 (ANHQ Real Hacienda, caja 37, f.163). Chantal Caillavet, in "Los mecanismos económicos de una sociedad minera: intercambios y crédito, Loja: 1550–1630," *Revista Ecuatoriana de Historia Económica,* 2:3 (1988), 21, has also noted this date. Previous authors had followed Federico González Suárez, who gave the founding of Zaruma as 1560 (*Historia General de la República del Ecuador,* 12 vols. [Quito: Daniel Cadena, 1931], 3:437).

14. Blackpowder blasting does not seem to have been used in the Audiencia of Quito before the late eighteenth century despite the existence of a large factory at Latacunga (see ANHQ Minas, caja 4, 26-ii-1795). Such mines were referred to as *desmontes* (literally, "clearings") in Zaruma, and in 1592, they prevailed over underground works, or *minas de socavón.* See Ponce Leiva, *RHGQ* 1:492. An anonymous relación of 1592 described primitive hydraulicking at Zaruma, especially during the wet months between December and March. Ponce Leiva, *RHGQ* 1:498.

15. Ponce Leiva, *RHGQ,* 1:492, "haciendo ciertas albercas y soltando el agua se llevo la tierra que alla le llaman desmonte y queda el metal el cual se muele con ingenios y con azogue se benefician." (Diego de Ortegón)

16. Ibid., 1:516 (1592 relación of Fr. Gerónimo de Éscobar). Zaruma's sulphide ores are found in extensive veins 0.5 m to c. 2 m thick. See H. Putzer's summary of Zaruma

district geology in Walther Sauer, *Geologie von Ecuador* (Berlin: Gebrüder Borntraeger, 1971), 272; Paul Billingsley, "Geology of the Zaruma Gold District of Ecuador," *Mining and Metallurgy* (Transactions of the American Institute of Mining and Metallurgical Engineers) 6:228 (December 1925): 615–18; and George Sheppard, *The Geology of South-Western Ecuador* (London: Thomas Murby, 1937), 195–97. Billingsley, "Geology of the Zaruma Gold District," 618, found that some mines in the district ran two to three ounces of silver per ounce of gold.

17. Encomendero Pedro González de Mendoza in Ponce Leiva, *RHGQ*, 1:546–47, 1592, "Las vetas, aunque a la superficie no son muy ricas, suelen dar en mucha riqueza, y mientras mas se ahondan, prometen a veces mas riqueza." This suggestion seems to be supported by the reconnaissance of irregular, lens-shaped oreshoots undertaken by Billingsley, in "Geology of the Zaruma Gold District," 617.

18. Ponce Leiva, *RHGQ* 1:495, my emphasis.

19. Galo Ramón, "Loja y Zaruma: Entre las minas y las mulas, 1557–1700," *Revista Ecuatoriana de Historia Económica* 7 (1990), 119.

20. Quito and Zaruma were linked by family ties, as in the case of Quito alderman Diego de Arcos and Rodrigo de Arcos, a Loja-based Zaruma mill owner. Apparently the latter used Quito connections to secure several cash loans in the late 1580s, mortgaging what must have been a substantial mill, since he claimed to have paid 5,500 pesos in gold for it (along with associated tools) some years earlier (ANHQ PN 6:3 SH, 10-xi-1587, f.77v, cf ff.4, 24). Two mills sold for 3,200 "silver" pesos in 1594 Zaruma, but they required 1,000 pesos' worth of repairs (ANHQ PN 1:5 DBL, 9-xii-1594, f.51v). In both cases the mills cost more than the largest landed estates sold in contemporary Quito.

21. Roberto Levillier, ed., *Gobernantes del Peru, Cartas y papeles, siglo XVI; documentos del Archivo de Indias*, 14 vols. (Madrid: Sucesores de Rivadeneyra, 1926), 6:181. According to one Spanish observer, milling at night was better than during the day, since "the water comes colder and heavier and gives more force as it hits the wheel." Ponce Leiva, *RHGQ*, 1:498.

22. Quito audiencia judge Francisco de Auncibay (the same man who proposed a slave utopia in chapter 2) claimed by 1592 that Zaruma's vein miners routinely "founded" gold with mercury (Ponce Leiva, *RHGQ*, 1:534: "se funde por asogue"). Lead cupellation and cementation, though known practices, are not mentioned in the records. One clever method of gold recovery mentioned in 1590s Zaruma seems to have been directly borrowed from a foreign manual. This was the catchment of milled fines in cloth strips *(paños, frazadas)*, described and illustrated by the sixteenth-century German metallurgist Georgius Agricola. It entailed the attachment of tilted, cloth-lined wooden channels of about 4–5 m length, like sluice boxes, to the stamp basin. Ground ore was scooped out from under the stamps and into the sloping channels, which ran with a thin stream of water diverted from the mill-wheel. Flowing water

carried off lighter waste material and the denser gold, even the tiniest of particles, remained snagged in the rough surface of the cloth. At the end of the day the cloths were carefully rolled and taken to a basin to be washed of their gold content (after several uses one could afford to burn them and collect gold from among the ashes). The water was then poured off from the basin and the gold collected and separated from the inevitable black sand, or iron oxide, with mercury. Ponce Leiva, *RHGQ*, 1:496. See illustration in Agricola, *De re Metallica*, 331.

23. See Levillier, *Gobernantes del Peru*, 6:181–83; and Caillavet, "Los mecanismos económicos de una sociedad minera," 19–62. In 1591 mine and mill owner Rodrigo de Arcos sent a direct request for sixty mitayos to the Indies Council in Madrid with Antonio Freile (ANHQ PN 1:3 DLM, f.207, 16-ii-1591). The workers were to come from the villages of Guachanama and Garrochamba.

24. See G. Ramón, "Loja y Zaruma," 111–43.

25. ANHQ PN 6:2 SH, 6-ix-1583, f.1016; and 6:2 SH, 13-ix-1583, f.264v (marked "267"). Martín Hederr ceded water rights worth five hundred pesos to Zaruma mill owner Alexo Martínez (ANHQ PN 6:2 SH, 31-vii-1583, f.1025v) "con las que yo beneficiava las minas que yo tenia en el dicho asiento de Çaruma."

26. Ramón, "Loja y Zaruma," 116; the others were native mitayos from Palta (140) and Cañar (100), taken from AGI Quito 27, f.16.

27. Slaves were still present in Zaruma after 1625, as an incident of slave theft by a rival dueño is mentioned in ANHQ Fondo Especial, caja 1, no. 66.

28. Anne Christine Taylor and Cristóbal Landázuri, eds., *Conquista de la Región Jívaro (1550–1650) relación documental* (Quito: Abya-Yala/IFEA/MARKA, 1994), 94.

29. Robert C. West, *Colonial Placer Mining in Colombia* (Baton Rouge: Louisiana State University Press, 1952). "Oro de Jelima" also appears in Popayán notary records and Quito smeltery ledgers in the 1590s.

30. ACC Notarías, t.1. See also Guido Barona, "Estructura de la producción de oro en las minas de la Real Corona: Chisquío (Cauca) en el Siglo XVII," *Anuario Colombiano de Historia Social y de la Cultura (ACHSC)* No. 11 (1983): 5–42.

31. The precise location of Matarredonda remains unknown. See AGI Quito 24:36 (8-iv-1596), Captain Juan de Mideros to Indies Council.

32. Gold from Almaguer appears in small quantities in Quito's 1601 smeltery ledgers (ANHQ Real Hacienda, caja 1 [11-ii-1601], f.12v).

33. West, *Colonial Placer Mining*, 14. See also Ponce Leiva, *RHGQ*, 1:26–29. This 1559 census listed 3,520 native Andean residents in Almaguer, 634 of whom were actively engaged in gold mining.

34. ACC Notarías, t.1.

35. Setting out from Quito in 1599, Padre Rafael Ferrer and fellow Jesuits established small missions among the Cofán, Omagua, and neighboring "infidel" groups, to be followed shortly after by Quito-based Franciscans. As in many other frontier districts of Spanish America, settlers would subsequently target rather than support these missions in their search for tributaries and gold mine laborers. See Newson, *Life and Death in Early Colonial Ecuador,* 325–30.

36. Velasco, *Historia Moderna,* 13–118. See also González Suárez, *Historia General de la República del Ecuador;* Pérez T., *Las Mitas en la Real Audiencia de Quito;* and Vargas, *La economía política del Ecuador.*

37. See Jaime Vicens Vives, *Economic History of Spain* (Princeton, N.J.: Princeton University Press, 1969), 323; and Earl J. Hamilton, *American Treasure and the Price Revolution in Spain, 1501–1650* (Cambridge, Mass.: Harvard University Press, 1934), 36–42.

38. Exceptionally penetrating studies in Jívaro ethnology include Philippe Descola's works on the Achuar of southeast Ecuador: *In the Society of Nature: A Native Ecology in Amazonia,* trans. N. Scott (Cambridge: Cambridge University Press, 1994); and *Spears of Twilight.* See also Pita Kelekna, "Achuara Trade: Counterpoise and Complement to War," in *Political Anthropology of Ecuador: Perspectives from Indigenous Cultures,* ed. Jeffrey Ehrenreich (Albany: Society for Latin American Anthropology/State University of New York, 1985), 217–56. On the Aguaruna, see Michael F. Brown, *Tsewa's Gift: Magic and Meaning in an Amazonian Society* (Washington, D.C.: Smithsonian Institution Press, 1985). The modern Shuar are discussed by Janet Wall Hendricks, *To Drink of Death: The Narrative of a Shuar Warrior* (Tucson: University of Arizona Press, 1993). Also indispensable is an understanding of neighboring lowland Quechua speakers, the Canelos Quichua. See the various studies by Norman and Dorothea Whitten, particularly his *Sacha Runa: Ethnicity and Adaptation of Ecuadorian Jungle Quichua* (Urbana: University of Illinois Press, 1976), and *Sicuanga Runa: The Other Side of Development in Amazonian Ecuador* (Urbana: University of Illinois, 1985).

39. Ponce Leiva, *RHGQ,* 1:99, 104. Mercadillo, who is also credited with founding Zaruma, was from the city of Zamora in north-central Spain.

40. Incredibly, the ill-fated Alonso de Sosa of Toledo makes a last appearance in the 1560s account books of Zamora's royal smeltery, dutifully paying taxes on gold; see Jorge Garcés, ed., *Las Minas de Zamora: Cuentas de la Real Hacienda, 1561–1565* (Quito: Archivo Municipal, 1957), 67.

41. Ibid., 101.

42. See Archivo Municipal de Quito (hereafter cited as AMQ) Miscelánea No. 104, Minas de Zamora, ff.125v–126.

43. An encomendero who visited the mines in 1556 or 1557 differed, claiming that "in the time of the Incas [these mines] were theirs, worked by them and for them, the

source, it is said, of most of the gold they carried and possessed." He went on to suggest that upon hearing of Spanish gold-lust at Cajamarca, native workers had sealed up the mines (Ponce Leiva, *RHGQ,* 1:549 [1592 relación of encomendero González de Mendoza]).

44. Alfonso Anda Aguirre, *Zamora de Quito y el oro de Nambija* (Loja: Casa de la Cultura Ecuatoriana, 1989), 53–60.

45. See 1580 testimonies of Zamora residents in Taylor and Landázuri, *Conquista de la región Jívaro,* 132.

46. Ibid., 13.

47. Ponce Leiva, *RHGQ,* 1:57. Governor Salinas said that Zamora's Spanish vecinos had originally numbered thirty-five, but that the dearth of native men available for encomienda service had caused a drop to "little more than twenty" (ibid., 104).

48. Ponce Leiva, *RHGQ,* 1:115. With few exceptions census-type records for the many other gold camps scattered across the Gobernación of Yaguarsongo have not survived, but the rate of demographic collapse was undoubtedly more rapid here than in the neighboring highlands. See, for example, the 1581 records for Loyola, Valladolid, Nieva, and Santiago de las Montañas transcribed by Taylor and Landázuri, *Conquista de la región Jívaro,* 157–81.

49. Taylor and Landázuri, *Conquista de la región Jívaro,* 114.

50. Newson, *Life and Death in Early Colonial Ecuador,* 295–96.

51. Biblioteca Nacional, Madrid (hereafter abbreviated as BN), ms. no. 3044, ff.330–34v.

52. Taylor and Landázuri, *Conquista de la región Jívaro,* 65–71. One of the men present at the town's founding was Martín Hederr (67), the Zaruma slave-owner and miner mentioned above.

53. See Stephen Minta, *Aguirre: The Re-creation of a Sixteenth-Century Journey across South America* (New York: Henry Holt, 1993).

54. AGI Quito 76, no. 31, f.6v., 24-i-1580. See also *Documentos Americanos del Archivo de Protocolos de Sevilla, Siglo XVI,* 3:325 (no. 1347); here Tomas Ricarte of Sanlúcar de Barrameda had testimony of military service in the colonies written down, 14-xi-1580. He claimed to have aided Vargas Escalona against Juan de Landa and other rebels in Macas, then later fought indigenous rebels on the Río San Juan, Popayán district, before returning to Spain. See also AGI Quito 24:8, Juan de Escobar, Escribano de Minas of Zaruma, 15-xii-1593, letter requesting confirmation of title. His only outstanding service was in Logroño during an uprising of "Jíbaro" and mestizos (no year given).

55. AGI Quito 22:52, 1584.

56. ANHQ PN 1:8 FGD, 11-v-1599, f.613; drapery for "el tumulo de las onras del rey nro senor."

57. Descola, *Spears of Twilight,* 223–29 and 378–83.

58. The documents are transcribed in Piedad and Alfredo Costales, eds., *Los Shuar en la historia: Sevilla de Oro y San Francisco de Borja* (Quito: Mundo Shuar, 1978), 15–79. Although this collection includes a town-council document from Sevilla de Oro dated 1608, the authors do not question Velasco's story (recall he claimed the town was abandoned by terrified survivors in 1599).

59. See, for example, Descola, *Spears of Twilight,* 175–78. The term is *uunt* among the Shuar; see Hendricks, *To Drink of Death,* 6.

60. See, for example, "Information from the city of Cuenca regarding the uprising of the Jíbaros, 1606," signed Martín de Ocampo, Corregidor of Cuenca, 12 April 1606 (in Taylor and Landázuri, *Conquista de la región Jívaro,* 295–96).

CHAPTER 5

1. Testimonies in AGI Quito 21, 1:67 (1569); 2:13 (9-iii-1572).

2. Garcés, *Las Minas de Zamora,* 298 ("Pedro de Arroba" in Zamora on behalf of Pedro de Ibarra, 1 April 1564).

3. Some of these bequests reflected peninsular norms and mandates; see Carlos Eire, *From Madrid to Purgatory,* 33, 251.

4. AGI Quito 22:24, 11-ii-1580 letter of Lic. Auncibay; 22:39, 1582 letter from Lic. Venegas de Cañaveral.

5. AGI Quito 22:55, 21-iii-1585 letter from fiscal Morales Tamayo.

6. AGI Quito 23:14, 28-i-1588. For another example, in early 1581 Alonso Maldonado de Chávez died intestate in Portoviejo after being struck in the head by a lateen-sail boom. His goods were auctioned by audiencia officials in Quito, and the resulting two-hundred-odd gold pesos sent to Lima merchants like Antonio de Yllescas to pay debts (ANHQ PN 6:1 AN, f.241).

7. See for example the miner testimonies collected in Zamora in 1580 in Taylor and Landázuri, *Conquista de la región Jívaro,* 121.

8. ANHQ PN 1:6 DLM, ff.618–19. Goods were ordinarily marked up c. 33 percent for retail, according to a 1596 bill of sale ("con el tercio más de los precios ordinarios" [ANHQ Notaría 1:7 FGD, f.428]). A thorough inventory of a merchant shop is in ANHQ PN 1:9 GA, 21-viii-1597, ff.340–48.

9. In 1596, for example, a self-described Spaniard visiting from Trujillo (Peru) signed for a variety of garments in Quito, but lamented "the cost of the adornment of my person" (ANHQ PN 6:4 DRD, f.42v). In October 1598 merchant Diego de León Cieza outfitted Quito's new corregidor, General Diego de Portugal, with all manner

of clothing, boots, tack, and bedding, noting tailoring fees and payment to "an Indian woman" for manufacture of a small valise (ANHQ PN 1:7 FGD, f.379).

10. ANHQ PN 1:9 GA, ff.244–56v. The fourteen-thousand-peso deal was sealed in part by a six-thousand-peso surety. The latter amount was given in silver, but to be paid back in gold "at eighty-three percent"; the debt was cancelled in October 1602 (ANHQ PN 1:9 GA, f.258v).

11. ANHQ PN 1:9 GA, f.508.

12. Ibid., ff.566–67v.

13. ANHQ PN 1:6 DLM, ff.678v–689v.

14. By the early seventeenth century merchant-bankers had emerged in the mining sectors of Mexico and Peru, called variously *rescatadores* and *mercaderes de plata*. See Louisa Schell Hoberman, *Mexico's Merchant Elite, 1590–1660: Silver, State, and Society* (Durham, N.C.: Duke University Press, 1991), 76–82; and Peter Bakewell, *Silver and Entrepreneurship in Seventeenth-Century Potosí: The Life and Times of Antonio López de Quiroga* (Albuquerque: University of New Mexico Press, 1988), 45–55. An overview of merchant types is James Lockhart's "The Merchants of Early Spanish America: Continuity and Change" (1994), repr. in his book *Of Things of the Indies*, 158–82.

15. Martín appears in twenty-eight wine sales in one notary's records for the year 1600 (moving c. 530 botijas peruleras of vino de la tierra). He was explicitly referred to as "mercader de vino," ANHQ PN 1:13 ADV, f.1329. For his appearances in smeltery ledgers, see, for example, ANHQ Real Hacienda, caja 37, *fundiciones* 1595–97, ff.9, 49, 58v, 76v, 82, 87. In the short period between mid-January and the first week of May the naturalized Fleming registered 2,862,372 maravedís' worth of Popayán gold dust, or almost 5,000 pesos of fine gold. See ANHQ Real Hacienda, caja 1, fundiciones 14-i-1601 to 5-v-1601. Some of this gold was said to come from Mocoa, east of Pasto. On a single day in February 1603 Cristóbal Martín quinted over 1,500 pesos' worth of gold dust from the northern mines, and one suspects there would have been much more had fuller records survived (ANHQ Real Hacienda, caja 1, fundición fragment 1603, f.8v). It is fairly certain that by this time Martín was engaged only in commerce, but one of his rare appearances in the Protocols from July 1583 hints at an early stab at mining. We do not know if anything came of the venture, but here a Quiteño named Francisco Paredes gave power of attorney to Cristóbal Martín and a certain Cristóbal López to stake mining claims in Cañaribamba on his behalf (ANHQ PN 6:2 SH, f.937).

16. Interest rates are notably absent in Quito's contemporary "consumer" sales records; rather, buyers obligated themselves to repay merchants in full within a set time-period, after which the total would double, triple, and so on, or pledged goods would be repossessed and auctioned. Timely cancellations are so rare as to suggest a great deal of quiet wrangling over repayment schedules in order to avoid full penalty. For similar arrangements in contemporary New Spain, see María del Pilar Martínez López-Cano,

El crédito largo plazo en el Siglo XVI, Ciudad de México, 1550–1620 (México, DF: UNAM, 1995).

17. He is identified as Quito's "banco y banquero" in AGI Quito 28, no. 4, f.23.

18. ANHQ PN 5:1 JBM, 9-viii-1600, ff.644–53; also included were four *Reportorios del Zamorano,* apparently referring to the popular almanac of Seville cosmographer Gerónimo Chávez. *Reportorios de Chávez* are explicitly noted in ANHQ PN 1:18 FGD 10-i-1601, f.24v.

19. ANHQ PN 6:10 DRD, 24-v-1601, ff.486v, 580; 1:13 ADV, 14-x-1600, ff.1050v, 1097–1104 (includes multiple copies of Fray Luis de Granada's popular *Manual de diversas oraciones y spirituales exercicios*); 1:17 ALM, 24-ix-1601, f.478; 1:14 DBL, 9-ii-1600, f.51v notes a book entitled *Cien tratados del almirante.*

20. On *cuerpos,* see Irving Leonard, 1949 *Books of the Brave* (New York: Gordian Press, 1964), 179.

21. Carlos Alberto González Sánchez, "La cultura del libro en el Virreinato del Perú en tiempos de Felipe II," *Colonial Latin American Review* 9:1 (June 2000): 63–80. See also his "Los libros de los españoles en el Virreinato del Peru, Siglos XVI y XVII," *Revista de Indias* 56/206 (1996): 7–48; and Teodoro Hampe M., *Bibliotecas privadas en el mundo colonial* (Frankfurt/Madrid:Vervuert/Iberoamericana, 1996).

22. ANHQ PN 1:13 ADV, 20-xii-1600, ff.1254v–56. Cotocollao governor don Juan Chuquicondor and alcalde Felipe Pillajo commissioned master organ-maker Francisco de la Chica, promising 350 pesos in community funds, 100 to be paid in the form of 225 loads of charcoal (after roofbeams the tribute item most responsible for Quito-area deforestation).Vihuela strings were imported from Germany (ANHQ PN 1:16 ALM, 6-vii-1600, f.143v.; the same document notes a ballad collection, the *Romancero de Maldonado,* f.144v.).

23. For a contract between sculptor Antonio Hernández and Quito Augustinians to make a *custodia,* or monstrance, following an imported drawing, see ANHQ PN 6:10 DRD, 21-vii-1601, ff.595v–97; see also ANHQ PN 1:18 FGD, 12-v-1601, f.322. Antonio Fernández was also commissioned by a merchant sodality to paint a "Cristo Ecce Homo" six palms high (6:10 DRD, 23-vi-1601, f.558). Medoro appears in ANHQ PN 1:18 FGD, 19-viii-1601, ff. 521–22, 533; and "maestre de danza" Antonio de los Ríos in ANHQ PN 1:15 DLM, 24-i-1601, f.301v. A sale between merchants notes, alongside chirimiyas, flutes, a clavichord, and ten large maps, "a large oil painting of San Diego," another large oil of "The Exile of Christ," and a third depicting "The Descent from the Cross." The high prices of these paintings (seventy pesos) suggest they were imported (ANHQ PN 1:16 ALM, 16-v-1600, f.88v).

24. Claros was said to have lost his estate at cards, dominoes, and other games, and now suffered "a burdened conscience and inquiet spirit." He swore before God, the cross, and a Quito notary that "from this day forward I shall desist from all forms of gaming

both inside and outside this city." Claros was fined five hundred gold pesos and made to purchase Holy Crusade indulgences; recidivism would result in a public declaration of infamy, exile to the Chilean Front, and prosecution by the Lima Inquisition (ANHQ PN 1:17 ALM, 27-xi-1601, f.700v). Cards sold for ten reales/pack, and were locally produced by monopoly holders like Juan de Herrera; his will is in ANHQ PN 1:13 ADV, 16-xi-1600, ff.1200v–03v.

25. Quito hospital administrator Lic. Damián de Mendieta received two hundred pesos annually for serving as city "physician, surgeon, and pharmacist" (ANHQ PN 1:18 FGD 16-iv-1601, f.267). About the same time "Dr. Meneses," also an audiencia judge, made rounds among at least eleven prominent Quito families, charging twenty to thirty pesos each per year (ANHQ PN 1:18 FGD, 13-vii-1601). A native surgeon cured the wounds of indigenous alcalde don Mateo Yopanque for six pesos in late 1601; he had been trampled by an audiencia secretary's horse (ANHQ PN 1:17 ALM, 17-xi-1601, f.679). In one of the stranger agreements to be recorded in Quito's Protocols, a stonemason named Alonso Muñoz promised to pay one hundred pesos to surgeon Gaspar López Ajurto within two months for the repair of his face. This may have been a pioneering act of cosmetic surgery, but more likely entailed the control of dangerously infected wounds sustained in a fight with a certain Quito couple López had offended (ANHQ PN 6:4 DRD, f.307v).

26. ANHQ PN 1:8 FGD, 11-v-1599, ff.613–14; and Eire, *From Madrid to Purgatory,* 293.

27. ANHQ PN 1:7 FGD, ff.202–3v. A concise and insightful discussion of these sorts of documents in contemporary Mexico is Asunción Lavrin's "*Lo Femenino:* Women in Colonial Historical Sources," in *Coded Encounters: Writing, Gender, and Ethnicity in Colonial Latin America,* eds. Francisco J. Cevallos-Candau, et al. (Amherst: University of Massachusetts Press, 1994), 165–68. See also Susan Socolow, *The Women of Colonial Latin America* (Cambridge: Cambridge University Press, 2000), 82–84, 95–96.

28. ANHQ PN 6:5 DRD, ff.575v–76.

29. ANHQ PN 6:5 DRD, ff.628–34v. (Note also 400 pesos worth of 6 "paños de corte de figuras del rey azuero.")

30. ANHQ PN 6:9 DRD, f.968.

31. ANHQ PN 6:6 DRD, ff.173–76v; see also ANHQ PN 6:4 DRD, ff.271–71v. Likewise Francisca de Talavera's 1600 dowry was made up mostly of a gold disk and a slave, María Bran, but also included furniture, household items, and clothing, along with a pearl choker and other jewelry. Presumably her husband-to-be, a Seville-born goldsmith, would enhance her person further (ANHQ PN 1:13 ADV, f.882v).

32. ANHQ Popayán, caja 1 (20-viii-1607).

33. ANHQ Real Hacienda caja 38, v.4, f.38v, lists "Alonso Martín Paladinés y su muger" of Almaguer among those paying the *composición de estrangeros,* 1599–1600. They paid

1,148 pesos of "oro en polvo de la dicha ciudad" for themselves and a certain Juan López, "Palatine."

34. AGI Quito 16:37 (20-iv-1610), my emphasis.

35. Ibid.

36. ACC Notarías, vols. 1–3.

37. ANHQ Real Hacienda, caja 34, vol. 1, f.104v. Benalcázar's booty registries of the 1530s (AGI Contaduría 1536) probably also originated in part in Popayán.

38. See, for example, the Zaruma *obligación* in ANHQ PN 1:7 FGD, 9-vii-1598, ff.458–67v.

39. Szászdi, "Preliminary Estimate of Gold and Silver Production in America," 183. Szászdi notes that remissions from the caja real of Cuenca for the years 1596, 1598, 1599, and 1601–3 may be found in AGI Contaduría 1468, 1469, 1470, and 1862.

40. ANHQ Real Hacienda 37, f.194v.

41. ANHQ Real Hacienda, caja 1, 5-i-1603, fragment of libro de fundición for 25-i to 22-ii, f.8.

42. "As early as 1594, Brittany sent nearly a million linen cloths to the West Indies, while in 1601 it was confessed in Rouen that 'linen cloths are the true gold and silver mines of this kingdom, because they are developed only to be transported to countries where gold and silver are obtained'" (Jane Schneider [with quotes from Peter Kriedte], "The Origins, the Agrarian Context, and the Conditions in the World Market," in *Industrialism before Industrialization,* ed. Peter Kriedte, Hans Medick, and Jürgen Schlumbohm [Cambridge: Cambridge University Press, 1981], 35). "Rumpelstiltskin's Bargain: Folklore and the Merchant Capitalist Intensification of Linen Manufacture in Early Modern Europe," in Weiner and Schneider, *Cloth and Human Experience,* 181–82.

43. ANHQ PN 1:8 FGD, ff.636–40v.

44. A Chisquío contract notes a forge located next to a mine entrance (ACC Notarías 1:2, 29-x-1603, f.840v).

45. ANHQ PN 6:1 AN, ff.334–36v.

46. Ibid., ff.183–84v. On the Philippine iron connection, see Woodrow Borah, *Early Colonial Trade and Navigation between Mexico and Peru,* Ibero-Americana No. 38 (Berkeley: University of California Press, 1954), 117–18. A description of the sort of cast-iron pots, nails, sheet metal, and such like brought to Manila on Chinese junks circa 1599 is found in future Quito Audiencia President Antonio de Morga's *Sucesos de las Islas Filipinas* (Mexico: 1609) published as *The Philippine Islands, Moluccas, Siam, Cambodia, Japan, and China at the Close of the Sixteenth Century,* ed. and trans. Henry Stanley (London: Hakluyt Society, 1869), 336–43.

47. ANHQ Real Hacienda 1 (fragment 2-xi-1584), f.144, Real Hacienda 37, ff.24v., 44v, 49, 58, 59.

48. ANHQ PN 1:18 FGD, 24-iii-1601, ff.212–13.

49. A 1600 composición de estrangeros in Popayán (ANHQ Real Hacienda 1, fragment 22-ii-1600) brought Quito roughly two thousand gold pesos and a small amount of silver.

50. Witnesses confirmed that Ribadeneira had participated in the 1557 defeat of the French at St. Quentin and various campaigns in the Netherlands. In the Indies, besides, he had served in the River Plate and claimed to have helped put down the tax rebels in Quito (AGI Quito 25:36, 25-v-1600).

51. AGI Quito 25:40, 9-xi-1600.

52. The term "aristocrat-entrepreneur" was coined by Steve J. Stern to define a class of individuals like Ribadeneira in the central Peruvian context; see *Peru's Indian Peoples and the Challenge of Spanish Conquest: Huamanga to 1640* (Madison: University of Wisconsin Press, 1982), 80.

53. ANHQ PN 1:6 DBL, ff.22–22v.

54. Ibid., f.509, 8-vii-1597.

55. Ibid., f.520, cf. f.613v, 14-ix-1598.

56. John C. Super, "Partnership and Profit in the Early Andean Trade: The Experience of Quito Merchants, 1580–1610," *Journal of Latin American Studies* 11:2 (November 1979): 265–81.

57. ANHQ PN 1:6 DBL, f.572.

58. ANHQ PN 1:6 DLM, f.624v.

59. Ibid., f.631v. See also ANHQ 1:7 FGD, 19-i-1599, ff.412–16 (contract for Latacunga obraje to produce similar colors, all at 2 pesos, 5 reales/vara); and ANHQ 1:2 DLM, 20-ii-1586, f.455v.

60. The only evidence I could find of attempts to produce luxury fabrics for the elite market in Quito is in ANHQ PN 1:9 GA, f.359v. Here a merchant, Sebastián Delgado, sold local customers about ten yards of a cochineal-dyed woolen, four yards of local, black paño, and a smaller amount of velvet "dyed here." The result was apparently less than satisfactory in the second case, and the cloth was discounted as flawed. On the other hand, Quito leather workers incorporated varicolored Chinese silk into saddles exported to Potosí (ANHQ PN 1:16 ALM, 11-vii-1600, f.148v).

61. ANHQ PN 1:8 FGD, ff.492–97v, 505.

62. Ibid., ff.764–67. For comparison, an obraje administrator's annual wage in 1583 was listed as 150 pesos (ANHQ PN 6:2 SH, f.996v), comparable to a large estancia

majordomo's pay in 1597 (130 pesos plus board, ANHQ PN 6:7 DRD, f.802v).

63. Powers, *Andean Journeys,* 111, citing a 1598 letter of Bishop López de Solis: "the corregidor's wife undertook every morning to assemble all the Indian women of the town in a corral . . . to spin cotton for the corregidor."

64. ANHQ PN 6:1 AN, 12-i-1581, ff.219v–20v; obligation for seven hundred pesos' worth of textiles from the Latacunga obraje of encomendero Rodrigo Núñez de Bonilla, including paños in blue/black, green, "fly's wing," brown, and "friaresque."

65. ANHQ PN 6:2 SH, ff.1288v–95v.

66. ANHQ PN 6:6 DRD, f.679.

67. ANHQ PN 1:8 FGD, f.498. See also ANHQ PN 6:1 AN, ff.51, 268; 6:6 DRD, f.435, 6:9 DRD, ff.521, 686v; 1:10 DBL, f.727.

68. ANHQ PN 1:11 ADV, f.61v.

69. ANHQ PN 1:9 GA, f.569v, 577.

70. ANHQ PN 1:6 DBL, f.314. Apparently Alarcón had come a long way since 1588, when an inventory listed only four hundred sheep, the Pelileo land, and a small wheat estancia in Chillogallo, not far from the capital (ANHQ PN 1:3 DLM, ff.43–46); she offered to leave twenty 'obejas de Castilla' each to "Beatriz yndia" and her two daughters "que tengo en mi servicio."

71. ANHQ PN 1:6 DBL, 16-xi-1595, f.317v. An April 1596 codicil suggests Ynés de Alarcón was near death, and though she left part of her remaining estate to a son, Baltásar Alarcón, two slaves were to be sold to found a chaplaincy in her name. One, twenty-year-old Antonio Bañol, lived and worked on the Patate estate; the other, twenty-two-year-old Ysabel Biafara, took care of doña Ynés in her house in Quito's San Marcos parish (ANHQ PN 1:6, DBL, f.397).

72. ANHQ PN 1:6 DLM, f.654v; see also the large-scale shoe and leather sale in ANHQ PN 6:7 DRD, f.875, late 1597.

73. ANHQ PN 1:10 DBL, f.477v; see also another sale of 1,000 pairs of shoes in 1599 1:10 DBL, f.749v.

74. ANHQ PN 1:10 DBL, f.693.

75. Ibid., ff.493v, 508v; ANHQ PN 1:10 DBL, f.742v.

76. In mid-1598, for example, Quito church canon García de Valencia used one thousand pesos' worth of gold and silver ingots "to employ in this city in *paño de la tierra,* saddles, reins, footwear, and other things" to be traded in Lima for wine. He expected a 30 percent return within four months (apparently not an unreasonable time-frame in the relatively dry summer season) (ANHQ PN 6:9 DRD, f.703).

77. ANHQ PN 6:1 AN, f.151.

78. Ica wine, at 11 pesos/botija, is explicitly mentioned in ANHQ PN 6:1 AN, 2-i-1582, f.195v; vino blanco de Castilla sold for 16 pesos/botija in a 1586 deal (ANHQ PN 1:2 DLM, f.467). Peter Bakewell, in *Miners of the Red Mountain,* 194, notes that a botija of Peru wine sold for about twelve pesos of eight reales in 1599 Potosí.

79. Ponce Leiva, *RHGQ,* 1:84, ANHQ PN 6:2 SH, f.910v.

80. ANHQ PN 1:1 DLM, ff.454v–455, 476v.

81. ANHQ PN 1:3 DLM, f.32v.

82. ANHQ PN 5:1 JBM, f.1.

83. ANHQ PN 1:3 DLM, ff.66, 102, 113, 118, 124v; 6:1 AN, f.288 (a 1581 obligation for ten jugs signed by the tanner Pedro García); 1:3 DLM, 28-xii-1589, f.145, vino de la tierra at 12 pesos/botija.

84. ANHQ PN 1:6 DLM, f.281.

85. ANHQ PN 5:1 JBM, f.425v.

86. ANHQ PN 1:5 DBL, f.168v.

CHAPTER 6

1. Translated by Nina Gerassi-Navarro in *Pirate Novels: Fictions of Nation Building in Spanish America* (Durham, N.C.: Duke University Press, 1999), 44. Castellanos, a Tunja-based priest, wrote the "Discourse" as part of his larger historical epic, *Elegías de varones ilustres de Indias* (Madrid, 1589). The title appears in a Quito merchant deal from January 1601, but the Drake portion was probably absent since it had been censored and excised by Inquisition authorities in 1591 (ANHQ PN 1:18 FGD 10-i-1601, f.24, and Gerassi-Navarro, *Pirate Novels,* 40).

2. AGI Quito 25:5, 4-iii-1598. A witness and fellow pirate-fighter, Diego López Fajardo, agreed that Carillo Espínola had been right out front, fighting "valiantly, and for his troubles [taking] a musketball that broke his right femur." The wound was bad enough, in fact, that most of his companions had expected him to die without leaving the island.

3. AGI Quito 24:24, 5-vii-1594.

4. AGI Quito 25:42, 20-ii-1601.

5. ANHQ PN 6:2 SH, 9-vii-1583, ff.51v–52v; 1-viii-1583, ff.1007v–8. Here two merchants sued to recover gold and silver confiscated from Oxenham by Panama officials. The date of attack is given as 12 March 1577 (f.1007v, see fig. 40, p. 196).

6. Harry Kelsey, *Sir Francis Drake: The Queen's Pirate* (New Haven, Conn.: Yale University Press, 1998), 155.

7. On his son's career, see Adam Szászdi, *D. Diego Tomalá, cacique de la Isla de la Puná: un*

caso de aculturación socioeconómica (Guayaquil: Museo Antropológico/Banco Central del Ecuador, 1988).

8. BN 3044, ff.462–62v, my translation.

9. Francis Pretty, "The admirable and prosperous voyage of the Worshipful Master Thomas Candish of Trimley . . . ," in Richard Hakluyt, *Principal Navigations of the English Nation,* multiple vols. (1600; New York: AMS Press, 1965) 11:312–18. See also David B. Quinn, ed., *The Last Voyage of Thomas Cavendish, 1591–92* (Chicago: University of Chicago Press, 1975).

10. AGI Quito 23:10, 15-x-1587.

11. AGI Quito 24:7, 10-xii-1593.

12. The encomienda remained in the family for four generations. See Ortiz de la Tabla, *Los encomenderos de Quito,* 253–57. Encomienda rents were used to purchase slaves, which in at least one case were donated to a Quito convent as dowry capital (ANHQ PN 6:10 DRD, 28-v-1601, ff.501v–506v).

13. AGI Quito 24:12, 15-iv-1592.

14. See also AGI Quito 25:30, 1599 letter from Catalina de Valer, widow of Diego de Arcos.

15. AGI Quito 23:32, 19-ix-1590.

16. The story is related firsthand in Hakluyt, *Principal Navigations,* 11:202–27; the bishop's *relación* is in BN 3044, ff.416–18.

17. AGI Quito 23:17, 15-iv-1588.

18. The argument over coastal defense strategy in the Dutch period is discussed at length by Phelan, *Kingdom of Quito in the Seventeenth Century,* chaps. 1 and 5.

19. Unlike participants in the early wars of conquest in the Andes, as noted by James Lockhart, these men were actually called *soldados,* or "soldiers," in contemporary records (despite equally uneven training and experience). See Lockhart's *Spanish Peru, 1532–1560: A Colonial Society,* 2d ed. (Madison: University of Wisconsin Press, 1994), 155.

20. Lavallé, *Quito y la crisis de la alcabala,* 91–114. See also Pilar Ponce Leiva's cogent analysis of these events in *Certezas ante incertidumbre: élite y cabildo de Quito en el Siglo XVII* (Quito: Abya-Yala, 1998), 77–105.

21. Around the turn of the seventeenth century Peruvian writer Felipe Guaman Poma de Ayala provided this caption for a sketch of Quito, which he had probably not visited: "Los caballeros y vecinos y soldados son gente rebelde como la ciudad de Trujillo, Cuzco, y Guamanga, como se alzaron por no servir ni pagar lo de la alcabala. . . . Envían y vienen jueces sobre ellos por sus pecados y rebeldes y poco servicio de Diós y la corona real de su Magestad. De como es notorio desde la fundación de la

dicha ciudad, siempre ha tenido sospecha y entre ellos no se quieren y no se aman. Siempre tienen pleito y mala justicia, asi españoles como indios y negros en la ciudad" (in *Primer nueva corónica y buen gobierno,* ed. John V. Murra and Rolena Adorno [Mexico, D.F.: Siglo XXI Editores, 1980], 923). Interestingly, Guaman Poma describes the city of Popayán in perfectly inverted (i.e., wholly positive) terms (ibid., 918).

22. AGI Quito 25:29, 15-xi-1599. Like Yaguarsongo's Governor Salinas, Martín García de Loyola was another of the Jesuit founder's ill-starred warrior-relatives.

23. ANHQ PN 1:8 FGD, 9-x-1599, ff.741, 807v.

24. ANHQ PN 1:10 DBL, 1-ix-1599, ff.720v–23.

25. I have relied on R. C. Padden's classic 1957 article, "Cultural Adaptation and Militant Autonomy among the Araucanians of Chile," repr. in *The Indian in Latin American History: Resistance, Resilience, and Acculturation,* ed. John E. Kicza, rev. ed. (Wilmington, Del.: Scholarly Resources, 2000), 71–91. See also Kristine Jones, "Warfare, Reorganization, and Readaptation at the Margins of Spanish Rule: The Southern Margin (1573–1882)," in *South America,* ed. Schwartz and Salomon, Part 2, 138–87.

26. AGI Quito 25:45, 8: 1.

27. See ANHQ Real Hacienda, caja 39, *libro de acuerdos,* ff.8v–10v. The Tulcanazas were said to have ceded property rights to the slaves—which they claimed under the "laws of war"—out of goodwill, but the recently rescued Sánchez de Cuellar immediately tried to seize them for himself. Since Sánchez de Cuellar could not produce written evidence to support his claim (lost in the wreck), Dr. Barrio rejected it and justified crown ownership under the law of "unclaimed goods" *(bienes mostrencos).*

28. AGI Quito 25:45, 8:6.

29. "Pi," or "bi," signifies "water," or "river" in the Awá, or Kwaiker language of this region, and "Pos" may be a corruption of "Puis" or "Pius," an indigenous group name from contemporary documents. The Puis were said to occupy the middle Patía; see Henri Lehmman, "Les Indiens Sindagua (Colombie)," *Journal de la Société des Américanistes* (Paris) 38 (1949): 67–89.

30. Ibid. For a discussion of anthropophagy in the greater Popayán region that included Barbacoas, see Chantal Caillavet, "Antropofagía y frontera: el caso de los Andes septentrionales," in Caillavet and Pachón, *Frontera y poblamiento,* 57–109.

31. AGI Quito 25:45, 8:7.

32. AGI Quito 9:2.

33. AGI Quito 9:6.

34. AGI Quito 25:45. Again the component "puis" appears in a place-name associated with Alpan.

35. See Kris Lane, "Heads and Hunters: The Sindagua Wars of Barbacoas (Colombia), 1597–1635," forthcoming. Alpan was in fact named as one of several "Malaba" caciques held responsible for the destabilization of Esmeraldas c. 1611; see Monroy, *El convento*, 95 (transcription from *Libro de Visita*, 1598–1666, in Quito's Archivo del Convento de la Merced). To be "punished for betrayal" by Spanish or creole volunteers were: "the Malabas Indians subject to the caciques Fernando Quajiba, Juan Yamban, Pusin, Chaltipsu, and Alpan, more or less 300 on either side of the Mira River; those on the left bank are called Aguamalabas, Espíes, Pruces [Piuses], Niupes [Nulpes], Mingas, and Quasmingas [Guasmingas]." These groups were said to fight among themselves, but "against the Spaniards they all unite."

BIBLIOGRAPHY

PRIMARY SOURCES

The core arguments of this book have grown from my reading of three broad classes of documents: 1) local notarial registers, or Protocols; 2) crown ledgers, including smeltery account books; and 3) letters sent to Spain by crown officials, churchmen, and assorted others. Published collections such as Pilar Ponce Leiva's hugely valuable *Relaciones histórico-geográficas de la Audiencia de Quito* and others are listed below. Unpublished documents have been cited using the customs of each archive. The general ANHQ collection is organized by section, box *(caja)*, date of document and folio (for example, ANHQ Religiosos, caja 1, 16-x-1613, f.5). References to notary *protocolos* (Protocols) in the ANHQ are designated "PN," serially numbered, and also assigned individual notary initials. AMQ documents are arranged by section, number, and folio (for example, AMQ Miscelánea no. 12, ff.3–6v.). AGI and ACC collections are organized by "Legajo" and "Signatura," respectively, followed by number and folio (for example, AGI Quito 961, ff.30–31v, and ACC Notarías Sig. 862, f.5). Dates have been added when necessary.

ARCHIVES AND ABBREVIATIONS

ACC: Archivo Central del Cauca (Popayán)

AGI: Archivo General de Indias (Sevilla)

AMQ: Archivo Municipal de Quito

ANHQ: Archivo Nacional de Historia, Quito

BN: Biblioteca Nacional (Madrid)

Alcina Franch, José, and Remedios de la Peña. *Textos para la etnohistoria de Esmeraldas: trabajos preparativos.* 4 vols. Madrid: Universidad Complutense, 1976.

Benzoni, Girolamo. *La historia del Nuevo Mundo (Relatos de su viaje por el Ecuador, 1547–50).* c. 1570. Guayaquil: Banco Central del Ecuador, 1985.

Burgos G., Hugo. *Primeras doctrinas en la Real Audiencia de Quito, 1570–1640.* Quito: Abya-Yala, 1995.

Cabello Balboa, Miguel. "Verdadera descripción y relación de la provincia y tierra de las Esmeraldas." 1583. *Obras,* 1–76. Quito: Editorial Ecuatoriana, 1945.

Caillavet, Chantal. "Ethno-histoire écuatorienne: un testament indien inédit du XVIe siècle." *Caravelle* 41 (1983): 5–23.

Campo del Pozo, Fernando, and Felix Carmona Moreno, eds. *Sínodos de Quito 1594 y Loja 1596 por Fray Luis López de Solís.* Madrid: Editorial Revista Agustiniana, 1996.

Colmenares, Germán, ed. *Fuentes coloniales para la historia del trabajo en Colombia (transcripciones del Archivo Histórico Nacional de Bogotá).* Bogotá: Ediciones Universidad de los Andes, 1968.

Costales, Piedad y Alfredo, eds. *Los Shuar en la historia: Sevilla de Oro y San Francisco de Borja.* Quito: Mundo Shurar, 1978.

Documentos Americanos del Archivo de Protocolos de Sevilla, Siglo XVI. Multiple vols. Madrid: Tipografia de Archivos I. Olózaga, 1931–35.

Estupiñán Viteri, Tamara. "Testamento de don Francisco Atagualpa." *Miscelánea Histórica Ecuatoriana* 1:1 (1988): 9–67.

Freile-Granizo, Juan, ed. *Autos Acordados de la Real Audiencia de Quito, 1578–1722.* Guayaquil: Corporación de Estudios y Publicaciones, Sección de Investigaciones Histórico-Jurídicas, 1971.

Friede, Juan, ed. *Documentos inéditos para la historia de Colombia.* Vol. 10. Bogotá: Academia Colombiana de Historia, 1960.

Fuentes, M. A. *Memorias de los virreyes que han gobernado el Peru.* Lima: F. Baitly, 1859.

Garcés G., Jorge, ed. *Colección de documentos sobre el Obispado de Quito.* 2 vols. 1546–1594. Quito: Archivo Municipal, 1946–47.

———. *Las Minas de Zamora: Cuentas de la Real Hacienda, 1561–1565.* Quito: Archivo Municipal, 1957.

———. *Libros de Cabildo de Quito,* 9 vols. 1573–1574. Quito: Archivo Municipal, 1934.

Hawkins, Richard. *Observations of Sir Richard Hawkins, Knight, or Voyage into the South Sea.* 1622. New York: Da Capo Press, 1968.

Llanos, García de, Gunnar Mendoza and Thierry Saignes, eds. *Diccionario y maneras de hablar que se usan en las minas y sus labores en los ingenios y beneficios de los metales.* 1607. La Paz: Museo Nacional de Etnografía y Folklore, 1983.

Mercado, Tomás de. *Suma de Tratos y Contratos.* 1569. Edited by Nicolas Sánchez Albornoz. Madrid: Fábrica Nacional de Moneda y Timbre, 1977.

Monroy, Joel. *El convento de la Merced en Quito, 1534–1617.* Quito: Escuela Tipográfica Salesiana, 1931.

Navarro Cárdenas, Maximina. *Investigación histórica de la minería en el Ecuador.* Quito: Dirección de Industrias del Ejército, 1990.

Ortiz de la Tabla Ducasse, Javier, et al., eds. *Cartas de Cabildos Hispanoamericanos: Audiencia de Quito.* Seville: Consejo Superior de Investigaciones Científicas, 1991.

Otte, Enrique, ed. *Cartas privadas de emigrantes a Indias, 1540–1616.* Mexico City: Fondo de Cultura Económica, 1996.

Ponce Leiva, Pilar, ed. *Relaciones Histórico-Geográficas de la Audiencia de Quito (Siglo XVI–XIX).* 2 vols. Madrid: Consejo Superior de Investigaciones Científicas, 1991–92.

Rumazo González, José. *Libro Segundo de Cabildos de Quito.* Quito: Archivo Municipal, 1934.

———. *Colección de documentos para la historia de la audiencia de Quito.* 8 vols. Madrid: Afrodisio Aguado, 1948–50.

Taylor, Anne Christine, and Cristóbal Landázuri, eds. *Conquista de la región Jívaro (1550–1650): relación documental.* Quito: Abya-Yala/IFEA/MARKA, 1994.

SECONDARY SOURCES

Adelman, Jeremy, ed. *Colonial Legacies: The Problem of Persistence in Latin American History.* New York: Routledge, 1999.

Alchon, Suzanne Austin. *Native Society and Disease in Colonial Ecuador.* Cambridge: Cambridge University Press, 1991.

Anda Aguirre, Alfonso. *Indios y Negros bajo el dominio español en Loja.* Quito: Abya-Yala, 1993.

———. *Zaruma en la Colonia.* Quito: Casa de la Cultura Ecuatoriana, 1960.

———. *Zamora de Quito y el oro de Nambija.* Loja: Casa de la Cultura Ecuatoriana, 1989.

Andrade Reimers, Luis. *Las esmeraldas de Esmeraldas durante el Siglo XVI.* Quito: Casa de la Cultura Ecuatoriana, 1978.

Andrien, Kenneth J. *The Kingdom of Quito, 1690–1830: The State and Regional Development.* Cambridge: Cambridge University Press, 1995.

Andrien, Kenneth J., and Rolena Adorno, eds. *Transatlantic Encounters: Europeans and Andeans in the Sixteenth Century.* Berkeley: University of California Press, 1991.

Ayala Mora, Enrique, ed. *Nueva Historia del Ecuador*. mult. vols. Quito: Corporación Editora Nacional, 1983–2002.

Bakewell, Peter. *Miners of the Red Mountain: Indian Labor in Potosí, 1545–1650*. Albuquerque: University of New Mexico Press, 1984.

Barona B., Guido. *La maldición de Midas en una region del mundo colonial: Popayán, 1730–1830*. Cali: Editorial Facultad de Humanidades, Universidad del Valle, 1995.

———. "Estructura de la producción de oro en las minas de la Real Corona: Chisquío (Cauca) en el Siglo XVII." *Anuario Colombiano de Historia Social y de la Cultura (ACHSC)*, No. 11 (1983): 5–42.

Barrett, Ward. "World Bullion Flows, 1450–1800." In *The Rise of Merchant Empires: Long-distance Trade in the Early Modern World, 1350–1750*, edited by James D. Tracy, 224–54. Cambridge: Cambridge University Press, 1990.

Basile, David G. *Tillers of the Andes: Farmers and Farming in the Quito Basin*. Chapel Hill: University of North Carolina Press, 1974.

Borah, Woodrow. *Early Colonial Trade and Navigation between Mexico and Peru*. Ibero-Americana No. 38. Berkeley: University of California Press, 1954.

Bowser, Frederick P. *The African Slave in Colonial Peru, 1524–1650*. Stanford, Calif.: Stanford University Press, 1974.

Bradley, Peter T. *The Lure of Peru: Maritime Intrusion into the South Sea, 1598–1701*. New York: St. Martin's Press, 1989.

Burga, Manuel, and Rosemarie Terán, eds. *Historia de América Andina, vol. 2: formación y apogeo del sistema colonial (siglos xvi-xvii)*. Quito: Universidad Simón Bolívar, 2000.

Burkett, Elinor C. "Indian Women and White Society: The Case of Sixteenth-Century Peru." In *American Women: Historical Perspectives*, edited by Asunción Lavrin, 101–28. Westport, Conn.: Greenwood Press, 1978.

Caillavet, Chantal. "Los mecanismos económicos de una sociedad minera: intercambios y crédito, Loja: 1550–1630." *Revista Ecuatoriana de Historia Económica*, 2:3 (1988): 19–62.

Calero, Luis Fernando. *Chiefdoms under Siege: Spain's Rule and Native Adaptation in the Southern Colombian Andes, 1535–1700*. Albuquerque: University of New Mexico Press, 1997.

———. "Pasto, 1535–1700: The Social and Economic Decline of Indian Communities in the Southern Colombian Andes." Ph.D. dissertation, University of California at Berkeley, 1988.

Carroll, Patrick J. *Blacks in Colonial Veracruz: Race, Ethnicity, and Regional Development*. Austin: University of Texas Press, 1991.

Chacón Zhapan, Juan. *Historia del Corregimiento de Cuenca (1557–1777)*. Quito: Banco Central, 1990.

Christian, William A. *Local Religion in Sixteenth-Century Spain*. Princeton, N.J.: Princeton University Press, 1981.

Colmenares, Germán. *Historia Económica y Social de Colombia*. 3 vols. Bogotá: La Carreta, 1979.

———. *La provincia de Tunja en el Nuevo Reino de Granada: ensayo de historia social, 1539–1800*. 1970. 3d ed. Bogotá: Tercer Mundo Editores, 1997.

Cueva, Agustín. *Notas sobre la economía ecuatoriana en la época colonial*. Quito: Instituto de Investigaciones Económicas, n.d. (c. 1975).

Cummins, Thomas B. F., and William B. Taylor, "The Mulatto Gentlemen of Esmeraldas, Ecuador." In *Colonial Spanish America: A Documentary History*, edited by Kenneth Mills and William B. Taylor, 147–49. Wilmington, Del.: Scholarly Resources, 1998.

Cushner, Nicholas P. *Farm and Factory: The Jesuits and the Development of Agrarian Capitalism in Colonial Quito, 1600–1767*. Albany: State University of New York Press, 1982.

———. *Lords of the Land: Sugar, Wine, and Jesuit Estates of Coastal Peru, 1600–1767*. Albany: State University of New York Press, 1980.

Davies, Keith. *Landowners in Colonial Peru*. Latin American Monographs No. 61. Austin: University of Texas Press, 1984.

DeBoer, Warren R. *Traces Behind the Esmeraldas Shore: Prehistory of the Santiago-Cayapas Region, Ecuador*. Tuscaloosa: University of Alabama Press, 1996.

———. "Returning to Pueblo Viejo: History and Archaeology of the Chachi (Ecuador)." In *Archaeology in the Lowland American Tropics: Current Analytical Methods and Recent Applications*, edited by Peter W. Stahl, 243–62. Cambridge: Cambridge University Press, 1995.

Deler, Jean-Paul. *Ecuador: del espacio al Estado nacional*. Quito: Banco Central, 1987.

Descola, Philippe. *The Spears of Twilight: Life and Death in the Amazon Jungle*. Translated by Janet Lloyd. New York: The New Press, 1996.

———. *In the Society of Nature: A Native Ecology in Amazonia*. Translated by Nora Scott. Cambridge: Cambridge University Press, 1994.

Díaz, Zamira. *Oro, sociedad y economía: El sistema colonial en la Gobernación de Popayán, 1533–1733*. Bogotá: Banco de la República, 1994.

Eire, Carlos. *From Madrid to Purgatory: The Art and Craft of Dying in Sixteenth-Century Spain*. Cambridge: Cambridge University Press, 1995.

Elliott, John H. *Europe Divided, 1559–1598*, 2d ed. London: Blackwell, 2000.

Estupiñán Viteri, Tamara. *El mercado interno en la Audiencia de Quito.* Quito: Banco Central del Ecuador, 1997.

———. *Diccionario básico del comercio colonial Quiteño.* Quito: Banco Central del Ecuador, 1997.

Gade, Daniel W. *Nature and Culture in the Andes.* Madison: University of Wisconsin Press, 1999.

Gauderman, Kimberly. "Women Playing the System: Social, Economic, and Legal Aspects of Women's Lives in Seventeenth-Century Quito." Ph.D. dissertation, University of California, Los Angeles, 1998.

González Pujana, Laura. "Minería y trabajo indígena en los Andes, Guamanga y Zaruma." *Revista Complutense de Historia de América,* no. 18 (1992): 117–131.

González Sánchez, Carlos Alberto. "La cultura del libro en el Virreinato del Perú en tiempos de Felipe II." *Colonial Latin American Review* 9:1 (June 2000): 63–80.

González Suárez, Federico. *Historia General de la República del Ecuador.* 12 vols. Quito: Daniel Cadena, 1931.

Guerra Bravo, Samuel. *Nambija: los lejanos senderos del oro.* Quito: Banco Central, 1987.

Hamilton, Earl J. *American Treasure and the Price Revolution in Spain, 1501–1650.* Cambridge, Mass.: Harvard University Press, 1934.

Harner, Michael. *The Jívaro: People of the Sacred Waterfalls.* Berkeley: University of California Press, 1972.

Hemming, John. *The Conquest of the Incas.* New York: HBJ/Harvest, 1970.

Hoberman, Louisa Schell. *Mexico's Merchant Elite, 1590–1660: Silver, State, and Society.* Durham, N.C.: Duke University Press, 1991.

Jamieson, Ross W. *Domestic Architecture and Power: The Historical Archeology of Colonial Ecuador.* New York: Kluwer Academic/Plenum Publishers, 2000.

Jara, Alvaro. *Tres ensayos sobre economía minera hispanoamericana.* Santiago de Chile: Editorial Universitaria, 1966.

Jaramillo Alvarado, Pío. *Historia de Loja y su provincia.* 1955. Loja: Ilustre Municipio de Loja/Universidad Nacional de Loja, 1991.

Jijón y Caamaño, Jacinto. *El Ecuador interandino y occidental antes de la conquista castellana.* 2 vols. Quito: Editorial Ecuatoriana, 1941.

Kamen, Henry. *Crisis and Change in Early Modern Spain.* Norfolk, UK: Variorum, 1993.

Kellenbenz, Hermann, ed. *Precious Metals in the Age of Expansion.* Papers of the Fourteenth International Congress of Historical Sciences, San Francisco, Calif., 1975. Stuttgart: Klett-Cotta, 1981.

Knapp, Gregory. *Andean Ecology: Adaptive Dynamics in Ecuador.* Boulder, Colo.: Westview Press, 1991.

Landázuri, Cristóbal. *Los curacazgos prehispánicos: agricultura y comercio, Siglo XVI.* Quito: IOA/Banco Central del Ecuador, 1982.

Lane, Kris. "Mining the Margins: Precious Metals Extraction and Forced Labor Regimes in the Audiencia of Quito, 1534–1821." Ph.D. dissertation, University of Minnesota, Minneapolis, 1996.

Lara, Jorge Salvador. *Quito.* Madrid: Editorial MAPFRE, 1992.

Larson, Brooke, and Olivia Harris, eds., with Enrique Tandeter. *Ethnicity, Markets, and Migration: At the Crossroads of History and Anthropology.* Durham, N.C.: Duke University Press, 1995.

Lavallé, Bernard. *Quito y la crisis de la alcabala, 1580–1600.* Quito: Corporación Editora Nacional, 1997.

Leonard, Irving. *Books of the Brave.* 1949. New York: Gordian Press, 1964.

Lockhart, James. *Of Things of the Indies: Essays Old and New in Early Latin American History.* Stanford, Calif.: Stanford University Press, 1999.

———. *Spanish Peru, 1532–1560: A Colonial Society.* 2d ed. Madison: University of Wisconsin Press, 1994.

Marzahl, Peter. *Town in the Empire: Government, Politics, and Society in Seventeenth Century Popayán.* Austin: University of Texas Press, 1978.

McDowell, John H. *So Wise Were Our Elders: Mythic Narratives of the Kamsá.* Lexington: University Press of Kentucky, 1994.

McFarlane, Anthony. *Colombia Before Independence: Economy, Society, and Politics under Bourbon Rule.* Cambridge: Cambridge University Press, 1993.

Meggers, Betty J. *Ecuador.* Ancient Peoples and Places, vol. 49. London: Thames and Hudson, 1966.

Miño Grijalva, Manuel. *La protoindustria colonial hispanoamericana.* Mexico City: FCE, 1993.

Moore, John Preston. *The Cabildo in Peru under the Hapsburgs: A Study in the Origins and Powers of the Town Council in the Viceroyalty of Peru, 1530–1700.* Durham, N.C.: Duke University Press, 1954.

Murillo, Rodrigo. *Zaruma: historia minera, identidad en Portovelo.* Quito: Abya-Yala, 2000.

Newson, Linda A. *Life and Death in Early Colonial Ecuador.* Norman: University of Oklahoma Press, 1995.

Ortiz de la Tabla Ducasse, Javier. *Los Encomenderos de Quito, 1534–1660: orígen y evolución de una élite colonial.* Sevilla: EEHA, 1993.

Padilla A., Silvia, María Luisa López A., and Adolfo Luis González R., eds. *La encomienda en Popayán (tres estudios)*. Seville: EEHA, 1977.

Palmer, Colin. *Slaves of the White God: Blacks in Mexico: 1570–1650*. Cambridge, Mass.: Harvard University Press, 1976.

Pérez T., Aquiles R. *Las Mitas en la Real Audiencia de Quito*. 1947. Guayaquil: Universidad de Guayaquil, 1987.

Phelan, John L. *The Kingdom of Quito in the Seventeenth Century: Bureaucratic Politics in the Spanish Empire*. Madison: University of Wisconsin Press, 1967.

Poloni-Simard, Jacques. *La mosaïque indienne: mobilité, stratification sociale et métissage dans le corregimiento de Cuenca (Equateur) du XVIe au XVIIIe siècle*. Paris: Ecole des hautes études en sciences sociales, 2000.

Ponce Leiva, Pilar. *Certezas ante incertidumbre: élite y cabildo de Quito en el Siglo XVII*. Quito: Abya-Yala, 1998.

Powers, Karen Vieira. *Andean Journeys: Migration, Ethnogenesis, and State in Colonial Quito*. Albuquerque: University of New Mexico Press, 1995.

———. "The Battle for Bodies and Souls in the Colonial North Andes: Intraecclesiastical Struggles and the Politics of Migration," *Hispanic American Historical Review* 75:1 (February 1995): 31–56.

———. "Resilient Lords and Indian Vagabonds: Wealth, Migration, and Reproductive Transformation of Quito's Chiefdoms." *Ethnohistory* 38 (1991): 225–49.

———. "Indian Migration and Sociopolitical Change in the Audiencia of Quito." Ph.D. dissertation, New York University, 1990.

———. "Land Concentration and Environmental Degradation: Town Council Records on Deforestation in Uyumbicho," in *Colonial Lives: Documents on Colonial Latin American History*, 1550–1850, edited by Richard Boyer and Geoffrey Spurling, 11–17. New York: Oxford University Press, 2000.

Quishpe B., Jorge Marcelo. *Transformación y reproducción indígena en los Andes septentrionales: los pueblos de la provincia de Sigchos, Siglos XVI y XVII*. Quito: Abya-Yala, 1999.

Rafael, Vicente. *Contracting Colonialism: Translation and Christian Conversion in Tagalog Society under Spanish Rule*. Ithaca, N.Y.: Cornell University Press, 1988.

Ramón, Galo. "Loja y Zaruma: Entre las minas y las mulas, 1557–1700." *Revista Ecuatoriana de Historia Económica* 7 (1990): 111–43.

Rappaport, Joanne. *Cumbe Reborn: An Andean Ethnography of History*. Chicago: University of Chicago Press, 1994.

———. *The Politics of Memory: Native Historical Interpretation in the Colombian Andes*. Cambridge: Cambridge University Press, 1990.

Restrepo, Vicente. *Estudio sobre las minas de oro y plata de Colombia.* 1884. Bogotá: Banco de la República, 1952.

Romero, Mario Diego. *Poblamiento y sociedad en el Pacífico colombiano, Siglos XVI al XVIII.* Cali: Universidad del Valle, 1995.

Rueda Novoa, Rocío. "Sociedad negra y autonomía: La historia de Esmeraldas, Siglos XVI-XVIII." Tesis de Maestría, Universidad del Valle (Cali, Colombia), 1990.

Rumazo González, José. *La región amazónica del Ecuador en el Siglo XVI.* Seville: CSIC, 1946.

Salomon, Frank. *Native Lords of Quito in the Age of the Incas: The Political Economy of North Andean Chiefdoms.* Cambridge: Cambridge University Press, 1986.

———. "Indian Women of Early Colonial Quito as Seen through Their Testaments." *The Americas* 44 (1988): 325–41.

Salomon, Frank, and Stuart B. Schwartz, eds. *The Cambridge History of the Native Peoples of the Americas.* Vol. 3: *South America.* Cambridge: Cambridge University Press, 1999.

Saville, Marshall. *The Gold Treasure of Sigsig, Ecuador.* New York: Heye Foundation, 1924.

Sempat Assadourian, Carlos. "The Colonial Economy: The Transfer of the European System of Production to New Spain and Peru." *Journal of Latin American Studies* 24 (1992, Quincentenary Supplement): 55–68.

Sempat Assadourian, Carlos, Heraclio Bonilla, Antonio Mitre, and Tristan Platt. *Minería y espacio económico en los Andes, Siglos XVI–XX.* Lima: Instituto de Estudios Peruanos, 1980.

Socolow, Susan Migden. *The Women of Colonial Latin America.* Cambridge: Cambridge University Press, 2000.

Stern, Steve J. *Peru's Indian Peoples and the Challenge of Spanish Conquest: Huamanga to 1640.* Madison: University of Wisconsin Press, 1982.

Suárez Pinzón, Ivonne. *Oro y sociedad colonial en Antioquia, 1575–1700.* Medellín: SECA, 1993.

Super, John C. "Partnership and Profit in the Early Andean Trade: The Experience of Quito Merchants, 1580–1610." *Journal of Latin American Studies* 11:2 (November 1979): 265–81.

———. *Food, Conquest, and Colonization in Sixteenth-Century Spanish America.* Albuquerque: University of New Mexico Press, 1988.

Szászdi, Adam. "The Economic History of the Diocese of Quito, 1616–1787." *Latin American Research Review* 21:2 (1986): 266–75.

———. "The Depreciation of Silver and Monetary Exchange in the Viceroyalty of Lima, 1550–1610." *Journal of European Economic History* (Rome) 4 (1975): 429–58.

―――. "El Trasfondo de un cuadro: 'Los Mulatos de Esmeraldas' de Andrés Sánchez Galque." *Cuadernos Prehispánicos* (Valladolid, Spain) 12 (1986–87): 93–142.

Thornton, John. *Africa and Africans in the Making of the Atlantic World, 1400–1680.* Cambridge: Cambridge University Press, 1992.

Tovar Pinzón, Hermes. *El imperio y sus colonias: las cajas reales de la Nueva Granada en el Siglo XVI.* Bogotá: Archivo General de la Nación, 1999.

Twinam, Ann. *Miners, Merchants, and Farmers in Colonial Colombia.* Latin American Monographs no. 57. Austin: University of Texas Press, 1982.

Tyrer, Robson B. *Historia demográfica y económica de la Audiencia de Quito.* Quito: Banco Central del Ecuador, 1988.

Vargas, José María. *La economía política del Ecuador durante la colonia.* 1957. 2d ed., con estudio introductorio de Carlos Marchán R. Quito: Banco Central del Ecuador, 1980.

Velasco, Juan de. *Historia del Reino de Quito en la América Meridional.* 1789. Caracas: Biblioteca Ayacucho, 1981.

Vila Vilar, Enriqueta. "La sublevación de Portugal y la trata de negros." *Ibero-Amerikanisches Archiv* N.F. Jahrgang 2, Heft 3 (1976): 171–92.

―――. *Hispano-América y el comercio de esclavos: los asientos portugueses.* Seville: EEHA/CSIC, 1977.

West, Robert C. *Colonial Placer Mining in Colombia.* Baton Rouge: University of Louisiana Press, 1952.

―――. *The Pacific Lowlands of Colombia.* Baton Rouge: Louisiana State University Press, 1957.

West, Robert C., and Alan K. Craig, eds. *In Quest of Mineral Wealth: Aboriginal and Colonial Mining and Metallurgy in Spanish America.* Geoscience and Man, vol. 33. Baton Rouge: Louisiana State University Press, 1994.

Whitten, Norman E., Jr. *Black Frontiersmen: Afro-Hispanic Culture of Ecuador and Colombia.* 2d ed. Prospect Heights, Ill.: Waveland Press, 1986.

―――. *Sacha Runa: Ethnicity and Adaptation of Ecuadorian Jungle Quichua.* Urbana: University of Illinois Press, 1976.

Zaruma: Cuatro siglos de peregrinaje histórico (memorias de las XVI jornadas de historia social, Zaruma 27–29 agosto de 1992). Vol. 7. Quito: Colección Medio Milenio, 1992.

INDEX